Music & Copyright in America
Toward the Celestial Jukebox

Kevin Parks

Section of
Intellectual Property Law

AMERICAN BAR ASSOCIATION

The materials contained herein represent the opinions and views of the authors and/or the editors, and should not be construed to be the views or opinions of the law firms or companies with whom such persons are in partnership with, associated with, or employed by, nor of the American Bar Association or the Intellectual Property Law Section, unless adopted pursuant to the bylaws of the Association.

Nothing contained in this book is to be considered as the rendering of legal advice, either generally or in connection with any specific issue or cases. Readers are responsible for obtaining advice from their own lawyers or other professionals. This book is intended for educational and informational purposes only.

Printed in the United States of America

Library of Congress Cataloging-in-Publication Data

Parks, Kevin.
    Music & copyright in America : toward the celestial jukebox / Kevin Parks.
        p. cm.
    Includes bibliographical references and index.
    ISBN 978-1-61438-671-1 (alk. paper) —ISBN 978-1-61438-672-8 (alk. paper)   1. Copyright—Music—
United States.   I. Title.   II. Title: Music and copyright in America.
    KF3035.P37 2012
    346.7304'82—dc23

                                                                                            2012028769

16 15 14 13 12   5 4 3 2 1

Discounts are available for books ordered in bulk. Special consideration is given to state bars, CLE programs, and other bar-related organizations. Inquire at Book Publishing, ABA Publishing, American Bar Association, 321 North Clark Street, Chicago, Illinois 60654-7598.

www.ShopABA.org

CONTENTS

ABOUT THE AUTHOR

Kevin Parks is an intellectual property attorney, teacher and entrepreneur who lives in Chicago. *Music & Copyright in America* is his first book.

ACKNOWLEDGMENTS

This book could not have come to fruition without the efforts and support of many people.

First, I acknowledge the Center for Intellectual Property Law at The John Marshall Law School in Chicago, one of the leading intellectual property programs in the country. This book grew from the coursework I have had the privilege of presenting there as an adjunct since 2004. Thanks in particular to Executive Director Michele A. Bridges and Acting Director William T. McGrath for many opportunities over the years.

Numerous John Marshall students assisted with research and ideas. Among them, Jason Koransky merits special thanks. Jason began as a researcher, but became much more—a contributor, editor, critic and friend. In particular, Jason contributed solid early drafts of sections on movie theater and jukebox exemptions. I thank him again for his interest and efforts.

Thanks are also due to Jonathan Jennings, a fellow John Marshall adjunct and colleague in the Chicago IP bar, for planting the seed for this book with the American Bar Association. At the ABA I acknowledge Richard Paszkiet for bringing me into the fold and Jeffrey Salyards for keeping me there by riding herd on deadlines in a firm yet understanding way.

I am blessed with good friends. For sage advice and humor, I turn to Wendell Gibson. For inspiration, I look to John Stauffer, an accomplished scholar and author who graciously took time from his busy schedule at Harvard to review the initial and final manuscripts. John, both your general comments and specific edits improved the book immensely. Thanks for your support and enthusiasm, and for a pleasant stay in Cambridge during the final stages.

Finally, I say thank you to my wonderful wife, Mary Ann, our children Jessica, George and Margaret, and the extended families we are so lucky to enjoy. Without your continued love, support and patience, this book could never have been completed.

PROLOGUE: THE KING IS DEAD

On June 25, 2009, some of the earliest notes of man-made music echoed from the recesses of a cave in southwestern Germany, when archaeologists reported discovering flute fragments fashioned more than 35,000 years ago from vulture bones and mammoth ivory.[1] Scholars can only speculate as to what drove a cave-dwelling Neanderthal to design, craft, and perform on a musical instrument. Was it a non-communal, anonymous impulse, an individual way to satisfy an urge for creative self-expression? Or perhaps a means of connecting with his community in ceremony, ritual, or celebration? One thing is certain: It was not a commercial endeavor, for it would be thousands of years before modern man made the art of music into a business.

Later the same day the reports came streaming in: Michael Jackson was dead at age fifty. The passing of the self-proclaimed "King of Pop" was a massive global event. Networks groaned under the weight of news coverage, rumor, commentary, and tributes, not to mention the commerce, with Jackson becoming (posthumously) the first artist to sell more than one million digital song downloads in a single week. Fans also flocked to purchase Jackson's songs in more traditional formats, sending compact disc versions of his albums again to the top of the charts.

If an anonymous cave man fingering the notes of his handmade flute marked the humble, solitary beginnings of popular music, the death of Michael Jackson represented an endpoint of sorts—not of music altogether, of course, but of an era in the music *business* when small cadres of talented and well-promoted artists dominated the marketplace: the global superstars who fed the beast of the modern music industry. As one commentator put it, the commercial reaction to Jackson's death was "a clear reminder of the sort of sales that were possible before technology and choice fractured the listening public into a million little niches, when the mainstream still ran strong."[2]

Jackson came of age in a time when recorded music was still a physical "product"—a recording made at the expense and under the close supervision of a

---

1. John Noble Wilford, *Flutes Offer Clues to Stone-Age Music*, N.Y. TIMES, June 25, 2009.
2. Eliot Van Buskirk, *Michael Jackson First Artist to Sell Over 1 Million Downloads in a Single Week*, WIRED, *Epicenter Blog*, July 1, 2009.

corporation that owned the resultant art, had the means to create demand through heavy promotion, and, significantly, controlled the distribution of those physical objects of music entertainment (in Jackson's day, vinyl discs, tapes, and later CDs) to music retailers to complete the final link in the chain by selling to consumers. It was an opaque industry, controlled by monolithic corporations that could afford to remain blissfully disconnected from their ultimate customers. These so-called major music labels, along with a small class of recording superstars like Jackson, and the songwriters and music publishers who supplied raw material in the form of songs, were the major beneficiaries of the late twentieth century business of music.

But a new century had arrived, and in 2009 the mainstream no longer "ran strong." A decade had passed since digital music storage and file-sharing software combined to disrupt business as usual by taking the "physical" out of music product, enabling anyone with an Internet-linked computer to access and share—that is, "distribute"—music. "Disintermediation" had come to the music business, sending shockwaves through the industry.

Even the likes of U2, one of the world's premier rock bands, felt the effects of the new music economy. In March 2009, U2's *No Line on the Horizon* went to No. 1 in the U.S. but, despite a massive marketing blitz, sold less than 60 percent of its predecessor, 2004's *How to Dismantle an Atomic Bomb*. Few were surprised. Regardless of its artistic merit, the release entered a music retail environment that was a shadow of its former self, the latest example being the announced closing of the remaining six Virgin Megastore locations in the United States. At peak activity there had been twenty-three stores—true music "destinations" with events, star-studded promotions and rows of deep music catalog—generating $230 million in annual sales. Revenue had since dropped to $170 million, leaving the real estate venture that owned the chain to search for higher rents from new, non-music tenants. Moreover, repeating what had become a regular occurrence for star-level artists, U2's latest release had "leaked" onto file-sharing networks pre-release, where hundreds of thousands of perfect digital copies were snapped up, without payment, before the music was available in stores or through "legitimate" online channels.

The business of selling recorded sounds was not what it used to be, calling for more creative approaches to marketing, in some cases through the mass-retail chains that commanded an increased share of a dwindling retail market. Following a trend established at Walmart by the Eagles and AC/DC, proudly independent artists Pearl Jam and Prince announced that their latest releases would be available exclusively at Target stores. Prince had earlier raised the ire of his distribution partners by giving away CDs with concert tickets and bundled into newspapers, the latter as a means of promoting his series of sellout performances at London's O2 Arena. Others adopted similar tactics, "giving away" recorded music in the name of promotion. Fans who purchased a $15 "membership" to the rock band No Doubt's reunion tour received free downloads of the band's entire eight-album catalog, along with other perks. And up-and-coming artists discovered that giving away downloads through Web sites and social networking portals had the effect of *increasing* sales of those same tracks through retailers such as the Apple's iTunes store, which as of August 2009 was responsible for a full 25 percent of all recorded music sales in the U.S. The line between merely promoting and actually selling music had become blurred.

In the same post-Napster decade, music licensing had taken on a new complexion as well. The placement of songs—in television and film productions, and in advertising—had gone from a stigmatized afterthought to a royalty-generating and promotional strategy sought after by nearly every recording artist, label, songwriter, and publisher. At the time of Michael Jackson's death, the Jackson 5's 1970 No. 1 hit, "I'll Be There," was getting new exposure as the soundtrack to a State Farm Insurance commercial, the latest example of a trend established by the 1999 pairing of Sting's "Desert Rose" single with Jaguar, a synergistic placement widely credited with jump-starting the sales of the artist's *Brand New Day* release, and repositioning Jaguar as a Baby Boomer brand. The placement opened a floodgate of licensing activity, lending credibility to a practice followed in subsequent years by nearly every major act. For emerging artists, a national advertising placement became a Holy Grail of sorts, its promotional strength at least as valuable as royalty dollars.

Faced with recorded music revenues that had been cut in half to $6.3 billion over the course of a decade, music content owners—the labels who owned recordings, and the music publishers holding rights in underlying songs—pursued legal strategies intended to protect their interests.[3] Record labels the world over flexed their legal muscles in the form of copyright infringement suits, attempting to stem the file-sharing tide. In the spring of 2009, a Swedish jury returned a guilty verdict in music labels' latest litigation against a file-sharing platform, The Pirate Bay, handing down prison terms to company founders and levying a $3.5 million fine. International music trade group IFPI CEO John Kennedy, a trial witness, said the case "was about defending the rights of creators, confirming the illegality of the service and creating a fair environment for legal music services that respect the rights of the creative community."

Closer to home, the labels' powerful lobbying arm, the Recording Industry Association of America (RIAA), touted court victories over other file-sharing platforms, and also in trials against two individual users. In what was widely regarded as a public relations disaster, the RIAA was nearing the end of a massive copyright litigation campaign in which it sued more than 30,000 of its own customers for file-sharing infringements. Most cases settled quickly for a few thousand dollars,

---

3. According to a Forrester Research Forecast, based on RIAA numbers, the United States recorded music business fell from a high of $14.6 billion in 1999 to $6.3 billion in 2009, a 56% decrease.

but an occasional defendant refused on principle, and in early 2009 two cases came to trial. In the first case, Boston College student Joel Tenenbaum was found liable for willfully infringing thirty recordings, resulting in a $675,000 jury verdict, an eye-opening award of $22,500 per song.[4] The news was even worse for Minnesota homemaker Jammie Thomas-Rasset, whose unprecedented third file-sharing retrial resulted in yet another jury verdict of liability, this time for $1.5 million, $62,500 for each of twenty-four songs.[5] Debates raged over the industry's heavy-handed strategies, raising the larger question of whether the copyright system itself was "broken," too archaic to keep up with technical advances, and unable to strike the proper balance among content owners, artists, technologists and fans. But the legal bottom line was clear—copyrights were routinely upheld against the unauthorized commercial use of music.

Meanwhile, 2009 witnessed the meteoric rise of another "legitimate" digital music provider. Spotify, an advertising-supported music streaming service initially available only in Europe, quickly surpassed six million users, coaxing investments from each of the four major labels—Warner Music Group, EMI, Universal, and Sony Music Entertainment—as well as a consortium representing the independent music community. Spotify's supporters declared that the future of the music industry depended on moving from one primary source of revenue—CDs—to many different revenue streams, including new forms of Web-enabled broadcasting, paid for indirectly through advertisers, directly by consumers in the form of subscription fees, or, in the case of Spotify, both.[6] In the meantime, similar services were gaining traction (and RIAA's lawyers' attention) in the race to put music "in the cloud," dispensing music "as a service," instead of a physical product.

In this arena, and in the United States in particular, the *recorded* music industry was playing catch-up with music *publishers*—the owners of underlying songs—who had long enjoyed a larger bundle of copyrights, and consequently more streams of revenue, particularly in the all-important realm of "public performance," such as broadcasting. Indeed, in August 2009 BMI, a major collecting agency representing more than 400,000 songwriters, composers, and music publishers, announced its twenty-fifth consecutive year of growth, gathering more than $905 million in revenue based on the public performance of its members' songs in all media—traditional radio, television, cable, satellite, and the Internet. Along with its counterpart and competitor, ASCAP, these performing rights organizations collected an unprecedented $2 billion on behalf of their constituents.

---

4. The award was later declared unconstitutional by the trial judge, who reduced it by 90%. Both sides appealed. *See Capitol Records, Inc. v. Thomas-Rasset*, 799 F. Supp. 2d 999 (D. Minn. 2011).

5. The presiding judge declared the verdicts excessive, reducing the third award to $54,000—$2,250 per song. The RIAA appealed the reduced award and other aspects of the case going back to 2008. See *Sony BMG Music Intm't v. Tenenbaum*, 721 F. Supp. 2d 85 (D. Mass. 2010), *aff'd in part, vacated in part, rev'd in part*, 660 F.3d 487 (1st Cir. 2011).

6. Spotify made its much anticipated U.S. debut in the summer of 2011.

On the other hand, SoundExchange, a much newer collecting agency working on behalf of the owners of sound recordings (labels and recording artists), collected just over $100 million in 2009, based on a less generous right of public performance that applied to *digital* broadcasting only. As 2009 wore on, American labels and artists continued their long battle for broader rights, pressing Congress to pass the Performance Rights Act, designed to create an additional revenue stream based on traditional terrestrial radio broadcasting, in addition to digital performances. As it had done before, the National Association of Broadcasters dug in its heels, labeling the initiative a "performance tax" that would decimate radio stations and disrupt the "symbiotic relationship" the broadcasting and recorded music industries had known for decades. In the process, a seemingly endless series of hearings and debates focused again on the value of recorded music, and whether, and how much, broadcasters should be required to pay to use recordings in various forms of broadcast media.

What kind of music industry had Michael Jackson left behind? At the end of the first decade of the twenty-first century, the business of music was a roller-coaster ride of trends and countertrends, apparently adrift in a sea of controversy and unending litigation, facing an uncertain future.

The goal of this book is to provide context and clarity amidst the chaos of these moments. To do so, we explore the history of music and copyright in the United States, revisiting earlier watershed periods in which technology disrupted the industry, only to create long-term opportunities for growth. As we shall see, many of the current issues and challenges are not new at all, but rather variations on themes that have played themselves out in the not-so-distant past. We look back at the artifacts of American music copyright, representing the resolutions of earlier debates concerning music as both art and commerce, seeking guidance from earlier tugs-of-war between creators, business people, and the consuming public.

At the end of the day we will find ourselves within sight of the Celestial Jukebox, an idyllic future in which music lovers expect to enjoy unfettered, on-demand access to the entire universe of recorded music, at any time, through any device, at a reasonable cost. The lessons of the past hold the potential for a beautiful future where creative artists have incentive to bring music to life, in alignment with the commercial interests who transform art into commerce, serving the passionate devotees who form the most important link in the chain running from Neanderthal caves to Michael Jackson and beyond—technology-empowered fans, for whom music transcends commerce to form bonds, organize communities, and create shared histories that are the common threads in the fabric of our lives.

PART I

Music as American Commerce

America's first superstar of music,
songwriter Stephen C. Foster (1826–1864).
Foster Hall Collection, Center for American Music,
University of Pittsburgh Library System

1. Music as Property
—The Early Sheet Music Trade

By the early 1800s, a young American republic had gained footing on the eastern seaboard and turned its eyes to the western frontier. With the Louisiana Purchase in 1803, followed by the Lewis and Clark expedition to the Pacific and back ending in 1806, President Thomas Jefferson began to appreciate the diversity in and sheer size of the continent that was now America's dominion. In this environment, the notion of property meant *land*. As the frontier pushed westward, the yeoman farmer who claimed, cleared, and tilled his parcel became the ideal of the American property owner.

But America was also a place of ideas, where a man could make good with his brain as well as his back. The concept of *intellectual* property, products of the mind as opposed to physical labor, took root in America even before the colonies achieved independence. This was acknowledged as a founding principle of the new republic by the Constitutional Convention of 1787, which recognized, in Section 8 of Article I of the Constitution, that "Congress shall have the power . . . To promote the Progress of Science and Useful arts, by securing for limited Times to Authors and Inventors the exclusive Right to their respective Writings and Discoveries."

President George Washington opened the second session of Congress by observing that "[t]here is nothing that can better deserve your patronage than the promotion of science and literature." Congress responded with the nation's first copyright law, signed by Washington on May 31, 1790, "An Act for the encouragement of learning, by securing the copies of maps, charts, and books, to the authors and proprietors of such copies." The law provided a fourteen-year period of exclusivity (renewable for a like period) in which only the author could "print, reprint, publish or vend" copyrighted works, with the right also extending to the author's "executors, administrators or assigns." The statute not only created a federal law of copyright, but also recognized that this form of creative, purely intellectual property could be transferred to others through intestacy or sale.

Just like owners of "real property," authors could exclude those who would trespass or "infringe" upon their rights, and could sell their intellectual assets for value.[1] Equally important, the law provided a basis for "licensing" copyrighted

---

1. *See* William Lichtenwanger, "Music and Copyright Law in the United States," *in* MUSIC PUBLISHING AND COLLECTING: ESSAYS IN HONOR OF DONALD W. KRUMMEL 69–94 (David Hunter ed. 1994).

property—allowing a third party to "print" and "vend" copies of a work for a period of time, in return for the payment of royalties to the author/licensor. In this fashion, Noah Webster, a pioneer of American copyright, licensed his early work *Grammatical Institute of the English Language* to seven different booksellers for use in their respective territories, using the royalty earnings to finance his more famous and lucrative work, *An American Dictionary of the English Language*, known as *Webster's Dictionary*.[2]

"Maps, charts, and books," the items explicitly delineated as the subject matter of copyright, each had a direct connection to the "promotion of science and literature," as urged by the president and reflected in the Constitution. As a music lover and active concertgoer, Washington would likely have had music in mind when he urged Congress to promote literary endeavors, but the first Copyright Act did not specifically include music, particularly folk or popular songs, among protected works, as these had little to do with science or, arguably, "literature."[3] "Books" concerning music would qualify, as would song collections compiled for religious or educational purposes. But what of early works deposited for registration under the new law, such as *The Rural Harmony, Being an Original Composition, in Three and Four Parts* (1793); *The Kentucky Volunteer, A New Song* (1794), authored by a "Lady of Philadelphia"; or *The Green Mountain Farmer, A New Patriotic Song* by Thomas Paine (1798)? These works were deposited for registration in the first decade of the initial Copyright Act, but whether they were "books" qualifying for protection against infringement is open to doubt, a question that does not appear to have been tested in the courts.[4]

The notion of music as a business was still young and undefined at the turn of the nineteenth century. Traveling minstrels made a rough living on the road, and a small number of educators, instructors, and performers had livelihoods based on musical talent. But nothing existed of what we know of as the music business today—the crafting, promoting, distributing, and selling of music as a consumable product. Printed music (and eventually copyright recognition for music) would fill this gap.

In the late 1700s, publisher owners of printing presses or music type began operating as vanity presses of sorts. Composers were required to pay the costs of producing sheet music editions of up to a few thousand copies, the majority of which the publishers sold in their own stores or shipped to other dealers, keeping the proceeds. Writers were given a portion of the print run to sell for their own

---

2. Russell Sanjek, American Popular Music and Its Business, The First Four Hundred Years, Vol. II, From 1790 to 1909, 26 (1988).

3. Not a musician himself, Washington was a dedicated fan of the musical arts. Before the Revolution, in 1757 he spent a sizable sum purchasing a block of seats for the first public concerts staged in Philadelphia, and later supported the efforts of others in pursuing music lessons and education, including most notably his step-granddaughter, Nelly Custis, for whom he purchased a piano and arranged for lessons. *See* Barrymore Laurence Scherer, *What George Washington Heard*, Wall Street J., July 1, 2010.

4. Sanjek, *supra* note 2, at 26.

account to pupils or small, nonmainstream merchants. Only relatively well-to-do composers could afford to bear 100 percent of the risk in such arrangements, and only the most popular works generated meaningful profits for the writer.[5]

Beginning around 1805, improved engraving techniques made it possible to include imagery on sheet music, illustrations of a song's subject matter that would help transform music into a bona fide consumer product. Shortly thereafter, the introduction of lithographic printing dramatically reduced printing costs, truly opening sheet music to the realm of the graphic artist, as well as the budding composer. With these developments, music publishing enterprises grew into a cottage industry: During the first twenty-five years of the new century, more than 10,000 compositions were published in America.[6]

Having arrived on the American scene in the 1780s, "sheet music" (printed on large, folio-sized pages) was the most extravagant and expensive of several music formats available at the time. Oftentimes songs would appear initially as "broadsides"—single sheets of lyrics with no music notation, selling for two cents each. Other formats included "songsters"—pocket-sized lyric books, again without notation, selling for around twenty-five cents, and "anthologies"—larger groups of songs complete with musical notation. A successful broadside might warrant an upgrade to a release as sheet music, which commanded 12.5 cents per page, meaning that a two-page piece "could bring in 25 cents per copy . . . more than ten times what a broadside version would bring, and far more than its per-piece yield in any songster or anthology."[7]

During the first quarter of the nineteenth century, sheet music was something of a luxury, a symbol of status and taste in American homes, displayed atop the piano in the parlor, or in leather-bound portfolios. Much like later formats for *recorded* music (cylinders, discs, and tapes), sheets were prized collectors' items, treasured as much for their look and feel as the music they contained.

For publishers, the highly profitable "sheet" was the optimal music format, and by the 1820s they turned out more than 600 titles per year.[8] The economics of sheet music publishing favored foreign music, as foreign compositions were not subject to protection under the new American copyright law. Publishers could reproduce foreign songs without regard for payment to authors, and in this sense, the early American music business was built on what its European counterparts considered "pirated" editions of successful overseas material. Publishing American music, on the other hand, required either the acquisition of copyrights, or payment of license royalties, based on retail price (up to 10 percent) or a fixed amount per copy sold, usually two cents.[9]

---

5. *Id.* at 4–5.
6. *Id.* at 34.
7. RICHARD CRAWFORD, AMERICA'S MUSICAL LIFE 231 (2001).
8. *Id.* at 232, citing SANJEK, *supra* note 2, at 137–38.
9. *See* CRAWFORD, *supra* note 7, at 232.

A home-grown song needed to be that much "better" than the foreign competition to catch a publisher's eye. Thus, recognizing songs and songwriters with commercial potential became one of the publisher's four essential functions as the business of music took hold in America. Recognizing talent, what we now refer to as the "A&R" (for "artists and repertoire") function, was necessary to build a pipeline of new products and a healthy catalog of reprintable songs that could meet demand. In addition to finding talent, publishers prepared the musical notation and arrangements based on the instrument (typically piano) on which the song was to be rendered, and made the engraving and printing plates necessary to reproduce the song in different printed configurations—broadsides, songsters, and sheet music. Third, publishers had the burden of creating consumer demand for specific songs through marketing and promotion (an aspect of the business that would become competitive and cutthroat through the years), or by positioning music in key distribution channels, such as with music teachers, who purchased at discounted rates for sale to their student customers. And fourth, a publisher needed the logistical wherewithal to physically distribute music to those, other than itself, who could offer sheets for sale to individual customers.

2. Copyright in "Musical Compositions"

As shown by the steady increases in publishing ranks during the 1800s, it became apparent that there was money to be made in music. The business was plagued by uncertainty and risk, however, with publishers claiming that "all but a few of [their] products lost money."[10] One notable early publishing concern, Boston's Oliver Ditson & Co., complained that "Not one piece in ten pays the cost of getting up; only one in fifty proves a success."[11] Ditson issued a warning of sorts to the composer community, stating that no author should be surprised by a rejection of his or her song manuscripts, and for songs that were accepted, some writers would be required to "purchase a certain number of copies, to help defray the first expenses and introduce them to the public."[12]

To justify investments based on such odds, publishers looked for any means of hedging their bets. Investing in copyrights became such a tool. Song ownership provided a means of enforcing exclusivity, keeping potential copyists at bay and helping to preserve the profits flowing from popular songs. As the law did not specifically recognize music as a distinct category of copyright, however, these investments remained uncertain. With help from the book and dictionary author

---

10. *Id.* at 232.
11. *Id.*
12. *Id.* at 233.

and publisher Noah Webster, an early proponent of copyright expansion, the legislative landscape took a positive turn for early American songwriters and publishers.

Webster's Dictionary was a landmark work the author had published in 1828, at age seventy. The initial term of copyright protection was limited to fourteen years, and was renewable for an additional fourteen only if the author was still living at the end of the first term. Heirs had no right to renew. Unsatisfied with the law, and aware of his own mortality, Webster embarked on the first campaign to extend the term of U.S. copyright protection.

Webster recalled that in the autumn of 1827 (even before his famous work was publicly available), he applied to Representative Ralph Isaacs Ingersoll of Connecticut, urging him to "use his influence" to bring forward a new copyright bill, to which he "very cheerfully complied."[13] The bill died in the House, however, so before the next session of Congress (1829–1830), Webster prevailed upon William W. Ellsworth, also a representative from Connecticut and a member of its judiciary committee, "to make efforts to procure the enactment of a new copy-right law" that would extend the copyright term and expand authors' rights.[14] Ellsworth, a Yale-educated attorney who also happened to be Webster's son-in-law, wrote to lawmakers of the principal European nations, requesting information on the state of copyright in their countries, and from their responses fashioned a report and bill that was approved by the judiciary committee but never came before the House at that session. Frustrated, Webster "determined in the winter of 1830–1831 to visit Washington myself, and endeavor to accomplish the subject."[15] That he did. Staying in Washington for more than two months, Webster read lectures in the "Hall of Representatives," which had "no little effect" on a new law coming forward, and lobbied unrelentingly for a more robust copyright law.

On December 17, 1830, Ellsworth produced "Report No. 3" on "Copy-Right," reflecting on the first copyright act (and an 1802 amendment recognizing "prints" as a protected category) as a positive but incomplete step for authors. The report proposed revisions to remove "discrepancies," eliminate "useless and burdensome" provisions, and most important, "enlarge the period for the enjoyment of copyright, and thereby . . . place authors in this country more nearly upon an equality with authors in other countries."[16] Ellsworth's primary strategy, one often used to this day by copyright proponents, was to shame Congress into expanding rights to meet those recognized internationally. "While, for most obvious reasons," he reported, "the United States ought to be foremost among nations in encouraging

---

13. NOAH WEBSTER, A COLLECTION OF PAPERS ON POLITICAL, LITERARY AND MORAL SUBJECTS 177 (1843).

14. *Id.*

15. *Id.* at 178.

16. H.R. REP. NO. 3, 21st Congress, 2d Session (Dec. 17, 1830).

science and literature, by securing the fruits of intellectual labor, she is, in this thing, very far behind them all, as a reference to their laws will show."[17]

Ellsworth drew comparisons to establish "that the United States are far behind the States of Europe in securing the fruits of intellectual labor, and in encouraging men of letters." In Germany, Norway, and Sweden for example, copyright was deemed perpetual, and in Russia, valid for the life of the author plus twenty years. France had recently extended copyright terms to life of the author and fifty years beyond, and under English law, authors were granted a twenty-eight-year copyright term, extendable for life if the author was still living.[18] British law was the subject of additional commentary pertaining to music. "It has furthermore been claimed, and, it seems to your committee," reported Ellsworth, "that the law of copy-right ought to extend to musical compositions, as does the English law."[19]

The House took up a bill on January 6, 1831, with the primary debates centered on the proposed term extension to twenty-eight years, renewable by the author, or any heirs, for an additional fourteen. Objectors found such a lengthy "monopoly" difficult to justify, especially in light of the mere fourteen-year term granted to patented inventions. Further, they argued that authors had an "implied contract" with both booksellers and the buying public who, having supported the higher prices commanded by books under copyright, should have an earlier opportunity to distribute works at lower prices, as they fell into the public domain.

Defending the bill, Ellsworth fell back on national pride, insisting that the proposed law would "enhance the literary character of the country, by holding forth to men of learning and genius additional inducements to devote their time and talents to literature and the fine arts."[20] Similarly, Rep. Huntington supported the bill as an act of "pure justice," one that "would do honor to the country, and promote, in the most eminent degree, the advancement of all that ennobles and dignifies intellectual man." As an example of a work worthy of an extended term, he pointed, not surprisingly, to *Webster's Dictionary*, "that unrivalled work, that monument of learning," testimony to the "genius of its author."[21] Rep. Gulian Verplanck of New York went further still, arguing in Lockian terms that copyright was an author's "natural right" that should be enjoyed in perpetuity; the least that could be done was to extend the right as proposed. The bill was ordered for a "third reading" by a vote of 81 to 31, and eventually passed in the House. Noah Webster recalled that after two readings, the bill passed in the Senate "without debate," coming into force on February 3, 1831, upon the signature of President Andrew Jackson.[22]

---

17. *Id.*
18. *Id.*
19. *Id.*
20. HeinOnline – 7 Cong. Deb. 423–24 (1831); Gales & Seaton's Register of Debates in Congress, Jan. 6, 1831, 421–24.
21. Gales & Seaton's Register of Debates in Congress, *supra* note 20.
22. Webster, *supra* note 13, at 178.

If music publishers presented any organized support for the new act, it is not apparent from the congressional debates. Rather, it appears the fledgling music publishing industry received a gift of sorts, with the recognition of "musical compositions" coming in on the coattails of the term extension, the main objective of Noah Webster, his son-in-law, and their fellow revisionists of 1831.[23] The only mention of music was in Ellsworth's report, which asserted that American songwriters should gain parity with their British counterparts, an issue not debated by Congress.[24]

Unbeknownst to many of them, composers and publishers awakened to a new day on February 4, 1831. They were now beneficiaries of a new copyright law that recognized their art form specifically, granting the author of a "musical composition" the "sole right and liberty of printing, reprinting, publishing, and vending" such work for a period of twenty-eight years, renewable for a total of forty-two. Moreover, the new law provided strong remedies against infringement. Violators were required to "forfeit the plate or plates" from which illicit works were printed, deliver up all infringing inventory to the copyright holder, and pay one dollar (to be split evenly between the author and the government) for every copy found in their possession, or shown to have been "printed or published, or exposed to sale, contrary to the true intent and meaning of this act." Authors could also collect the "full costs" of prosecuting a successful suit for infringement.

With copyright protection confirmed for musical works, American songwriters and publishing entrepreneurs had the framework in place to build careers and businesses. Indeed, the esteemed music and copyright historian D.W. Krummel called the forty-five years "which began with the Jacksonian era and ended with the Reconstruction" the "crucial period in American music publishing," as output increased dramatically, and the industry spread west beyond the established centers of Philadelphia, Boston, and New York.[25] Beginning around 1845, published titles doubled to around 3,000 per year; they expanded further to 5,000 annually in the 1850s, and increased again to around 8,000 titles per year in the 1860s.[26] In

---

23. Ellsworth was made executor of Webster's estate upon the author's passing in 1843, and oversaw the sale of his copyright interests to the Merriam organization, from which the *Merriam-Webster's Dictionary* was born and lives to this day.

24. In stark contrast, recognition of a "composer's right" in the United Kingdom in 1777 came only after long years of hardscrabble lobbying and litigation, culminating in a case brought by Johann Christian Bach, the eighteenth child of Johann Sebastian Bach, in which Lord Mansfield held a "musical composition" to be a protectable "writing" within the Statute of Anne, the nation's first copyright law, enacted in 1710. This story is told in compelling fashion, and with thoughtful perspective on modern copyright issues, by Michael W. Carroll in *The Struggle for Music Copyright*, 57 FLA. L. REV. 907 (2005).

25. D.W. Krummel, *Counting Every Star; Or, Historical Statistics on Music Publishing in the United States (American Music Bibliography, IV)*, in 10 ANUARIOS INTERAMERICANO DE INVESTIGACION MUSICAL 180 (1974).

26. *Id.* With the country's population roughly doubling each decade between 1830 and the Civil War, it was an opportune time to market a reasonably priced consumer product like sheet music.

1859, *The Knickerbocker* magazine noted the emergence of an American song-writing voice. It proudly asserted that "[r]eprints of English works used to form the staple of a publisher's issues, but, with the increase of musical cultivation among us, multitudes of composers have been developed, and our sheet-music publishers now do mostly a copyright business. Many of these copyrights are very valuable."[27]

3. Music Goes to Court

In due course, copyright owners began asserting their rights under the new law. In 1844, the first reported decision involving infringement of a musical composition was resolved by the Circuit Court for the Southern District of New York, which upheld plaintiff William E. Millett's rights in "The Cot Beneath the Hill," a parlor song composed in 1841.[28] Millett charged that William Snowden had published the song in the June 1843 issue of his successful New York-based women's journal, the *Ladies' Companion*, a monthly magazine said to embrace "every department of literature, embellished with original engravings, and music, arranged for the piano forte, harp and guitar." Snowden readily admitted to the use, but claimed no wrongful intent, proving at trial "that the music had been copied from a Boston paper by the young man having charge of that department," that "neither [of them] knew of its being copyrighted," and that, in any event, the music had been changed slightly from the original.

The court was not moved, stating flatly that "intention could not be taken into view. If a copyright has been invaded, whether the party knew it was copyrighted or not, he is liable to the penalty." Moreover, "trifling" changes from the original did not "avoid the statute." The court also made clear that it had no discretion in fixing the penalty. If Snowden infringed the work, he owed one dollar for each sheet proven to be "sold, or offered for sale." The verdict was for $625.

Claiming that biased coverage of the trial had "been read by at least half a million in [New York] and immediate vicinity," Snowden used the pages of the *Ladies' Companion* to show his readers that "although acting innocently, and in all good faith, we have hazarded a large sum of money for their gratification." He did so as a demonstration of the publication's "chivalric devotion" to "the ladies of New York and America," and their "enlightened tastes." Snowden complained that his efforts to prove the full circumstances of the matter had been "ruled out by the court." For example, he pointed out that immediately upon discovering that the music was subject to copyright, a corrective notice was printed identifying Millett as the copyright owner and providing his address for purposes of obtaining a

27. EDITOR'S TABLE, 54 THE KNICKERBOCKER OR NEW YORK MONTHLY MAGAZINE, Dec. 1859, at 668, cited in KEN EMERSON, DOO-DAH! STEPHEN FOSTER AND THE RISE OF AMERICAN POPULAR CULTURE 242 (1997).

28. Millett v. Snowden, 17 F. Cas. 374 (No. 9600) (Circuit Court, S.D.N.Y. 1844).

proper copy of the sheet. Further, adopting what has become a common refrain of music copyright defendants for more than 150 years, Snowden asserted that his actions should be excused because the "infringement" had the effect of "promoting" sales of the original.

At trial, Snowden established that Millett himself had printed only 500 copies of the song, which, according to Snowden, "had scarcely been entered upon by purchasers." "Our publication of it did him good," he insisted, "and drew the public's attention to it. Every lady keeps her collection of music for the purpose of binding, and our pages could not be incorporated with those of regular music-sheets—consequently, if the composition were a superior one, every lady, (after our acknowledgment in our July number,) would send to Mr. Millett for a copy of his music, to be placed with her collection already accumulated. Thus we contend that Mr. Millett has been largely benefitted by the publication in the *Ladies' Companion* of 'The Cot Beneath the Hill,'—for which we have been, (very reluctantly I assure you!) made to contribute still further, by a direct tax upon our product. How far we have been to *blame*, in the business, we leave our readers to judge."[29] As Snowden and his colleagues quickly discovered, the new copyright law had teeth.

A year later in 1845, music copyright assumed a higher profile, when Supreme Court Chief Justice Roger Taney, sitting as a trial judge with the Maryland Circuit Court, presided over a jury trial in the case of *Reed v. Carusi*.[30] The case revealed the complexities that could arise from a seemingly simple proposition—the ownership and alleged infringement of "The Old Arm Chair," a tear-jerking sentimental ballad based on lyrics written by an English poet, Elizabeth Cook, in 1838, and set to music by the composer and performer Henry Russell. A Londoner, Russell promoted the song in New York and Boston area performances, bringing it to the attention of the music publishing firm of Oakes and Swan, who acquired the copyright in early 1840. In 1841, it transferred the rights to Benjamin W. Thayer of Boston, who in turn assigned the copyright to Boston music publisher George P. Reed in December 1842.[31]

Even before Reed purchased the copyright in Russell's version of the song, Samuel Carusi, an Italian-born musician, composer, and publisher operating in

---

29. LADIES' COMPANION, Vol. 19–20, available at http://books.google.com/books?id=PhkAAAAAYAAJ &printsec=frontcover&source=gbs_navlinks_s#v=onepage&q=&f=false.

30. Reed v. Carusi, 20 F. Cas. 431, 8 Law Rep. 410 (No. 11,642) (Circuit Court, D. Md.—Nov. Term, 1845). At the time, Supreme Court judges literally "rode circuit," sitting as trial judges in various federal circuit courts. Sitting in the same capacity in 1861, Chief Justice Taney delivered the decision in *Ex Parte Merryman*, rebuking President Lincoln's suspension of the writ of habeus corpus during the Civil War. Four years earlier, Taney had delivered the Supreme Court's decision in *Dred Scott v. Sandford*, ruling that African Americans could not be considered citizens of the United States, which was viewed by many to be an indirect cause of the war.

31. *See* Frank McCormick, *George P. Reed v. Samuel Carusi: A Nineteenth Century Jury Trial Pursuant to the 1831 Copyright Act*, (Digital Commons@University of Maryland School of Law) (Jan. 10, 2005), *available at* http://digitalcommons.law.umaryland.edu/mlh_pubs/4/.

Washington, D.C., and Baltimore, had created his own arrangement of "The Old Arm Chair," by arranging Cook's lyrics to the tune "New England," a song written by I.T. Stoddard and owned by Carusi. Carusi registered the copyright in his version of "The Old Arm Chair" in late October 1842.[32] Soon thereafter, Reed discovered Carusi's version in the market, and prepared to sue for infringement, hiring John H.B. Latrobe as counsel, a prominent attorney known for representing the Baltimore and Ohio Railroad Company, with personal connections to leading politicians and jurists, including Chief Justice Taney. The suit came to trial in November 1845, with Carusi represented by William Frick and Francis Brinley. Instead of the near literal copying at issue in *Millett*, the complaint alleged that Carusi's version of "The Old Arm Chair" was "substantially the same" as Reed's. Reed sought $2,000 in damages.

Chief Justice Taney was joined by Judge Upton S. Heath in conducting the trial, but Taney led the proceedings and eventually delivered the "instructions" (equivalent to an opinion) of the court. A legal observer of the day concluded that in "disclosing the views of the chief justice, upon a statute but little subject of judicial exposition, as to musical compositions, it is an interesting case."[33] Indeed, the testimony unfolded in interesting fashion, with both sides presenting expert witnesses to opine on the degree of similarity between the arrangements. Further, over Carusi's objection, Taney allowed John Cole, a professional singer, to sing both versions in open court for the jury's consideration.

Carusi first argued that the plaintiff did not own an "original" composition, asserting that Russell borrowed his song from two older tunes, "The Blue Bells of Scotland" and "The Soldier's Tear." Second, even assuming a valid copyright, Carusi maintained that his version was sufficiently different from Russell's to avoid infringement, as it was based on Carusi's own copyrighted tune, "New England." Both arguments were based on the "derivative" nature of popular song, another refrain asserted by copyright defendants over the years.

In accordance with local practice in Maryland, at the close of the evidence the attorneys presented "prayers," the legal propositions supporting their client's position. In *Reed*, Chief Justice Taney rejected both sides' prayers and drafted his own instructions for the jury to follow in evaluating the facts. First, Taney held that "the defendant is not liable to this action, unless the jury find that Russell was the author of the musical composition" (i.e., that the song was "original" to Russell and not copied from earlier works). Assuming original authorship, Taney opined that Carusi could not be liable for infringement unless the "main design" of the songs was the same, or that Carusi had altered Russell's composition with the intent of evading the law. Further, even if the songs were materially the same, Carusi could avoid liability by proving independent creation—that his song "was the effort of his own mind, or taken from an air composed by some other person, who was not a plagiarist of Russell." Turning to the statute of limitations, Taney instructed that Carusi could be

---

32. *Id.* at 4.
33. Reed v. Carusi, Note 1, from 8 Law Rep. 410.

liable only if the action was brought within two years of the infringement, and (contrary to the statute) advised the jury that in determining damages, they should find the number of copies printed "within two years before the suit was brought."

The jury reached its verdict on November 8, 1845, finding Carusi liable for $200. *Reed v. Carusi* was widely viewed as a significant test of the copyright law as applied to musical compositions, establishing important precedent still looked to for guidance.[34] Able counsel had represented both parties before the Chief Justice of the Supreme Court, in groundbreaking litigation as to the standards for originality, infringement, viable defenses, and damage awards. Indeed, in a rare showing of post-verdict solidarity, Reed's counsel supported Carusi's request for a pardon of the government's half of the damage award. In crafting a recommendation on the issue, William S. Marshall, U.S. Attorney for the District of Maryland, noted that "the case was one which excited the curiosity of the bar" in general, and gave his personal view that Carusi had acted in good faith. On February 3, 1846, President James K. Polk pardoned Carusi's debt of $100 to the United States, finding him a "fit subject for executive clemency."[35]

4. The First Superstar of American Song

Surviving as a professional songwriter in the mid-nineteenth century was a difficult proposition. John Hill Hewitt, author of popular songs from the 1820s through the Civil War, maintained that songwriting was not worthwhile "[f]or the simple reason that it does not pay the author," not to mention the fact that "the publisher pockets all, and gets rich on the brains of the poor fool who is chasing that *ignis fatuus*, reputation."[36] Making music pay was even more difficult for nonperformers. As composer Henry Russell recalled, "There was no such thing as a royalty in those days, and when a song was sold it was sold outright. Had it not been that I sang the songs myself, and so in a certain measure conduced to their popularity, the payment for their composition would have meant simple starvation."[37]

---

34. The *Reed* decision has been cited as recently as 1998 in the majority opinion in Feltner v. Columbia Pictures Television, 523 U.S. 340 (1998), in support of the proposition that juries, not judges, should measure statutory damages in copyright cases.

35. McCormick, *supra* note 31, at 18–19.

36. John H. Hewitt, Shadows on the Wall or Glimpses of the Past. A Retrospect of the Past Fifty Years 66 (1877), cited in Emerson, *supra* note 27, at 139–40.

37. Henry Russell. Cheer! Boys, Cheer! Memories of Men and Music 198–99 (1895), cited in Emerson, *supra* note 27, at 140. Handbills promoting 1841 concerts by New Hampshire's Hutchinson Family Singers asked the question: "When foreigners approach your shores, You welcome them with open doors, Now we have come to seek our lot, Shall native talent be forgot?" Early performances did not draw enough interest to earn a profit (at twelve-and-a-half cents a ticket), but like bands in the modern era, the group persevered through difficult times by staying on the road, honing their performing and writing talents, as well as their image. By 1843 the group had positioned themselves (quite legitimately given their background as four—of sixteen!!—siblings) as promoting the virtues of family and

Despite these odds, during this time the growing American music industry produced the first superstar of American popular songwriting—Stephen Collins Foster. Born near Pittsburgh on July 4, 1826, the eighth of ten children, by the time of the 1831 Copyright Act (recognizing "musical compositions" as a distinct category of copyright) Foster was showing signs of a budding musical talent, marching around the family home banging a drum and whistling "Auld Lang Syne."[38] Foster's musical education began by eavesdropping on his sisters' lessons, and by age ten he was a capable performer on the flageolet (a small woodwind) and piano. He soaked up a variety of musical influences, ranging from orchestrated music to the "Jim Crow" performances of Thomas Dartmouth "Daddy" Rice, whose blackface minstrel shows Foster experienced in Pittsburgh and as a riverboat traveling companion to his mother on visits down the Ohio River to see friends in Cincinnati, Louisville, and points between.

Foster was especially close to his older brother Morrison, and the two attended a variety of cultural events. In early 1843, they went to hear Henry Russell, the famous ballad singer and composer of "The Old Arm Chair," a performance that left a lasting impression on Stephen, inspiring his first efforts as a songwriter.[39] Russell's favorite American writer was George P. Morris, the author of numerous poems including "Open Thy Lattice, Love."[40] After hearing Russell in concert, sixteen-year-old Stephen set "Lattice" to a lilting romantic melody, and sent the results to music publisher George Willig in Philadelphia, probably paying for the privilege of publication. Willig issued a two-page sheet, without title page, misspelling the writer's name as "L. C. Foster." In this inauspicious fashion Stephen Foster debuted as a published songwriter (coincidentally, at about the same time George Reed, owner of the copyright in Russell's arrangement of "The Old Arm Chair," was proceeding to trial against Samuel Carusi). Foster's art, and the law that would enhance its commercial value, were coming of age together.

At the age of twenty in 1846, Foster moved to Cincinnati, acting as bookkeeper for Irwin & Foster, his brother Dunning's partnership with Archibald Irwin, Jr., a brokerage of sorts that arranged for shipping of cotton and other goods on the Ohio River.[41] Stephen was a meticulous record keeper, and the position suited him well. The bustling city also provided plenty of exposure to the melting pot of musical influences that traveled the river along with the hard goods of traditional com-

---

religion, and against the vices of alcohol and sins of slavery. The Hutchinsons struck a broad enough nerve to succeed as uniquely "American" antebellum performers, and after adopting a more overt abolitionist stance in 1843, went on to achieve phenomenal success as performers (and songwriters) in the 1840s and 1850s. Deeply researched and tautly written, Scott Gac's SINGING FOR FREEDOM: THE HUTCHINSON FAMILY SINGERS AND THE NINETEENTH-CENTURY CULTURE OF REFORM (2007) tells the Hutchinsons' story in fine style.

38. JOHN TASKER HOWARD, STEPHEN FOSTER: AMERICA'S TROUBADOUR 368 (1934).

39. *Id.* at 115.

40. SANJEK, *supra* note 2, at 73.

41. EMERSON, *supra* note 27, at 111–12.

merce. Before long, Foster struck up a relationship with William C. Peters, a music publisher with locations in Cincinnati and Louisville. Foster began turning out a steady stream of songs, including the successful "Uncle Ned," and in 1848 his first runaway hit, a "glorious bit of nonsense"[42] that would become one of the most performed and (later) recorded songs in the entire American repertoire, "Oh! Susanna." Foster's relationship with Peters was not exclusive, and Foster had given out numerous manuscript copies of the song to minstrel performers and others. As a result, between 1848 and 1851 no fewer than twenty-one versions of "Oh! Susanna" were entered for copyright by an array of purported owners, including many of the leading publishers of the day—William Peters, William Millet (who had enforced his copyright in "The Cot Beneath the Hill" in the first reported court decision addressing musical compositions), Oliver Ditson, and C. Holt. Foster received payments from some, but certainly not all of the versions that flooded the market. His first hit served as an object lesson against the practice of distributing too many manuscripts before publication.

On the other hand, the distributed manuscripts served as effective promotion, and soon the highly infectious "Oh! Susanna" appeared in the repertoire of virtually every traveling minstrel show. Written in dialect and including lyrics that would be deemed racist and offensive today, the song was tailored to blackface minstrel performers, and was soon embraced by high- and low-brow audiences alike. But what took the song to unprecedented levels was its association with the California gold rush. In January 1848, gold was discovered at Sutter's Mill, followed by the treaty with Mexico that ceded California and New Mexico to the United States. The rush was on, and by the following year the trails were packed with westward travelers with a gleam in their eye and a single song in the heart, as "Oh! Susanna" became the unofficial anthem of the forty-niners, a connection still firmly in place as late as 1923, when the song was featured as the theme of *The Covered Wagon*, Paramount studios' filmed version of the pioneer movement, heralded as the first truly epic Western film. And the pioneer band sang,

> It rained all night the day I left;
> The weather it was dry,
> The sun so hot I froze to death;
> Susanna, don't you cry.
>
> Oh! Susanna, don't you cry for me,
> For I've come from Alabama wid—
> My banjo on my knee.[43]

---

42. Howard, *supra* note 38, at 144.

43. The film's promotional program reprints Foster's original lyrics, including the shocking second verse: "I jumped aboard de telegraph, and trabeled down de ribber; de 'lectric fluid magnified, and killed five hundred nigga."

In early 1849, Foster reached out to additional publishers. He was not yet an established writer, but the novelty of "Oh! Susanna" was ringing in the ears of every American, and making its way around the world, from Germany to as far away as the wandering minstrel singing in the streets of New Delhi—exotic places Stephen himself would never visit.[44] Foster interested a leading New York publisher, Firth, Pond & Company, in his work, selling them two songs in 1849, in return for payment in the form of fifty copies of each for the author to sell on his own account.[45] Things went smoothly, and later in the year Foster entered into the first of several agreements with Firth, under a more favorable two-cent royalty arrangement. At about the same time, Stephen made a similar agreement with F.D. Benteen of Baltimore. With these contracts in hand, Foster left Cincinnati and returned home to Pittsburgh, a capable young songwriter on the verge of true success. His confidence and potential must have made him a more attractive bachelor, and after a short courtship he married Jane McDowell on July 24, 1850. Almost nine months later, a daughter Marion was born on April 18, 1851, the couple's only child.

Initially, the pressures of a young family motivated Stephen further, and he entered a period of great productivity. During the first half of 1850 he produced eleven songs, including "Camptown Races" (published originally in dialect as "Gwine to Run All Night"), another rollicking novelty along the lines of "Oh! Susanna," wisely promoted through the live performances of E.P Christy, the composer, singer, and impresario whose name became synonymous with minstrel shows. Christy's Minstrels performed in blackface, an excellent fit for Foster's tunes, many of which were written in Negro dialect and positioned as "plantation songs." The following year, the same combination of a dialect song written for and promoted through Christy made "Old Folks at Home (Swanee River)" the third massive hit of Foster's burgeoning career, and another of America's best known melodies.

By September 1852 Firth, Pond & Co. boasted that "Old Folks at Home" was "one of the most successful songs that has ever appeared in any country," sales having reached 40,000 copies. Firth offered some perspective on these sales figures in a paid advertisement in *The Musical World*: "When the reader takes into consideration the fact, that, fully one half of all the sheet music published proves to be a total failure—that three thousand copies of an instrumental piece and five thousand copies of a song, is considered a *great sale*, he can form some idea of the surpassing popularity of the 'Old Folks at Home.'" Two years later Firth updated the numbers, claiming sales of more than 130,000 copies of "Old Folks at Home," plus 90,000 of "My Old Kentucky Home," 74,000 of another dialect tune, "Massa's In the Cold Ground," and 48,000 for "Old Dog Tray," the latter in less than six months.[46]

---

44. Howard, *supra* note 38, at 144–45.
45. *Id.* at 153.
46. *Id.* at 207.

These regular and sustained successes led to renewed contract negotiations with Firth, Pond & Co. In May 1853, the parties signed an agreement that provided increased royalties for Foster, in return for exclusivity. The arrangement did not last: In December 1854 another agreement was reached, eliminating Firth's exclusivity and giving Foster the most favorable terms of his career—10 percent (2.5 cents) on most previously published songs, and all future compositions published through Firth, with the publisher to pay for (and not recoup) all expenses associated with bringing the sheets to market. Firth was also obligated to pursue infringers, splitting any proceeds with Foster. In return, the contract allowed the publisher to register copyrights in its own name, and provided explicitly that Firth was to have the "sole and exclusive right of proprietorship over the music published according to this contract."[47] The agreement marked the height of Foster's career, reflecting terms available only to the most successful writers.

Foster apparently enjoyed working with Firth, Pond & Co., for, despite their nonexclusive arrangement, he gave Firth all but one of his songs penned during the contract period. The exception was the beautiful, yet haunting, "Comrades, Fill No Glass for Me," published through Miller & Beacham of Baltimore on November 23, 1855. "Comrades" was a temperance song, demonstrating Foster's awareness of the dangers of alcohol. By this time, he had learned of such dangers firsthand, having separated from his wife and family for nearly a full year (before reuniting), a rift caused, at least in part, by Stephen's drinking. Foster biographer John Tasker Howard chose to believe that Stephen was not yet a confirmed alcoholic in 1855, and simply wrote a tune "he knew would strike a chord in the so-called temperance circles."[48] A more objective conclusion is that the song was Foster's public acknowledgement of a demon he could not control, the title asking his friends ("boon companions") to refrain from serving him, though he was too often serving himself.

There is little doubt that alcohol began to dominate Foster's life by 1855, putting a strain on family relations as well as finances, leading to questionable decisions concerning his valuable copyrights.[49] For several years, a steady stream of royalties had provided ample income, but Foster was spending even more, often taking advances against anticipated quarterly earnings. In January 1857, he made a dramatic move by taking stock of his previously published songs, determining their earnings to date, then bundling and selling his future royalties to Firth, Pond & Co. for a discount to their estimated value. The transaction netted Foster $1,872.28.[50] He then went through the same process with F.D. Benteen publishers, netting an additional $200 for the future value of the sixteen songs previously published with them. Foster appears to have been prudent with the proceeds, paying off bills and

---

47. *Id.* at 244–50.
48. *Id.* at 253.
49. *See* EMERSON, *supra* note 27, at 203–04.
50. HOWARD, *supra* note 38, at 270.

supporting his family. But his marriage was strained, and by the middle of the year Stephen and Jane had separated again.

In February 1858, Foster negotiated another deal with Firth, Pond & Co. His leverage had diminished, and though he maintained a royalty rate of 10 percent on future songs, Firth demanded, and received, exclusivity. In addition, there were safeguards intended to limit advances, but Foster still managed to get himself in debt to Firth, his advances far outweighing royalties from songs actually delivered. By early 1860, the situation had become dire, and Foster saw another royalty bundling and sale as his only option. On August 9, 1860, he again assigned to Firth all his future interest in the sixteen songs published under the existing contract for $100 each. Soon thereafter, Foster moved to New York, closer to his regular source of income, but without his family and with his drinking problem growing more extreme. By this time, Foster had earned a little more than $15,000 as a professional songwriter, an average of nearly $1,400 annually since 1849. He had little to show for it.

Virtually all personal and direct accounts of Foster's activities ceased after his move to New York, and rumor and myth cloud his final years. He clearly was not well-suited to big city life, which enabled his drinking and caused his health to deteriorate steadily. Some claim to have observed Foster writing and selling songs on demand for "paltry sums," to satisfy an "insatiable appetite for liquor."[51] As the Civil War raged, Foster hunkered down with a bottle in his Manhattan cocoon, writing music. If nothing else, he was prolific in his final years, with more than half of his published songs written between 1860 and 1864. Few were worth more than the small sums paid for them, but there were striking exceptions, including one more American classic, "Beautiful Dreamer," written in the final period of his life and copyrighted posthumously by William A. Pond & Co. (a successor to Firth) shortly after Foster's death on January 13, 1864. Foster had suffered a fall in his modest room in the Bowery, gashing his neck and bruising his head. His first friends on the scene plied him with alcohol, "which seemed to help him a lot," and got him to Bellevue hospital for professional treatment.[52] But it was too late. Life had caught up with Stephen Foster at the age of 37.

On hearing the news, brother Morrison and widow Jane hurried to New York. Morrison paid $1.25 for Stephen's medical care and to retrieve his belongings—a coat, pants, vest, hat, shoes, overcoat, and a small leather purse containing thirty-eight cents and a piece of scrap paper bearing five handwritten words, "Dear friends and gentle hearts," perhaps the last song fragment that appeared in the mind of Stephen Foster.

Having bundled and sold his royalty streams, Foster died without any ongoing interest in his songs, so he had nothing to will to Jane and daughter Marion. But legal issues arose when Foster's copyrights came up for renewal in succeeding years,

---

51. *Id.* at 314.
52. *Id.* at 342.

bringing an unexpected windfall to his heirs. Many of Foster's copyrights had changed hands due to publisher buyouts and mergers. Most significantly, Firth, Pond & Co. dissolved in 1863, with Stephen's works going to its successors, Firth, Son & Company and William A. Pond & Company.[53] Firth remained in business for only a short time before selling out to the growing publishing powerhouse, Boston's Oliver Ditson & Company. Thus, when Foster's copyrights approached the end of their initial term, Ditson and Pond controlled many of the songs. Among those controlled by Ditson was "Old Folks at Home," for which the authorship was less than clear, due to the publication of the work originally in association with blackface performer E.P. Christy, who was credited as the writer in early editions. (Such arrangements were not unusual, since public performances were acknowledged as the best, if not the only, kind of promotion for stimulating sales of sheet music. Foster and his publishers had developed relationships with E.P. Christy and others for precisely this reason.)

Foster's songs had become popular through widespread performances, but even hit songs faded over time. There was no "oldies" radio format to keep a song alive and in front of new generations of buyers. When live performances waned, sales did too. And so it was with Foster's songs, even the mega-hits that had brought him fame and fortune. As it happened, however, fortune was not done smiling on the songs of Stephen Foster.

In the fall of 1870, Swedish prima donna Christine Nilsson made her first trip to America, giving regular concerts for the next two years, returning in 1873–1874, and in succeeding years until her retirement in 1888. As reported in the music trades, Nelson heard "Old Folks at Home" soon after her arrival in America. Struck by the "plaintive melody and touching words," she learned and began performing the song in her concerts, giving "renewed interest" to a song published nearly twenty years earlier, when Nilsson was just eight years old.[54] Oliver Ditson capitalized immediately, issuing a special edition of the sheet, featuring a portrait of the singer. Its economic interest peaked by the resurgence in sales, Ditson looked more closely at the copyright term and saw an opportunity for renewal income. Thus, in the spring of 1879, Ditson corresponded with Foster's widow, Jane (by then remarried, to Matthew Wiley), seeking to clarify ownership of "Old Folks" (even the Nilsson reissue claimed authorship by E.P. Christy). The publisher offered participation of three cents per copy (more than Foster himself had ever received) should she be willing and able to assist with copyright renewal.[55]

Copyrights of the day were valid for twenty-eight years, but could be renewed for another fourteen by the author or his heirs. With "Old Folks At Home" set to expire in July 1879, Ditson offered Jane the royalty or a flat upfront payment of $100.

---

53. *Id.* at 350.
54. *Id.* at 349–50.
55. *Id.* at 350–51.

She wisely turned the letter over to Morrison, who responded by confirming his brother's authorship of "Old Folks," and by pointing out that "the copy rights of a number of his best songs run out next year, and each year for several years yet."[56] On behalf of Jane and Marion (then married to Walter Welsh), he offered to renew the copyrights and allow Ditson to continue publishing the titles it held, in return for an advance of $100 against a royalty of three cents per sheet. Ditson readily agreed.[57] Morrison followed the same course with William A. Pond & Company, which after significant haggling agreed to the same terms of $100 in advance against a three-cent royalty, in return for renewal rights in more than twenty compositions they controlled, including "My Old Kentucky Home" and "Hard Times Come Again No More." It gave Morrison great pleasure to administer his brother's renewed copyrights on behalf of Jane and Marion, which he did until the final $.45 cents of royalty receipts trickled in from sales of "Gentle Annie" in 1898, when the last of the renewal terms expired. By this time, the songs had generated more than $4,000 for Stephen's heirs.[58]

The structure of early American music copyright emerges in the career and legacy of Stephen Foster. Foster's genius was embodied in valuable copyrights, which, although owned by publishers, provided a steady stream of royalty revenue for the author, predictable income that served as the basis for creative (if ill-advised) financing in the form of bundling and selling future earnings, an early form of securitization. Although Foster sold his future interests for immediate cash, the law did protect longer-term interests by allowing copyright renewals only by the author or his heirs. Not everything he penned was renewed: the wheat was separated from the chaff of his songwriting after a song's initial term of twenty-eight years. Many of his works, however, had value well beyond their day. Accordingly, publishers came calling at renewal time, and Foster's heirs were rewarded for their participation. By the end of the century, the balance of Stephen Foster's incredible oeuvre fell into the public domain, where the songs continue to resonate today, one of the greatest contributions to American popular culture.

---

56. *Id.* at 352.
57. *Id.*
58. *Id.* at 354–55.

5. High Tech Hellion
—John McTammany's Organette

On January 27, 1888, Judge LeBaron Bradford Colt[59] of the Circuit Court for the District of Massachusetts rendered a brief opinion in *Kennedy v. McTammany*,[60] dismissing the plaintiff's claim that his copyrighted musical composition, "Cradle's Empty, Baby's Gone," was infringed by the manufacture of "perforated papers [rolls] which, when used in organettes, produce the same music." The brevity of the opinion belied the extent of the music business interests at stake.

John McTammany, Jr. was born in Scotland in 1845, and came to the United States as a teen, just in time to serve with the Union forces in the Civil War. After hostilities subsided, he spent time teaching music and tinkering with various innovations before finding his focus as an inventor of mechanical music machines, beginning with organettes and player reed organs, precursors to the player piano. McTammany's organette was a small, hand-cranked organ of sorts, with no keyboard. In essence, it was a glorified music box, but with key differences as far as the use of music was concerned.

Music box technology had been around for centuries, the typical mechanism consisting of a simple metal coil that a key could wind tightly. When released, the coil unwound, causing a drum to spin slowly. Depending on the style, the drum might be visible or hidden, in either case having Braille-like, protruding metal nibs that plucked the teeth of a metal comb, yielding a musical note as the narrow metal bands vibrated back into position. In this way a music box played back the single tune that had been built into the mechanism itself—usually a shortened version of a lullaby or classical work that accompanied a spinning ballerina or other appropriate scene. More sophisticated "disc" music boxes came equipped with several different discs that, with some degree of care, a user could switch out, yielding different songs. No consumer market existed for the discs themselves; boxes were promoted for their craftsmanship and mechanical sophistication, not music content.

The same was true of barrel organs—mechanical instruments known at least as early as the sixteenth century in Europe, using a barrel-and-pin mechanism that, when turned by a crank or a system of weights and pulleys, activated a set of organ pipes or metal tongues. A barrel might be up to several feet in length, encoded with pins representing the notes of one or more (up to as many as twenty) tunes. Barrel organs were used most commonly as musical accompaniment to hymn and psalm singing in church settings. They later served secular audiences as well, sometimes

---

59. Judge Colt was the nephew of Samuel Colt, the famous maker of firearms, including the "Colt 45."
60. Kennedy v. McTammany, 33 F. 584; 1888 U.S. App. LEXIS (Circuit Court, D. Mass. 1888).

outside vaudeville theaters, as a means of attracting the public's attention. They were not consumer products, however, and as with music boxes, musical compositions were "hard-coded" onto the barrel, integrated into the hardware itself. A user could change barrels to introduce new songs, but only with significant effort. In essence, the music was an integral component of the mechanical playback device.

With the introduction of the organette, however, music was suddenly separated from the playback device, both conceptually and practically. In contrast to organ barrels or metal music box drums, perforated paper music rolls were portable and easily switched, giving the user a choice of tunes for playing, enabling a "deejay"-like musical environment in which small groups could enjoy a series of songs. Moreover, like sheets, rolls were made of inexpensive paper, raising the prospects of mass production and sale to a broad consumer audience. The organette represented the beginning of the dichotomy between music hardware (the organette itself) and software (the roll)—a consumer product not only in the playback mechanism, but also, separately, in the *music* to be played via the device.

Organette rolls represented a brand new music format, standing in stark and high-tech contrast to the traditional sheet. Rolls held music, but the "notes" were perforations that could be "read" only by machines, not the human eye. Even more dramatically, by the use of organettes and rolls, songs could be rendered mechanically, without a musician in the room! Miraculously, and thanks in large part to John McTammany, *anyone* could "play music" with the simple turn of a crank.

According to the Pianola Institute, "If anyone can be hailed as the 'father' of perforated music, then it is probably John McTammany, Jr., who seems to have been the first to have invented practical musical instruments that were played pneumatically with the aid of paper rolls."[61] After securing numerous patents for various aspects of his device, McTammany began marketing his organettes in Cambridge, Massachusetts, in the late 1870s. McTammany's advertising focused on the inventor's technical prowess, claiming that the proprietor was "the greatest musical inventor of any age," "the first person in the world to make and exhibit a reed instrument operated by perforated paper." It went on, deriding competitors as thieving second-comers: "His instruments are superior to every other make, and contain features which others cannot produce, while all others contain imitations and thefts of his rights." The "No. 1" model, selling for $10, featured an ebony case and gold trim, while, for an additional $4, the "No. 2" also included an attachment for easily rewinding music rolls following playback. The feature that caught the watchful and wary eye of the music publishing community went to the musical content. McTammany included six music rolls with the purchase of either model, and offered additional compositions for 20 to 50 cents apiece. Knowing that McTammany had not requested licenses for this purpose, music publishers regarded his incorporation of their musical compositions into organette rolls as blatant acts of copyright infringement.

---

61. www.pianola.org.

Notable among concerned publishers was Boston's Oliver Ditson & Co., owner of the copyright in "Cradle's Empty, Baby's Gone," a parlor song written by Harry Kennedy in 1880, one of the many tunes McTammany used to supply rolls for his organettes. Ditson sued for infringement, marking the music industry's first attempt to enforce its copyrights against a form of "copying" enabled by advancing technology, the organette. As posed by the court, the "sole question in issue [was] whether these perforated sheets of papers are an infringement of copyrighted sheet music." Judge Colt tipped his hand by observing early in his opinion that "[t]o the ordinary mind it is certainly a difficult thing to consider these strips of paper as sheet music. There is no clef, or bars, or lines, or spaces, or other marks which are found in common printed music, but only plain strips of paper with rows of holes or perforations." Having stated the obvious, the court's conclusion seemed inevitable: "I cannot convince myself that these perforated strips of paper are sheet music, within the meaning of the copyright law."

The plaintiffs had argued "forcibly" that rolls were essentially the same as sheet music, which could consist of musical notation rendered in "different characters or methods," of which rolls were just another example. The court, however, looked to the "purpose" of the finished object in rejecting the analogy. Rolls "are not designed to be used for such purposes as sheet music," Judge Colt concluded. Rather, "they are a mechanical invention made for the sole purpose of performing tunes mechanically upon a musical instrument . . . Their use resembles more nearly the barrel of a hand organ or music box."

It is hard to argue with the court's logic, but the analysis seems based on the wrong premise. The boxes did not copy "sheet music," as opposed to a "musical composition" protected by statute. Judge Colt recognized that a song was an "intellectual production," but took a narrow and circumscribed view of its metaphysical nature, refusing to see that it could be fixed or rendered in different ways, "played back" by human musicians in one instance, or by a mechanical device in another. In either case, it was the same "musical composition." As a case of first impression, the judge noted that he had not found any "decided cases which, directly or by analogy, support the position of the plaintiffs." The determining fact seemed to rest on the nature of the playback device: If human, an infringement had occurred; if mechanical, there had been no unlawful copying.

The result could not have come as a surprise to Oliver Ditson & Co. or the other music publishers who had anxiously awaited the outcome. After all, the 1831 statute protecting "musical compositions" delineated an author's rights narrowly, as the "sole right and liberty of printing, reprinting, publishing and vending" the copyrighted work. The terminology addressed the sheet music business; it was a stretch to argue that the statutory language applied to the manufacture of organette rolls, the components of a mechanical device. Indeed, by the time of the decision in *Kennedy*, copyright protection for musical compositions had been on the books for nearly sixty years. During that time, it had served songwriters and publishers well, protecting against the printing of illicit sheets by willful copyists, and even by well-meaning, innocent infringers such as Samuel Carusi and before him, William Millet, publisher of the *Ladies' Journal.* Suddenly, amidst the Industrial Revolution, at the dawn of the age of mechanically reproduced music, the law seemed archaic and out of step. Copyright owners were powerless to prevent the wholesale, unrestricted copying of their compositions for use in connection with the latest high-tech gadgetry, organettes. The winds of technology were swirling, and the law was falling behind. For copyright owners, things would get a whole lot worse before they got better.

6. "After the Ball"

In 1893, Chicago mounted its first World's Fair—the Columbian Exposition—a gargantuan production celebrating the 400th anniversary of Columbus' discovery of America. The fair also announced Chicago's Phoenix-like rise from the ashes of its Great Fire of 1871, to become not only the gateway to the American West, but one of the premier cities of the world.[62] The fair represented the nation's coming of age as well. Having settled the land within its own geographic borders, the United States now opened its arms to the world.[63] The Exposition proved a huge success, but there were elements of the production that exposed the city's (and country's) split personality, an inferiority complex relative to the European guests that flocked to Chicago to see what America's upstart city could offer. First there were the fairgrounds themselves, a gleaming "White City" built in classical European style, fully electrified and lighted at night like a beacon on the shore of Lake Michigan. Just north of the grounds lay the real Chicago, the gritty, dirty urban center of a city coming to terms with the Industrial Revolution.

The dualities extended to the Exposition's cultural and entertainment offerings. For instance, William F. "Buffalo Bill" Cody, one of the most popular and successful showmen of the era, having toured the U.S. and in Europe (performing for the Queen of England) telling the uniquely American story of the conquering and settlement of the West, was deemed too "low-brow" by fair organizers, and excluded from the official grounds. Cody's response was to stage his Wild West extravaganza on a rented plot adjacent the fairgrounds, where he proceeded to sell more than three million tickets during the course of the Exposition, netting more than $1 million in profit, still one of the most profitable runs in live entertainment

---

62. For a wonderfully readable narrative of Chicago's rise in the nineteenth century, *see* WILLIAM CRONON'S NATURE'S METROPOLIS (1991).

63. Indeed, in presenting his famous paper, *The Significance of the Frontier in American History*, at the historical congress convened in connection with the Columbian Exposition, University of Wisconsin historian Frederick Jackson Turner reflected on the "closing" of the American frontier.

history. Many who witnessed Cody's spectacle left with the impression that they had seen the fair, never making it onto the official grounds.[64] Popular (as in the "people's") entertainment won the hearts and dollars of fair visitors.

A similar dichotomy played itself out with regard to music. As one observer put it, "At issue throughout the duration of the fair was the clash between advocates of the so-designated artistic programs presented by the Exposition Orchestra and proponents of the popular programs given by concert bands."[65]

Theodore Thomas, the conductor recruited from New York to establish the Chicago Symphony Orchestra in 1891, oversaw the fair's music programs. He spared no expense in organizing the 150-piece Exposition Orchestra, which presented its programs primarily in the Music Hall, a 2,500-seat pavilion located at the north end of the Peristyle, part of the grand structure fronting on Lake Michigan that welcomed visitors to the Exposition. The Peristyle featured forty-eight Corinthian columns, each three stories high and representing every state and territory in the nation, along with a double row of rooftop statues extending from the Columbian Arch at the center. The Music Hall was a place for serious music, where, for an additional one dollar, patrons could hear performances of classical repertoire, from Handel's "Messiah" to Beethoven's "Ninth Symphony" and Gounod's "Redemption." But the public was not particularly interested. In the first months of the fair, only about one-fourth of 1 percent of patrons paid to hear the classical concerts. Soon they were discontinued, and even the free concerts that took their place were thinly attended. Before the fair officially ended, the classical concerts were abandoned altogether and the orchestra dismissed.[66]

At the other end of the musical spectrum was the popular repertoire, programs featuring everything from Colonial American folk tunes to current sentimental ballads, parlor songs, and marches performed by the concert bands that played in bandstands erected in the public areas, and along the vast Midway Plaisance. They mingled with the exotic acts organized by music promoter (and future U.S. congressman) Sol Bloom, including musicians from around the world—Algeria, Tunis, Egypt, Turkey, Persia, China, Java, Samoa, and Africa. (Indeed, some of the first cylinder recordings of "world" musicians were made at the fair.)

The concert bands curried great favor among fairgoers, particular that of John Philip Sousa, whose fifty-piece band played daily on the Midway and elsewhere during the first months of the fair. Sousa was unique in his ability to bridge the gap between classical and popular music making (he was engaged by Theodore Thomas to play concerts at the Music Hall as well), and because of this he was well-positioned

---

64. Louis S. Warren, Buffalo Bill's America: William Cody and the Wild West Show 419 (2005).

65. Sandy R. Mazzola, *Bands and Orchestras at the World's Columbian Exposition*, American Music 407–24 (Winter 1986).

66. *Id.* at 413.

to participate in promoting what became the biggest popular music success of the nineteenth century.

John Philip Sousa was born in 1854 and studied music and violin as a youth, before joining the U.S. Marine Band on June 9, 1868. He registered the copyrights in his early compositions during his second enlistment in 1873, before the age of twenty. Following an honorable discharge in 1874, Sousa continued touring the country as a music director and bandleader, then came to prominence as conductor of "The President's Own" (the U.S. Marine Band) under presidents Hayes, Garfield, Arthur, and Cleveland between 1880 and 1892.

On the heels of another honorable discharge, Sousa was invited to perform with his civilian band at dedication ceremonies for the Columbian Exposition buildings on October 21, 1892. He stayed on in Chicago and performed in the early months of the fair, where he catered to the mainstream musical tastes of those who crowded his Midway performances, playing his Sousa Band renditions of the popular songs of the day. Stuffier bandleaders looked down their noses at popular songs, claiming it was "prostituting the sacred art of music to play such rot."[67] But Sousa found it futile to deny popular taste, and "foolish to try to play above the heads of one's listeners. The audience at big outdoor concerts is composed of the masses and they love light and pretty tunes that have a dash to them." By May 1893 newspapers were reporting that Sousa's band "has met with more popular favor than [Theodore] Thomas' orchestra."[68]

Charles K. Harris, a songwriter from nearby Milwaukee, approached Sousa at the Columbian Exposition, his newest composition in hand, "After the Ball," which was enjoying an initial surge of popularity. With Sousa's backing, the song was poised to become the sales success of the century.

Born in 1867 in Poughkeepsie, New York, Harris had grown up in Saginaw, Michigan, where he was self-taught on the banjo after receiving a used instrument from performer Billy Carter as he passed through town. Harris never learned to read music, always relying on hired musicians to write down his melodies in notation, and to arrange the tunes to his vast supply of tear-jerking, sentimental lyrics. At age fourteen, Harris' family of twelve moved to Milwaukee, where his musical interests broadened, and he began teaching banjo and performing at local events for what he considered "the munificent sum of five dollars a night."[69] In an initial attempt at songwriting, Harris and a colleague, Charles Horwitz, wrote "Since Maggie Learned to Skate," and persuaded the actor and singer Nat Goodwin to incorporate it into the show in which he was starring, *The Skating Rink*. The song proved a moderate success, and though Harris never saw any royalties, his writing

---

67. *Id.* at 416.

68. *Id.* at 408.

69. CHARLES K. HARRIS, AFTER THE BALL: FORTY YEARS OF MELODY 8–10 (1926). *See also* http://parlorsongs.com/bios/ckharris/ckharris.php.

partner may well have. Publisher T.B. Harms issued the sheet music in 1885, attributing sole authorship to Horwitz.

Harris was undaunted, and continued to write a steady stream of what he called "heart-story" and "home-loving" ballads, always with a fitting moral message. His initial foray into songwriting also taught him a valuable lesson in the promotional power of public performance. Harris "knew that music publishers would create a demand for their numbers by having prominent performers of the stage sing them; and once a song registered with the public, it would invariably seek out the first music store and purchase copies. Therein," he concluded, "lay the secret."[70]

Harris focused on writing songs for specific performers and shows, in time gaining an introduction to David Henderson, manager of the Chicago Opera House and producer of popular shows including *Ali Baba and the Forty Thieves*, featuring the comedian Eddie Foy. According to Harris, his initial songs for Foy and others were so well-received that Henderson footed the bill for a songwriting residency at the Palmer House Hotel, Chicago's finest of the day, sending Harris home to Milwaukee with an envelope stuffed with $200 in cash.[71] At eighteen, he was on his way as a songwriter, understanding that "the real start at popularizing a song is to sell it to the performers. If it strikes their fancy, they will surely sing it for the public. Common sense tells one that the bigger the reputation and ability of the performer whose assistance the author and composer enlist, the more chances of its success in catching the public's favor."[72] Harris targeted performers with obsessive single-mindedness, making speculative trips by steamer down to Chicago, seeking introductions to performers and their managers. He believed that a "new song must be sung, played, hummed and drummed into the ears of the public, not in one city alone, but in every city, town, and village, before it ever becomes popular."[73] In the days before radio, traveling performers were the only means of reaching a regional or national audience. Currying their favor was critical to a songwriter's prospects for success.

Despite the debacle with "Since Maggie Learned to Skate," Harris continued to work with Charles Horwitz, who agreed to include a new Harris composition, "Hello, Central, Hello!" in Horwitz's performances with the Ray L. Royce Comedy Company. Harris would engrave the plates and print the sheets, which Horwitz would purchase for sale on the road at $10 per hundred. Harris scraped together the $45 necessary to pay upfront costs, and sent the first hundred to Horwitz in Kansas City. He was a publisher. At the same time, he continued his attempts to publish his songs through others, but royalties were middling, and he soon concluded that, for him, acting as his own publisher would be the only road to success. Lacking the capital to start a business on his own, he brought in two partners

---

70. HARRIS, *supra* note 69, at 15–16.
71. *Id.* at 35.
72. *Id.* at 36.
73. *Id.* at 40.

who contributed $500 in capital to found Charles K. Harris & Co. in 1891. For his part, Harris agreed to contribute all the songs he wrote during the first year, and act as operations manager. The three would split profits equally.

On New Year's Day, 1892, Harris called a company meeting. During their first year in business, the company had generated profits of $1,000 per partner, but Harris, always an independent, felt he was doing more work than his passive investors. He proposed a long-term arrangement, on the condition that the others work full-time for the business, as he was. The partners balked, and eventually agreed to sell their interests to Harris, who became and continued as the sole owner of his namesake business until 1924.

Later in 1892, Harris attended a gala ball in Chicago, an event that changed his personal and professional lives forever. Across the room, he spied and fell in love at first sight with Cora Lerhberg, who soon became his wife. Amidst their giddy affection, they noticed a less fortunate couple, engaged in a lover's quarrel, inspiring Harris to reflect on the fact that "Many a heart is aching after the ball." Around this line, Harris built a sentimental ballad about love going unrequited due to mistaken identity. The lyrics and melody for "After the Ball" were composed in less than an hour's time, and included a "goodly dose of sentiments," the kind he "purposely injected" in all his songs.[74] As always, Harris paid ($10 in this case) to have the music arranged, then printed promotional, or "professional" copies and, thinking he had a winner on his hands, resolved to "tackle every singer, male or female, who appeared in Milwaukee" to persuade them to sing it.

Following several rejections, Annie Whitney of Clark's Burlesquers became the first professional to adopt "After the Ball." Whitney's performance in Providence, Rhode Island, exposed the song to May Irwin, who then caused a "tremendous sensation" singing it in New York.[75] Soon thereafter, Harris attended the opening performance of *A Trip to Chinatown* at Milwaukee's Bijou Theater, in which the renowned baritone James Aldrich Libby was the featured vocalist. Harris would bristle at the characterization, but after gaining an introduction to Libby he arranged a "payola"-type transaction, perhaps one of the first in popular music. Harris claimed to have traded a mere write-up of the show in the *New York Dramatic News*, for which he was a local correspondent, for Libby's agreement to insert "After the Ball" into his performance. Others have reported, more realistically, given Libby's stature, that Harris paid a placement fee of $500 plus a percentage of sales for the singer's cooperation.[76] In either case, Libby's performances pushed the song to its first success. Again according to Harris, following Libby's initial rendition the "entire audience arose and standing, wildly applauded for fully five minutes," compelling Libby to "sing the chorus at least six times over." Immediately

---

74. *Id.* at 62.
75. *Id.* at 69.
76. Sanjek, *supra* note 2, at 321; Crawford, *supra* note 7, at 479.

following the show, Julius Witmark, another upstart publisher with New York's Witmark & Sons, offered Harris $10,000 for complete rights to the song. Harris demurred, thinking that if it was worth that amount to the Witmarks, "it should be worth double that amount to me."[77]

As *A Trip to Chinatown* left Milwaukee to tour in the East, orders for "After the Ball" poured in. Oliver Ditson Company of Boston offered to purchase 75,000 copies for $14,250, sending Harris scrambling to find a printer who could handle such an order. Thereafter, he ordered 100,000 more to keep up with the demand created by the song's continued presence in Libby's performances. Soon he had packed away $75,000 in the company vault, and money continued to pour in at the rate of $1,000 a day.[78]

Still dizzy from the financial impact of his first substantial hit, but looking for even bigger paydays, Harris ventured to the Columbian Exposition in Chicago, where he introduced himself to Sousa, one of the few performers with even more clout than Aldrich Libby. According to Harris, Sousa met him with the good-natured greeting: "Confound you, Harris, the playing of your song has tired me out!"[79] There is no question that the tune was already popular in the spring of 1893, but in all likelihood their meeting was more businesslike, including a gentlemen's deal struck to guarantee further performances. According to one report, Harris claimed to have paid fifty singers between $5 and $50 each per week to include "After the Ball" in their shows, and there is no reason to believe that Sousa was not among them.[80] In any event, Sousa continued to play his arrangement of "After the Ball" to the throngs of fairgoers who crowded the Midway, and those performances sent sales skyrocketing further. "I never failed to give John Philip Sousa due credit for popularizing my song," Harris said, "for there were thousands of visitors to the World's Fair who heard Sousa's band play the song as only he could render it. They would then invariably buy copies in Chicago's music stores to take back home with them, to show the home folks the reigning song success of the World's Fair. That was one of the reasons why the song spread throughout the world as no ballad of its kind had ever done before."[81]

Harris was not known for his modesty; indeed, his autobiography reveals a boastful, gloating, and conceited man, ruminating on his financial successes, determined to prove himself right, and others wrong, in nearly all his dealings. Surprisingly, however, he does not divulge sales numbers for "After the Ball," other than confirming its first 200,000 units. Estimates have varied dramatically, but it is clear that the song was a multimillion-selling national and international hit, whose initial success was compounded by the repeated public performances of a

---

77. HARRIS, *supra* note 69, at 73.

78. *Id.* at 80.

79. *Id.* at 86.

80. DAVID SUISMAN, SELLING SOUNDS: THE COMMERCIAL REVOLUTION IN AMERICAN MUSIC 30 (2009).

81. HARRIS, *supra* note 69, at 87.

signature artist, Sousa, in the venue that provided an unprecedented opportunity for true mass exposure. "After the Ball" represented a cultural inflection point: The coming of age of the American popular song, and its triumph over the higher art that fair organizers had attempted to dictate to the masses. To music publishing entrepreneurs, it revealed even more—the limitless commercial potential of the well-placed, well-promoted pop song.

The incredible success of "After the Ball" allowed Harris to expand his business, and he soon opened a New York office on 28th Street between Broadway and Sixth Avenue, the block that would become known as Tin Pan Alley, the cradle of American popular song publishing. Over the course of his career, Harris remained on the cutting edge of the business, demonstrating genius in the art of promotion. Along the way, he navigated situations in which the value of music, versus the power and value of promotion, were called into question. Recognizing the value of a performer's image, he "conceived the idea of placing photographs of prominent singers on the title pages of my songs." One might conclude that the use of a celebrity likeness was worth paying for, but Harris viewed the photographs as providing "considerable free advertisement" for performers. Even so, he "made a five-year agreement with [James Aldrich Libby] that no other photograph than his should adorn the title page of 'After the Ball.'"[82] Who was advertising for whom? Who should pay for the privilege, and how much?

In many, if not all cases, the performer held the leverage in this equation. Harris himself recalled the early days of Tin Pan Alley, when the song pluggers would converge on singers right in the street, stuffing their pockets with cash and other goodies to gain their attention and keep their loyalties. In time publishers "were paying the singers all kinds of money for singing their compositions," along with orchestra leaders and others associated with the theatrical business, who demanded charitable donations and support from the publishing community. Eventually, Harris recalled, "the business was in a state of chaos. Something had to be done."

That something turned out to be the formation of the Music Publishers' Protective Association in 1914,[83] essentially a cartel of the most influential publishers, whose bylaws imposed a $5,000 fine on any member caught paying performance payola. Harris maintained that the organization eliminated "advertising graft" for a time, but ultimately self-regulation was no match for the creativity of publishers who found ways to make it worth a singer's while to perform their songs.[84] Payment for public performance promotion remained rampant in the Tin Pan Alley of the 1910s and 1920s.

A similar value proposition presented itself in the form of the "illustrated song," a precursor to the modern music video, in which painted canvases and, later, glass

---

82. *Id.* at 127–28.
83. Later, and currently, known as the National Music Publishers Association, NMPA.
84. HARRIS, *supra* note 69, at 212, 295–97.

slides, were used as visual background for live performances, depicting the important scenes of a song. In contrast to purist publishers who did not care for the practice, Harris "found it was the quickest and easiest way to popularize a ballad before the phonograph, player piano, and radio came into existence."[85] What about the advertising potential flowing from the depiction of commercial products in such productions? According to Harris, one owner turned down his request to photograph the interior of a telephone exchange to illustrate a song, but another readily took up the offer and thanked him for the "wonderful advertisement."[86] Similarly, Harris claimed to have declined at least one offer of $10,000 to write a song touting the efficacy of a certain hair restorer.[87] Even in the twilight of his career, in the mid-1920s, Harris confronted the promotional value of the latest technological advance to sweep the country, radio. The "burning question" of the day, he said, was to determine "how the radio will affect composers in the future. Will it help to popularize or will it destroy a song? Only time will tell."[88] Similar questions are "burning" again in the twenty-first century, as performance right legislation is bandied about in Congress, and royalty rates are established for music performed through different broadcast formats, from traditional radio to satellite and Internet deliveries.

7. Century's End

Appropriately, the Chicago World's Fair coincided with the internationalization of U.S. copyright. As if to prepare for the world's visitors, and the revolution in popular music that the fair would propel, in 1891 Congress passed the International Copyright Act.[89] It extended copyright protection to foreign copyright owners who satisfied three conditions. First, U.S. copyright owners had to receive protection in the foreign author's country on "substantially the same basis" as that country's own citizens. Second, the foreign copyright owner had to comply with those copyright formalities, such as notice and deposit, applicable to works by U.S. authors. Finally, foreign authors were required to have their works printed from type set "within the limits of the United States," or "from plates made therefrom, or from negatives, or drawings on stone made within the limits of the United States, or transfers made therefrom." Reciprocity and the "manufacturing clause" together guaranteed equivalent treatment of domestic and foreign authors.[90] "After the

---

85. *Id.* at 181.
86. *Id.* at 193–95.
87. *Id.* at 185–86.
88. *Id.* at 364.
89. Act of Mar. 3, 1891, 51st Cong., 26 Stat. 1106. The law was passed pursuant to the 1886 Berne Convention, which, as it turned out, the United States would not join until 1989.
90. The manufacturing clause was later held inapplicable to musical compositions in Oliver Ditson Co. v. Littleton, 67 F. 905 (1st Cir. 1895).

Ball" was an early beneficiary of the broadened rights: Copyright followed the song around the world, as it was translated into dozens of foreign languages, each yielding another revenue stream for songwriter and publisher Charles K. Harris.

As if to punctuate its influence on the course of popular music, the Columbian Exposition also spawned the first music case to reach the Supreme Court in 1896. In *Press Publishing Company v. Monroe*,[91] Chicago resident Harriett Monroe sued the publisher of *The World* newspaper, alleging violations of her rights in a "lyrical ode" commissioned by a committee of the Columbian Exposition, and licensed by the author for use as part of the opening ceremonies of the fair on October 21, 1892. Ownership of the ode remained with the author, but despite her attempts to prevent the "piratical" schemes of newspapers, *The World* "surreptitiously" obtained and published the work prematurely on September 25. This subjected the author, she claimed, to "shame, mortification and great personal annoyance," not to mention "alleged damages in the sum of $25,000" (twenty-five times the amount of the original commission).

Ms. Monroe dutifully proved her case and the jury returned a verdict of $5,000, which the Circuit Court of Appeals upheld. The newspaper appealed to the Supreme Court, arguing that the plaintiff's copyright was defective, and that the publisher had acted within its rights in obtaining an advance copy of the composition from the Exposition committee. The Supreme Court never addressed the substance of these intriguing questions. Noting that the complaint had been couched in terms of equity, and not under the copyright statute, the court concluded that it did not have jurisdiction to hear the appeal. The Court of Appeals' decision stood as the final word.

Music's first trip to the Supreme Court proved anticlimactic,[92] but even its fleeting presence before the nation's highest tribunal reflected its increased stature as a component of American commerce. In a century's time, music publishing had grown from humble beginnings into a cottage industry, and then a more substantial market that, by century's end, contributed $2 million per year to the American economy. Along the way, nineteenth century publishing enterprises established patterns, structures, and practices still followed in the music business 150 years later. Early on, publishers recognized the commercial advantage of separating songs from their creators and establishing direct ownership of the copyrights in musical compositions. In accordance with what became "standard" contract terms, songwriters transferred copyrights to publishers in return for royalty payments based on retail or per unit pricing of the end product, sheet music. Publishers also required writers

---

91. Press Publishing Company v. Monroe, 164 U.S. 105; 17 S. Ct. 40; 41 L. Ed. 367; 1896 U.S. LEXIS 1846.

92. In terms of "firsts," the *McTammany* decision was in fact appealed to the Supreme Court in 1888, but dismissed without a hearing pursuant to "Rule 10," essentially for want of prosecution. Although it, too, was eventually dismissed on a technicality, lack of jurisdiction, *Press Publishing* was the first "music case" to be considered in substance by the Supreme Court.

to purchase sheets of their own compositions, as a means of defraying printing and promotional expenses, a practice giving way, as time went on, to "advancing" money to artists, to be recouped from future royalties. Moreover, music was a "hit"-driven business from the very beginning. Publishers based their business planning on the assumption that only one in ten songs would break even, and only 2 percent—one in fifty—would bring significant profits, enough to subsidize the vast majority that were destined for commercial failure. In short, music became a commodity, but one with the unique quality of being exploitable for profit—through sales and licensing— over long periods of time, without parting with ownership.

Songwriters relied completely on their publishers to promote, distribute, and account for sales of their compositions. Distribution of the physical product—the sheet—was a key function of publishers, which grew in importance as transportation and mail systems improved, opening the first truly "national markets" for music. In addition, publishers developed preferred marketing and distribution partners (then music teachers, now mass retail merchants) who enjoyed favorable pricing and terms, due to their critically important place in the distribution chain as the final link to the pocketbook of the individual consumer.

Early publishers also showed a knack for finding the most profitable formats for delivering music to consumers, developing and promoting the "sheet" over other forms of printed music. And perhaps their most important marketing lesson was the realization that public performance was the most effective means of advertising and promoting new music. From "Old Folks at Home" to "After the Ball" and beyond, consumers needed to hear music before they could be expected to buy it. Accordingly, publishers sought out and paid dearly for the privilege of having their songs incorporated into the shows and concerts of the taste-making performers of the day.

Interestingly, and although its full impact would not be realized for many years, before the century was out one final revision to the copyright law transformed public performance from a promotional tool into something much more—a copyright owner's dream, a revenue stream in and of itself.

8. Before and after *The Mikado* —The Exclusive Right of Public Performance

On March 20, 1897, a grand dinner was held at New York's famed Delmonico's restaurant (even then in its sixtieth year), celebrating the final copyright revision of the nineteenth century—passage of the Cummings Copyright Bill, by which the owners of "dramatic" and "musical" compositions were granted the exclusive

right of "public performance." The hosts were members of the American Dramatists Club; its president, Bronson Howard, presided over a gathering of 150 distinguished guests, including Abram Jesse "A.J." Dittenhoefer, an active Republican
who had helped elect Abraham Lincoln to the presidency and served as a local
judge during the Civil War, before rising to prominence as one of the nation's leading theater lawyers.[93] As the primary architect of the legislation, Dittenhoefer took
a prominent seat at the guest table, along with various luminaries from theatrical
society. Until well after midnight, they toasted, glad-handed and backslapped,
praising one another's efforts, speaking in reverence to the wisdom of their com-
mander in chief, President Grover Cleveland, who had signed the bill into law, to
Congress, and even the judiciary, whose decisions had pointed out the need for
new legislation.[94] And yet, as historian Zvi Rosen has noted, "despite the celebratory mood and all the toasts given, not one speaker . . . mentioned the fact that the
battle for the right of public performance *for music* had been successful."[95]

Lawmakers had included "musical compositions" in the legislation, but only as
an afterthought. The primary advocates driving the legislative agenda were playwrights and dramatists, who had been agitating for fifty years for copyright changes
that would allow them to enjoin unauthorized performances and productions of
their works. The cauldron from which the victors were served their celebratory
dinner in 1897 had been put on to boil a half-century earlier by Philadelphia congressman Charles Jared Ingersoll.

Ingersoll declared his intention to introduce copyright legislation in 1843.
Copyright recognition for music was still young, having been granted just twelve
years prior, in 1831, the same year Henry Russell's concert performance of "The
Old Arm Chair" inspired a youthful Stephen Foster to take up songwriting. There
can be no doubt that the song's publisher, George Reed, was thrilled to have his
songs included in Russell's repertoire, since name-artist performances were powerful and proven promotional tools. Foster, like other music fans, bought sheets of
the songs he heard in concerts and vaudeville houses, generating profits for publishers and their writers. Among music publishers, there was no cause for concern
about public performances; to the contrary, performances were so highly desirable
that publishers were already engaged in forms of what would later be called "payola," compensating performers to keep songs in their shows and concerts. Music
industry proponents had little incentive to seek an exclusive right of public perfor-

---

93. *See* Abram J. Dittenhoefer, How We Elected Lincoln: Personal Recollections (University of Pennsylvania Press 2005, with a foreword by Kathleen Hall Jamieson) (1916).

94. *Copyright Act Welcomed*, N.Y. Times, Mar. 21, 1897.

95. Zvi S. Rosen, *The Twilight of the Opera Pirates: A Prehistory of the Exclusive Right of Public
Performance for Musical Compositions* 24 Cardozo Arts & Ent. L.J. 1157, 1216 (2007) (emphasis
added). Until publication of Mr. Rosen's excellent narrative history in 2007, the history of performance
rights in music copyright was essentially untold. The article fills the gap in fine style, and is recommended reading for all students of performance rights.

mance with respect to their works; for them, the notion of being paid, as opposed to paying *for* performances, was counterintuitive.

Plays and dramatic pieces (including operas) were different animals altogether. For owners of such works, the primary monetary reward lay in production and presentation (that is, public performance), not in the sales of physical printed product. In essence, the production *was* the product. Naturally, playwrights (and their producer partners) were sensitive to the proliferation of "unauthorized" productions, which by midcentury were becoming more sophisticated and efficient. The trouble for copyright owners was that this activity, while abhorrent to them, was legal. Copyright law provided redress against the illicit copying and printing of written works, but not their dramatization. Thus, dramatists led the charge for recognition of an exclusive right to publicly perform their works. Music interests tagged along for the ride, seemingly oblivious to the boon that the public performance right would deliver them in a half-century's time.

Charles Ingersoll was himself a writer of historical and dramatic works, making him a natural copyright advocate. In early 1844, he introduced a wide-ranging bill intended to benefit copyright owners. The measure wound up in committee, which accepted amendments directed to public performance, specifically providing that the author of any "tragedy, comedy, play, opera, farce, or any other dramatic piece or entertainment, song, or musical composition . . ." would have "the sole liberty of representing, or causing to be represented or performed, at any place or places in the United States, any such production . . . ."[96] As it turned out, the bill was too ambitious; during the course of the committee's deliberations detractors came forward, most notably John Quincy Adams, whose personal dislike for Ingersoll was amplified by their deep political differences. Adams led the opposition that sealed the fate of the first legislative effort to bring an exclusive right of "public performance" into copyright law. The bill died in committee.[97]

Lobbying efforts for a *dramatic* public performance right in particular picked up steam again in the early 1850s.[98] The poet, playwright, and later, diplomat, George Henry Boker published his best-remembered play, *Francesca da Rimini*, in 1853, a tragedy based on Dante's *Inferno*. Boker represented a new breed of American dramatist, intent on earning recognition of playwrights as legitimate professionals, raising their status to that enjoyed by other authors, and in this fashion encouraging the production of original American dramatic works. Recognizing that he could not legally prevent others from staging his plays, even without his authorization, Boker focused a new initiative to gain a public performance right. Boker wisely enlisted the influential New York Senator William Henry Seward to assist

---

96. *See id.* at 1159–67, *citing* H. Journal, 28th Cong., at 30 (1st Sess. 1843); H.R. 9, 28th Cong. (1844) as amended Jan. 18, 1844.

97. Rosen, *supra* note 95, at 1166–67.

98. *See* O. Bracha, *Commentary on the U.S. Copyright Act Amendment 1856, in* Primary Sources on Copyright (1450–1900) (L. Bently & M. Kretschmer eds. 2008), www.copyrighthistory.org.

in his efforts, who introduced legislation to the Senate on April 10, 1856. There was essentially no opposition or serious debate, and the measure passed on July 16. The House followed shortly, and the Copyright Act Amendment of 1856 was signed into law on August 18, granting to the author or owner of any "dramatic composition" not only the sole right to "print and publish" the work, but "also to act perform or represent the same . . . on any stage or public place."

The 1856 Amendment was significant in many respects. As the first recognition of a public performance right in U.S. copyright law, the measure signaled an expanded conception of copyright in general, from the literal and constricted right to "copy" or "reprint," to a broader view of authorship as producing intangible, intellectual works that could be exploited in additional, nonmaterial ways, such as public performance, which should also be recognized and protected as exclusive rights. The amendment also marked the first time minimum "statutory damages" were included in the federal copyright law, providing that violations were to be assessed at "not less than one hundred dollars for the first, and fifty dollars for every subsequent" infringing performance. And yet, despite the groundbreaking aspects of the bill, it lacked one important element—the power to *enjoin* unauthorized performances. The amendment specifically reserved an author's right to pursue "equitable" remedies, such as an injunction, "in any court," but did not itself create a basis for injunctive relief. Thus, its statutory damages provisions notwithstanding, the 1856 Amendment did little to stem the tide of unauthorized dramatic productions, many of which were local or regional, itinerant affairs that found it easy enough to stay one step ahead of infringement litigation.

The recognition of a performance right for dramatic compositions meant little to composers and publishers of music, whose rights were unaffected. But the *dramatists'* efforts to find a means to enjoin unauthorized productions eventually pulled music back into the public performance sphere. Retracing these efforts requires a detour into the doctrine of so-called common, non-statutory law.

Under nineteenth-century law, an author kept all his rights so long as a work remained in "manuscript," or "unpublished" form. Pursuant to "common law" principles, in the prepublication stage, a work of authorship was private property, with an author retaining all rights to dispose of as he saw fit. Following publication, however, statutory law took over, and authors had only those rights specifically delineated in the Copyright Act. For some works, like books, publication was a bright-line event, but for others, notably dramatic and operatic works, the move from manuscript into the public sphere was much less clear. Beginning around 1880, a series of cases involving operettas and their musical scores, many authored by the British creative team of librettist W.S. Gilbert and composer Arthur Sullivan, explored the dichotomy between common law and statutory copyright, and the legal meaning of an author's "publication," all in the context of the authors' efforts to enjoin "piratical" productions of their works.

Gilbert and Sullivan collaborated on fourteen comic operas between 1871 and 1896, their first major success coming in 1879 with the *H.M.S. Pinafore*, followed by *The Pirates of Penzance*, later *Iolanthe* and finally, their most famous and enduring work, *The Mikado, or the Town of Titipu*, first performed in London in 1885. *The Mikado* represented not only a creative zenith, but also the last judicial word on whether the unauthorized performance of a musical drama could be enjoined under U.S. law.

As British citizens working prior to the International Copyright Act in 1891, Gilbert and Sullivan had gone to great lengths to bring *The Mikado* under the ambit of U.S. copyright law. They arranged for a Boston musician, George Tracey, to create and copyright a piano score of the musical, thus having an "American copyright" to use in the attempt to enjoin the U.S. productions that sprouted up as soon as the work became a success in London. In addition, the authors asserted a "common-law right of public representation," based on the theory that the work had not been published in America. One of the more sophisticated unauthorized productions was being developed for the stage by the Duffs, a father-son production team operating in New York. The Duffs had negotiated for the right to present an official production of *The Mikado*, but when negotiations fell through, they decided to move forward alone. Using their manager and producer, Richard D'oyly Carte, as the named plaintiff, Gilbert and Sullivan launched a preemptive litigation attack against the Duffs, seeking a pre-performance injunction that, if successful, could be used as a template for suits against the dozens of other illicit productions popping up across the country.[99]

Despite what the court called an "ingenious" litigation strategy, combining common law and statutory claims, Gilbert and Sullivan's case faced numerous obstacles. The Duffs were ably represented by A.J. Dittenhoefer, who carved away at the claims, arguing successfully that the London performances of *The Mikado* amounted to publication of the work, through which the authors, as foreign citizens, had dedicated their dramatic opera to the public. Thus, no basis for relief existed based on common law principles. That being the case, the authors could seek protection only as owners of the U.S. copyright in the piano score, under the strict language of the statute. Because the piano score was a "musical composition" (not a "dramatic" one), the statute barred unauthorized "printing and publishing," but not public representation or performance.

In denying the motion for an injunction, the court displayed a good deal of judicial discomfort, reluctantly acknowledging that the Duffs' actions were "lawful, however unfair commercially or reprehensible in ethics [the] conduct may be." Noting that the result would be different under British law, the court found "much to be regretted" in the fact "that our statutes do not, like the English statutes, protect the author or proprietor in all the uses to which literary property may

---

99. Carte v. Duff *(the Mikado Case)*, 25 F. 183 (C.C.S.D.N.Y. 1885).

be legitimately applied." Nevertheless, it was "not the judicial function to supply the defect"—that would have to come from Congress.[100]

The legislative fix would not arrive for another twelve years. In the meantime, the best method for combating "piracy" was to compete in the marketplace, exactly as Gilbert and Sullivan did following their legal defeat. The duo mounted their own production of *The Mikado*, which opened in New York just days before the Duffs', with Sir Arthur Sullivan himself leading the orchestra. Before the performance, Sullivan expressed to the opening night crowd his hope that the United States would someday recognize a more complete set of rights for the man "who employs his brains in literature," but "even when that day comes" he would "trust mainly to the unerring instinct of the great public for what is good, right and honest."[101] His trust was well-placed: Gilbert and Sullivan's "legitimate" New York production of *The Mikado* was a runaway success, while the Duffs' "piratical" version was virtually ignored and soon closed.

As we have seen, the next copyright revisions came in 1891, when U.S. law recognized the rights of foreign authors whose countries provided reciprocal protection to Americans. Sir Arthur Sullivan undoubtedly appreciated the effort, but his frustration with the inability to protect his dramatic musical productions in the burgeoning U.S. market remained. The next attempt to fill this gap came from an unlikely source—William M. Treloar, a one-term U.S. representative from Pike County, Missouri. Treloar was a composer, teacher, and music publisher of some renown: At the time of his election in 1894 he was enjoying the brisk sheet sales of his song, "Sleigh Ride," a seasonal favorite that sold more than 250,000 copies between 1890 and 1908.[102] As such, in 1896 he introduced a wide-ranging copyright bill intended to correct what he considered shortcomings in existing law, including, among many other things, the absence of a robust public performance right.

Treloar was naïve enough to believe that his bill could pass on the strength of good ideas alone. The political realities proved quite different. Treloar soon found himself at odds with the powerful Authors and American Publishers Copyright Leagues, the unofficial gatekeepers of copyright law who had ushered in the international copyright legislation in 1891. Dubbed by these interests as the "Wild Missourian," Treloar came under attack for what was sarcastically labeled "Pike County Copyright"—the discriminatory notion that good ideas on such sophisticated matters as copyright policy could come only from experienced and influential politicians from the urban east. Despite initial support from the newly formed Music Publishers Association of the United States, the detractors prevailed by waging a brutal, personal campaign against Treloar, by then a lame duck soon

---

100. *Id.* at 186–87.
101. Rosen, *supra* note 95, at 9.
102. *Id.*

to be on his way back to Pike County. The Treloar bill never made it out of committee.

Even as Treloar faded into obscurity, another piece of copyright legislation, one with considerably more political clout, continued to percolate. The Cummings Copyright Bill had been introduced to the House by New York representative Amos J. Cummings on April 24, 1894, and to the Senate shortly thereafter. The bill's pedigree started with its author—A.J. Dittenhoefer, the prominent jurist and litigator who had successfully defended the Duffs in the landmark litigation over their production of *The Mikado*, confirming that existing copyright law did not provide an adequate basis for enjoining unauthorized stage productions. Now, as the principal author of the Cummings Copyright Bill, Dittenhoefer sought to "supply the [legislative] defect" recognized in the court's opinion.

The bill was crafted to curb "play piracy" by granting the owners of "dramatic or operatic" works the exclusive right to perform those works in public. The law included stiff monetary penalties, up to a year's jail time for the criminal "misdemeanor" of willful infringement, and, importantly, the ability to obtain injunctions against unauthorized performances; these could be issued by any federal court with proper jurisdiction (an essential enforcement tool in the case of traveling shows). Further, injunctions could issue "ex parte"—without prior notice to a defendant, who would then have the unenviable burden of proving that the injunction should be lifted. Through the powerful American Dramatists Club, the country's leading playwrights, producers, managers, and actors lent their immediate support, which carried the bill through an initial period of debate, into the 54th Congress in December 1895, and onto hearing calendars in early 1896.

The House Committee on Patents favorably and unanimously reported the Cummings Bill in March 1896, but with a subtle, yet significant amendment that would change the face of the music business in the years to come. Instead of the "dramatic or *operatic*" works covered in Dittenhoefer's draft, the amended language made the law applicable to "dramatic or *musical*" compositions. The Committee's report concluded that the omission of musical compositions from the 1856 Amendment "was doubtless the result of oversight," there being "no reason why the same protection should not be extended to one species of literary property of this general character as to the other. . . ."[103] The House Committee's conclusion and reasoning are open to serious doubt, however. First, the conclusion that the drafters of the 1856 Amendment, working forty years before, had merely overlooked musical compositions was a grand assumption indeed. The 1856 Amendment focused solely on "dramatic" compositions, its genesis being in addressing problems of "play" piracy. At the time, copyright recognition for "musical compositions" had been in place for only twenty-five years, and no one in the nascent music publishing industry had expressed the need for a public performance right.

---

103. Rosen, *supra* note 95, at 21.

Similarly, Judge Dittenhoefer, a leading theater lawyer and copyright scholar, had crafted the original Cummings Bill specifically and exclusively as a more effective means of thwarting unauthorized *dramatic* productions. All indications are that his omission of musical compositions from such a measure was quite deliberate.[104]

Moreover, the notion that "dramatic" and "musical" works were of the same "general character" is dubious, particularly with regard to the right of public performance. As noted previously, public performance was the primary means of exploiting a dramatic work for profit—it was the dramatists, after all, who had spearheaded decades of judicial and legislative efforts to gain and then strengthen a right of public performance. To the extent music figured in this equation at all, as in *The Mikado* litigation, it was only as a component of a larger *dramatic* work. For pure "musical compositions" (popular songs and ballads), on the other hand, performance was merely a method of creating demand, a means to the end of selling hard goods— sheet music. Music publishers and songwriters had little, if any, expectation of receiving compensation for the public performance of their songs. Indeed, their practice of paying *for* such exposure was well established. Given these distinctions, there would have been perfectly valid policy reasons for treating dramatic and musical compositions differently in terms of the right of public performance.

Some of these underlying issues emerged during the House debates of December 10, 1896, the final substantive discussions of the Cummings Bill.[105] After reading the bill and the House Committee's report into the record, Committee Chairman William F. Draper of Massachusetts suggested there was no "need of discussing the measure at length," and called for an immediate vote. Several representatives intervened with questions and concerns that prompted considerable debate. Much of the discussion focused on the due process issues related to the scope of the remedies provided in the bill, including the availability of ex parte injunctions, and the potential for jail time in cases of willful infringement. In the end, the enforcement provisions survived, with the exception of the ex parte measure, which was eliminated pursuant to an amendment offered by Representative James A. Connolly, who, along with his Illinois colleague, Representative Albert J. Hopkins, had expressed concern over what they viewed as a "stretch of Federal authority" reflected in the bill.

It fell to New Jersey representative James F. Stewart to probe on the music issue. As an attorney, Stewart was familiar with copyright principles, and became curious as to the eleventh-hour inclusion of "musical compositions" in a bill aimed at play piracy. He asked, "Does not this preclude any person from singing a topical

---

104. It seems likely that Dittenhoefer simply acquiesced in musical compositions being brought into the bill, even at a late date and on dubious grounds, as the inclusion did not affect the rights being afforded the dramatists, his main constituents and the primary intended beneficiaries of the legislation.

105. 29 Cong. Rec. 85 (1896).

ballad if it is copyrighted?" Chairman Draper replied, "of course. It would include the performance of anything that was the property of another, without authority." At this point Draper became frustrated, noting that the bill had "awakened more discussion than I expected." Thus he yielded the floor for "ten minutes" to the bill's sponsor, but Representative Cummings was interrupted by an amendment proffered by George Hulick of Ohio. In response to Hulick, Cummings launched into a lengthy, seemingly prepared speech about the state of the theater industry, its value to the economy, and the dire need for an effective means of preventing unauthorized performances. He railed against piratical companies whose inferior productions "mangle and mutilate" dramatic works, causing "irretrievable damage" to the erstwhile playwright. If the thief were to steal a hog, he maintained, "he would probably be shot or hanged, but he can steal the product of another man's brain and be virtually protected by defective laws."

When Cummings finished his speech, Representative Stewart promptly resumed probing on the issue of music. "The penalties of the bill apply to musical compositions publicly played or performed, either with or without hire. Take a musical ballad, for instance, that is sung upon the street by boys and girls, or played upon an organ without compensation, the provisions of this bill would apply to that, would they not; and if so, ought there not to be an amendment to except such cases?" Cummings did not see the need: "I will say to my friend that the author of a popular ballad is always too glad to have it sung upon the streets or played by a hurdy-gurdy, because that brings it into public notice." Stewart went on: "That is true as a matter of sentiment, but does not this bill apply to cases where ballads are sung publicly in that way?" Cummings' reply was surprising: "I think not," he said, quickly adding, "I have not examined it carefully. It is not the bill that I introduced. It is the one that the Senate has passed. There may be a slight difference."

When taken out of the comfort zone of a canned speech, Cummings seemed to know little about the legislation he had sponsored. His comments made it clear that he knew nothing at all about the reasoning behind the inclusion of "musical compositions" in the bill. Seeing as much, Stewart offered an amendment to "meet the case" he had just described, the singing of popular ballads in public. After a short exchange, Cummings said he had no objection to Stewart's amendment, "although I think it entirely unnecessary." Stewart formally offered the amendment, but withdrew it when reminded there was already an amendment pending. Having gathered himself, Cummings offered his further comments: "I will say, Mr. Speaker, that I do not think such an amendment is necessary, because I do not think any trouble will ever arise in the case the gentleman from New Jersey [Stewart] mentions. I know that when it is desired to perform 'The Banker's Daughter,' or any other play at a church festival, the permission of the author is always given; in fact, the author is glad to give such permission, because it makes his composition more popular, and thereby enhances its value."

He then reverted to his rehearsed comments: "Finally, Mr. Speaker, I say that it is a disgrace to the Congress of the Untied States to have the dramatic authors and musical composers of the country coming here year after year praying for relief and asking simple justice for the protection of their property—such protection as you give to cabinetmakers, machinists, and breeders of razor-backed hogs." Whereupon applause erupted in the chamber, the hammer fell, and once again attention was diverted from the subject of music.

Though he had little knowledge of copyright, Cummings' practical reaction to Stewart's proposal made sense. Playwrights may have taken a different view, but it was unlikely that any song publisher would object to a public performance, because that was how a song became popular. If the promotion argument was correct, however, it begged the larger question of why musical compositions had made their way into the bill at all. Reading between the lines, Stewart seems to have directed his proposal specifically toward what he called "ballads"—popular songs, as opposed to the musical scores incorporated into operas and musical plays. These distinctions, however, never came to light, as Stewart withdrew his amendment and the discussions progressed in different directions.

Eventually, music came back into the discussion when Iowa Representative John F. Lacey offered an amendment that displayed his (and several of his colleagues') fundamental misunderstanding of copyright principles. The amendment, which would have essentially negated the essence of the bill, proposed that "the printing, publication, and sale of such dramatic or musical composition by the proprietor thereof shall be deemed sufficient consent to the public performance or representation thereof." In other words, there could be no "bundle" of copyright privileges—exploitation in one fashion, through publication, dedicated the work to the public domain for all other purposes, such as performance. The House defeated the amendment by a wide margin.

The debates shed little light on the questions of why, how, and at whose behest "musical compositions" had come into the bill. Rosen suggests that the Music Publishers Association, established in 1895, could have had some influence, but acknowledges that there is no hard evidence of its involvement.[106] We do know that prominent songwriter and bandleader John Philip Sousa was lurking in the shadows of this process, noted as one of the "dramatists" who had asked for the legislation. Sousa certainly knew the promotional power of public performance, as he was still fresh from his experience at the Columbian Exposition in Chicago, where his renditions of "After the Ball" propelled the song to national and international prominence. But no evidence has been revealed showing Sousa making the case for a right of public performance in music. As it stands, who and what prompted the "musical composition" amendment to the Cummings Copyright Bill remain a mystery. But one thing is clear: The unseen machinations of the

---

106. Rosen, *supra* note 95, at 17, 21.

House Committee on Patents, along with some "narrow misses" in the House debates, combined to bestow a substantial gift upon the nascent music industry. In what Zvi Rosen characterizes as a "central irony" of the legislation, musical compositions were included in the law only as an afterthought, and without anything but a conclusory, questionable justification or foundation. The extent of the irony would not become fully apparent until an incredible new medium—radio—created opportunities for public performance that could scarcely have been imagined by the celebrants attending the Delmonico's dinner in 1897. It was a rare instance in which copyright law was in fact *ahead* of technology, albeit by accident.

9. Transitions

The close of the century marked seven decades of American music copyright. Recognition of the songwriter's art provided the backbone of a business that had grown from humble beginnings to produce in growing numbers a familiar staple of the American household—the sheet music on the parlor piano. Along the way, America had produced its first superstar of popular music in Stephen Foster, whose songs, nurtured by Congress' extension of copyright terms, provided continuing income for his heirs well beyond the author's early demise.

In 1891 Congress extended international copyright protection to authors in reciprocating nations, which, along with the power of public performances at the Chicago World's Fair in 1893, provided the twin platform for songs like Charles K. Harris' "After the Ball" to become international megahits, heralding the arrival of a bona fide business called music publishing, an industry worth nearly $2.3 million annually in wholesale value by 1900.[107]

At century's end, Congress had taken a significant step forward by recognizing a public performance right in both "dramatic" and "musical" works, reflecting the beginnings of a new and expanded conception of copyright as a bundle of distinct rights, not just the singular and literal right to make "copies" of printed pages. But the performance legislation had been driven by the dramatists, whose works (and livelihoods) were dependent on public performance as the primary means of exploiting their works. For music publishers, whose habit was to pay *for* the favor of public performance, the full and significant measure of the new right would not become apparent for many years.

Over the years the courts had done their part to put teeth into the law of music copyright, enjoining infringements and discouraging would-be pirates with the threat of monetary awards. But as far as rights holders were concerned, not all had

---

107. SANJEK, *supra* note 2, at 399. Doubling this figure to approximate retail value, and dividing by the average sheet music price of 25 cents, yields estimated annual sheet sales of 9,200,000 units in 1900.

gone well with the judiciary. Particularly troubling was the *McTammany* decision,[108] holding that newfangled organette rolls were not unlawful copies of musical compositions, a narrow reading of the law that sent chills down music publishers' collective spine. McTammany and the "mechanical people" were coming. Was copyright ready for the mechanical age?

---

108. *See* Chapter 5.

PART II

The End of the World as We Know It, Part 1—Rolls, Cylinders, and Discs

The Aeolian Co.'s attempt to corner the
piano roll market led to the U.S. Supreme
Court in 1908 (*White-Smith v. Apollo*) and
the "mechanical license" in 1909.
Author's Collection

10. *Stern v. Rosey*

As far as music publishers were concerned, the twentieth century could not have been ushered in on a more dissonant note than the U.S. Court of Appeals for the District of Columbia's decision in *Stern v. Rosey*, rendered February 13, 1901.[1] Just as the U.S. Circuit Court in Massachusetts had done in its *McTammany* opinion[2] twelve years earlier, the court failed to protect publishers from what they felt was a clear and unadulterated form of copying their songs in connection with newfangled music playback technology. John McTammany's copies took the form of the perforated music rolls used in his organette. George Rosey's transgressions were even more profound, as he incorporated publishers' copyrighted songs into perfect "master recordings" that could be played back on a new mechanical instrument know as the "phonograph."

The inventive genius of Thomas Edison made Rosey's business possible. As part of his focus on technologies related to Alexander Graham Bell's invention of the telephone in 1876, Edison turned his attention to the concept of a "talking machine" that could record incoming messages, or serve as a dictating machine. In late 1877, his team of engineers yielded the phonograph, consisting of a foil-wrapped cylinder turned by a hand crank. On one side of the cylinder, a mouthpiece connected to a thin metal diaphragm with a steel stylus (needle) attached. Shouting at the contraption (while turning the crank) vibrated the diaphragm, causing the stylus to etch sound waves into the foil. On the other side of the cylinder, a corresponding stylus and diaphragm "read" the indentations and regenerated the sounds, "playing back" the recording.

When the invention was first demonstrated for the public on December 6, 1877, its novelty created an uproar, but in its original form the device lacked commercial potential. Edison paid little attention to the phonograph in the succeeding years, though other inventors, most notably Alexander Graham Bell and his cousin Chichester Bell, experimented further with recorded sound, making improvements such as using a wax-coated cylinder, yielding what they dubbed the "graphaphone." The Bells approached Edison with their improvements in 1886, but Edison summarily rejected their proposed partnership. Yet Edison's interest in the phonograph was renewed, and he soon produced an improved machine powered by an electric motor, which incorporated both the wax cylinder and an "eartube" for easier listening.

---

1. Stern v. Rosey, 17 App. D.C. 562; 1901 U.S. App. LEXIS 5029.
2. *See* Chapter 5.

At about the same time Emile Berliner introduced the "gramophone," which worked on the same principles, but employed a platter or "disc" instead of a cylinder. Others followed suit and the competitive rush was on, even though no well-defined market existed for the "talking machine." Edison still envisioned a business application—recording dictation—as the primary purpose of the phonograph. Others imagined a wide range of consumer products, from talking dolls and speaking cash registers to automatic, coin-in-the-slot phonographs for public use in amusement arcades. It was the latter notion of using the phonograph for *entertainment* that would give birth to the recorded music industry.[3]

A coin-operated phonograph was made available to exhibitors in 1889, modified to include multiple "eartubes," allowing for simultaneous listening by up to fifteen customers. The machines required content, thus creating the initial market for cylinder "records," which operators purchased in lots of one dozen, containing an assortment of spoken word, instrumental, and vocal music performances by anonymous artists. In general, independent entrepreneurs owned the exhibition phonographs. They positioned them in arcades or other public spaces—shops, train stations, hotels—changed the "record" once every day or two for variety, and collected the deposited nickels. The novelty of recorded performances made the machines successful, with at least one, located in a San Francisco saloon, generating $1,000 in its first five months of operation, averaging more than 130 nickel performances per day.[4]

The success of amusement phonographs led Edison, and others, to the conclusion that significant profits could be made by selling recorded content, cylinders, as well as the machines themselves. Edison set about experimenting with different methods of production that would satisfy the growing demand for recordings, generated by both amusement operators and individual consumers eager to have the latest entertainment technology in their homes, complemented by a library of owned recordings. By 1900, Edison was supplying prerecorded cylinders en masse. The profit margins were significant, around 43 cents on each cylinder retailing for 50 cents.[5] The industry exploded: between 1897 and 1900, U.S. sales of recorded music (in cylinder and disc formats) rose from 500,000 to nearly 3 million, and continued its steady growth into the new century.[6]

For the first time, the "music industry" became a duality, comprised of the publishers and composers who owned copyrights in musical compositions, on the one hand, and those who manufactured and sold playback hardware, and the recorded music to go along with it, on the other.

---

3. For a detailed and thoughtful history of the development of recorded sound, *see* ANDRE MILLARD, AMERICA ON RECORD: A HISTORY OF RECORDED SOUND (1995).

4. *Id.* at 43.

5. *Id.* at 49.

6. *Id.*

In its early days, as now, the recorded music business was dominated by a few major producers—Edison, the Victor Talking Machine Company (founded in 1901), and Columbia, of Washington, D.C. Other eager and opportunistic entrepreneurs also worked on the fringes of the burgeoning industry, including small-scale recording outfits and cylinder replicators like George Rosey.

Music publishers observed the proliferation of recordings flooding the marketplace with great trepidation. Their copyrighted songs were being recorded and sold, but they earned no compensation. With an exploding market passing them by, they turned again to the courts in an effort to protect their interests. The major manufacturers, loaded with their own manufacturing patents and the resources to litigate, were not good targets, as compared to the upstart business of Rosey.

The Joseph W. Stern Co., a New York-based publisher founded in 1894, held copyrights in the parlor ballads "Take Back Your Gold" and "Whisper Your Mother's Name," which had seen success in sheet sales. Rosey recorded and reproduced both songs in his fledgling business. As described by the court, he "inserted smooth wax cylinders in the said phonograph and, whilst they were being revolved therein under a metal horn or megaphone, caused the music to be played upon some musical instruments, and the words of the songs to be sung by some person. These were received and transmitted through the megaphone to what is called a sapphire recording point, having a sharp even surface, which engraved upon the revolving cylinders a record of both the music of the composition and the words of the songs as received. Obtaining in this way a satisfactory record, which is called a 'master record' [apparently the first judicial use of this term of art], the defendant would place it in a machine called a 'double phonograph,' and immediately below it another smooth or blank wax cylinder. The machine would revolve both and by means of a double sapphire recording point the engravings upon the master record would be reproduced upon the blank cylinder. In this way defendant has produced as many as five thousand copies of the 'master record' of the [plaintiff's] music and songs, which are intended for use in the phonographs. He has sold many of these and realized large profits from said sales."

The facts were clear and undisputed, making it easy for the appellate judges to affirm the lower court's finding of no infringement. Confirming that copyright claims were based "wholly" on the language of the statute, the court looked to the specific rights provided to copyright owners—namely, "the sole liberty of printing, reprinting, publishing, copying, executing, finishing and vending same." Rosey's operation had done none of these things.[7] As the court reasoned, "[w]e can not regard the reproduction, through the agency of the phonograph, of the sounds of musical instruments playing the music composed and published by the [plaintiffs],

---

7. Nor did his activities violate the right of public performance in "musical compositions," recognized in 1897.

as the copy or publication of the same within the meaning of the act. The ordinary signification of the words 'copying,' 'publishing,' etc., can not be stretched to include it."

The court likened wax cylinders to "the metal cylinder of the old and familiar music box," which had never been regarded as infringing. The court acknowledged that the "precise question here presented . . . is a novel one because of the comparatively recent innovation of the phonograph." Nevertheless, a "close analogy" existed to two prior cases—the *McTammany* decision,[8] in which the U.S. Circuit Court "held that the perforated paper used in organettes were not copies"; and, portending the next technology-generated controversy to face U.S. music publishers, the English Chancery Court's decision in *Boosey v. Whight.* The *Boosey* decision held that "perforated papers, used in an Aeolian [player piano], which represented the instrumental music of certain songs, were parts of the instrument and not sheets of music within the act."[9]

As Rosey breathed a sigh of relief, the Edison, Victor and Columbia factories belched with delight. So too did John McTammany and the growing number of organette manufacturers, who supplied a steady stream of music rolls for their customers' expanding collections. But even these developments paled in comparison to the magnitude of piano rolls pouring forth from New York's Aeolian Company, which had quickly become the country's leading manufacturer of player pianos, and the complementary musical content, piano rolls.

Technology ran wild, and music publishers' attempts to harness the landslide into a revenue stream had encountered nothing but futility and frustration.

11. The Mechanical People Invade Tin Pan Alley

Frenchman Henri Fourneaux invented the player piano, which he exhibited for the first time at the Philadelphia Centennial Exposition in 1876. Also marketed as the "pianola" or "pianista," such players were driven by a pneumatic motor, which moved a paper "roll" through the instrument. As with the organette, musical notation was encoded into the roll as a series of perforations, like the "tabs" on a voting card or exam paper.

Piano rolls did not literally "record" or reproduce "sounds." Rather, the perforations in the roll comprised a set of instructions, which, when "read" by the machine (instead of a performer), depressed the keys, yielding the song. The result

---

8. *See* Chapter 5.

9. Boosey v. Whight [1899] 1 Ch. 836. "These rolls are strictly part of a machine, and cannot be brought within the scope of the Copyright Acts."

was a new "performance" with each use, as opposed to "replaying" a previously recorded performance, as with phonograph records or cylinders.

Player pianos did require some degree of human contribution, as they were equipped with foot pedals to pump the pneumatic motor, and controls to adjust speed and volume. But no "musical" training was necessary to operate the instrument—the machine did the work. It was literally "machine made," or "mechanical" music. The high-tech contraptions magically made music on their own by "reading" the chad-like perforations, triggering a mechanism that depressed a piano key and rendered a note, all without the touch of a human hand.[10]

At the turn of the century, the Aeolian Company of New York City dominated the player-piano industry. William Tremaine founded the Mechanical Orguinette Company, a producer of reed organs, in 1878, then created Aeolian (named for Aoelus, Greek God of wind) in an effort to capitalize on the growing market for player pianos. Tremaine's son Harry, a disciplined businessman and a born promoter and marketer, took over the business in 1898. Built upon an unwavering commitment to advertising, as well as an impressive portfolio of acquired[11] and pooled patents, Aeolian propelled itself into a leading position, both in the U.S. and internationally through multiple subsidiaries.[12] The company was responsible for a majority of the 75,000 player pianos sold in 1902, and, having purchased the physical plant of a Boston-based roll manufacturer, a large portion of the 1 million piano rolls then sold annually.[13]

As Aeolian came to dominate the player piano (and roll) market, disc and cylinder makers busily competed among themselves in the first "format war" of the nascent recorded-music business. By 1901, the Victor Talking Machine Company had acquired Emile Berliner's disc-playing gramophone business, and the "Victrola" player challenged Thomas Edison's cylinder phonograph. Discs were easy to handle, package, and store, and had ample room on their labels for colorful graphics, company logos, and artist information, all advantages over awkward, can-shaped cylinders. Then, in 1902, a promising young Italian tenor named Enrico Caruso made his first recordings for Victor's associated British enterprise, the Gramophone Company (now known as EMI). Caruso moved to New York in 1903, gained a contract with the Metropolitan Opera (where he would remain for seventeen years), and signed directly with Victor in the U.S., publicly committing himself to recording on discs exclusively. Caruso's talent, together with Victor's

---

10. *See* Mark Sommer, *The Day the Music Died; QRS Has Ended Production of Player-Piano Rolls*, Buffalo News Blog, January 3, 2009, 7:03AM, updated August 20, 2010 7:32PM, http://www.buffalonews.com/incoming/article134934.ece.

11. Acquired patents included those pertaining to John McTammany's organette. *See* Russell Sanjek, American Popular Music and Its Business, The First Four Hundred Years, Vol. II, From 1790 to 1909, 380 (1988).

12. David Suisman, Selling Sounds: The Commercial Revolution in American Music 96–97 (2009).

13. Sanjek, *supra* note 11, at 381.

creative and tireless promotion, combined to create America's first *recording* star, and, in the process, further solidified the supremacy of the disc format among the buying public.

Edison remained dedicated to the cylinder format, introducing a sonically superior, longer-playing "Blue Amberol" cylinder as late as 1908, and continuing to manufacture cylinders for many years. But he unofficially conceded defeat in the first format war by introducing his own disc phonograph in 1912.[14] On the strength of its Victrola player, which was becoming a staple in American households—along with the bold promotion of both individual artists and the technical superiority of its recordings, all featuring its famous "Nipper" trademark (the white dog, ears perked and head cocked, dutifully listening to "His Master's Voice")—the Victor Talking Machine Company raced ahead of its competitors. By 1916, Victor claimed that its sprawling recording and manufacturing complex in Camden, New Jersey, was "the greatest musical center in the whole world."[15]

And so it was in the early years of the twentieth century. A flood of technological advances generated new consumer markets for a variety of music machines, from the phonograph to the graphophone, and from the organette to the more sophisticated player piano. Each playback device had its corresponding music software—wax cylinders, discs, organette, and piano rolls. Consumers enjoyed the latest innovations, which afforded greater opportunities to enjoy music in the comfort of their homes. On the other hand, the established music trade—the publishers and composers ensconced in the traditional sheet music industry—did not care for such disruptive developments. For them, the manufacturers were "mechanical people," like robots from outer space, sent down to destroy the music business with their "canned," machine-made music.

The mechanical people were not the only ones acting like industrialists, however. A new breed of music publisher had emerged in the late nineteenth century, led by namesake entrepreneurs like the Witmark Brothers, Joseph Stern (the unsuccessful plaintiff in the *Rosey* case), Tom and Alex Harms, Maurice Shapiro, and Leonard Feist. Concentrated on the west side of Manhattan between 14th and 28th Streets—soon to be dubbed "Tin Pan Alley" for the constant jangling of piano keys—these fierce entrepreneurs took cues from American big business (Aeolian and Victor included) to create a new approach to creating and selling songs. Tin Pan Alley represented the birth of the modern music business, the mass production of commercial culture in the form of the American popular song. According to David Suisman, "what distinguished Tin Pan Alley from other modes of making music was that the *primary* motivation for writing a song was to sell it, not to express some inherently human feeling or musical impulse." He adds: "Songwrit-

---

14. Mark Coleman, Playback: From the Victrola to MP3, 100 Years of Music, Machines, and Money 24 (2003).

15. Suisman, *supra* note 12, at 101.

ers in this regime were workers, not artists, and their output was a vehicle for the amusement of others, not for personal expression."[16]

In the new business of music, publishers employed songwriters whose job it was to turn out predictable, accessible melodies within formulaic guidelines. Yet, regardless how mechanized songwriting became, a fundamental distinction remained between music and other kinds of industrial output; each musical product was unique and therefore highly speculative. Try as they might, publishers could not simply "assemble" songs in the manner of a true commodity, enhancing marginal profits through more efficient manufacturing and marketing. To the contrary, there was no inherent demand for the latest tune. Publishers had to promote every new song from scratch to a fickle buying public, based on that song's own characteristics. As a result, the business became even more hit-driven. Publishers modeled their enterprises on the assumption that proceeds from only a few blockbusters could balance the vast majority of songs that would make no profit at all.[17] The modern model also contemplated a steady stream of new material that, naturally, lived within shorter "windows" or cycles of popularity. Just like commodity manufacturers who relied on natural or even "planned" obsolescence of consumer products, music publishers had to keep the pipeline full of "new" and "improved" songs.

In this system, more sophisticated and aggressive marketing methods were necessary to compete. Marketing techniques employed earlier by the likes of Charles K. Harris for his 1893 hit song, "After the Ball," became common, mainstream practices. Song-plugging—hiring musicians to perform songs in public spaces—and the placement of songs with singers and vaudeville performers for use in their shows, became more intense and broader in scope, as the vaudeville circuit created the first regional and national promotion and distribution networks for new music.[18] Publishers showered notable performers with free "professional copies" of new songs, and popular vaudeville singers received cash and gifts for adding and keeping songs in their performance playlists—pure "payola," to use the term that came into vogue in the late 1930s, in reference to turn-of-the century Victrola phonographs.[19]

Trade advertising for specific songs also became common, and publishers devoted more resources to using graphic designs and performer photographs in their sheets, to create visual appeal. Further, despite their significant production costs, the use of "song slides"—still images projected on a movie screen while a song played—became more prevalent as a promotional tool, as these precursors to music videos made a lasting impression on audiences, exposing the song along with a built-in set of visual references to establish mood and theme, encouraging purchase.

---

16. *Id.* at 22.
17. *Id.* at 44.
18. *Id.* at 79.
19. *Id.* at 84.

Publishers' promotional efforts (and expenses) also extended to the retail level, particularly as large department stores installed "music counters," sometimes using deeply discounted sheets as loss leaders to lure consumers into stores in the hopes of selling them more expensive, profitable products.[20] Music counters were staffed by impressionable young (mostly female) sales clerks, whom publishers showered with gifts ranging from perfume to cash, pleasant bribes meant to keep a certain publisher's songs top of mind when customers needed recommendations.[21]

While increased promotional expenses drove up overhead costs and heightened competition among firms, it also helped to identify publishers' mutual interests and the need for organizing and mobilizing against common "enemies" like the mechanical people. Now that the industry was more concentrated geographically, publishers organized more efficiently for purposes of pursuing a collective agenda in Washington, D.C. As we have seen, earlier copyright revisions benefiting music firms—the recognition of music copyright in 1831, and a performance right in 1897—were put in place without controversy, and with little direct input from the music community.[22] As they faced the onslaught of a new century's technology, and the powerful corporate interests behind it, however, publishers realized they could no longer remain naïve to politics.

Trade organizations were initiated or reorganized to serve collective interests. The Board of Music Trade had existed since 1855, with a narrow focus on maintaining sheet music prices. On June 11, 1895, the organization was reborn as the Music Publishers Association, with seventeen original members, including the Witmark brothers.[23] It agreed to a broad agenda, which included providing support for any "action toward a revision and improvement of the administration of the present copyright system, with the view of making it an adjunct of greater value to the publishing interests in this country than it is now."[24] With regular advice and counsel from a young show business attorney named Nathan Burkan, the Music Publishers Association kept a steady eye on music roll, cylinder, and disc manufacturers, who continued to use the publishers' music royalty-free.[25] Individual composers and performers like Victor Herbert[26] and John Philip Sousa contributed to the process, lending their "artist laborer" images in support of the publishing agenda, while railing against the evils of mechanical music.[27] One commentator called the Tin Pan Alley of the early twentieth century "the most effi-

---

20. Much as "big box" and mass retailers do with respect to recorded music today.

21. SUISMAN, *supra* note 12, at 64.

22. *See* Chapters 2 and 8.

23. For insight into the Witmarks' political endeavors, *see* IDORE WITMARK AND ISAAC GOLDBERG, FROM RAGTIME TO SWINGTIME (1939).

24. SANJEK, *supra* note 11, at 394.

25. *Id.* at 397, 400.

26. Herbert also acted as president of the Authors and Composers League of America.

27. Sousa was an interesting figure whose motives and allegiances were not always clear. He had railed against the evils of "canned music" in congressional hearings and in a 1906 APPLETON'S MAGA-

cient music machine the world had yet seen."[28] The music industry's ability to act as a group in Washington completed the final components. With a political agenda in place and the resources to pursue it, the machine was complete.

In this fashion, a turn-of-the-century perfect storm of copyright conflict brewed within the business of music. Manufacturers wished to continue developing new technologies without the costly constraint of paying for access to content. Along with their composers, employees, and partners, publishers cried out for protection of their own commercial interests. Though sometimes discussed in terms of the "art" of songwriters and publishers versus the "commerce" of manufacturers, in reality the conflict was the clashing of well-organized commercial interests on both sides of the music industry. The conflict would play itself out in court and in Congress during the first decade of the new century.

12. *White-Smith v. Apollo*

Though blinded by an eye infection at the age of eight in 1863, German-born Adam Geibel overcame his disability to become a successful gospel and popular songwriter, conductor, organist, music teacher, and publisher. After coming to the United States, Geibel was educated at the Pennsylvania Institute for the Blind in Philadelphia, earned an honorary degree from Temple University, and was chief organist for the John Stetson Mission Sunday School. He founded a publishing house to manage his own music properties, and in time assigned the copyrights in many of his compositions to the White-Smith Music Publishing Company of Boston, where two of them became the subject of music's second trip to the nation's highest court.

Like its fellow publishers, White-Smith was concerned by the uncompensated use of its copyrighted compositions in piano rolls. One of the leading culprits, in its eyes, was the Apollo Company, part of the Melville Clark Piano Company, founded in 1900 in DeKalb, Illinois. Clark introduced the Apollo Piano Player in 1901, along with rolls featuring the leading popular compositions of the day, including two of Adam Geibel's more popular secular tunes, "Kentucky Babe" and "Little Cotton Dolly." Sales were brisk.

Despite the recent *Rosey* and *McTammany* decisions, holding that cylinder recordings and organette rolls, respectively, did not infringe, White-Smith launched

---

ZINE article, *The Menace of Mechanical Music*. During the same period however, his name pops up among spokesmen for Aeolian and Victor.

28. Reebee Garofalo, *From Music Publishing to MP3: Music and Industry in the Twentieth Century*, 17 Am. Music 321 (Autumn 1999), quoted by Brendan Charney in *Congress and the Culture Industry: Copyright Law and the Development of the American Popular Music Business, 1890–1940*, p. 12 (Apr. 10, 2008) (Senior Thesis, History Department, Columbia University), available at www.columbia.edu/cu /history/resource-library/Charney_thesis.pdf.

litigation against Apollo, alleging that the manufacture of piano rolls violated its copyrights in the Geibel compositions.

The parties did not dispute the facts. The evidence established "quite convincingly" that "the single purpose of the perforated sheets [rolls] is to mechanically reproduce musical sounds, and that they are not like the sheet music, addressed to the vision, or intended to be read."[29] As such, the legal conclusion was inevitable. The principles enunciated in *Rosey* and *McTammany* were "fully applicable," and had established a "settled rule of statutory construction." Making, selling, and distributing piano rolls did not infringe musical compositions. Despite the clarity of the opinion, the publisher appealed, and a year later, in May 1906, the Court of Appeals for the Second Circuit issued a short affirming opinion, again striking fear into the heart of the publishing community. Piano rolls are not "copies," said the court, "[t]hey are mere adjuncts of a valve mechanism in a machine."[30] Nevertheless, in the face of the "settled rule of law" (and for reasons that later became apparent), White-Smith promptly appealed to the nation's highest court.

As the *White-Smith* case ambled its way through the courts, Congress was considering wholesale revisions to the country's copyright law. Music publishers, among many other groups, actively pushed for reforms that would expand copyright protection to cover the explosion of technologies that had come forth in the Industrial Revolution. As reflected in the House Report on the legislation that became the Copyright Act of 1909, "[t]he reproduction of various things which are the subject of copyright has enormously increased. The wealth and business of the country and the methods and means of duplication have increased immeasurably. The law requires adaptation to these modern conditions."[31] President Theodore Roosevelt delivered the same message in his December 1905, address to Congress, telling lawmakers: "Our copyright laws urgently need revision. They are imperfect in definition, confused and inconsistent in expression; they omit provisions for many articles which, under modern reproductive processes, are entitled to protection."[32]

In light of Roosevelt's message, the Librarian of Congress invited interested parties to take part in a series of conferences and hearings, conducted by the House and Senate Committees on Patents, to formulate a copyright bill. The debates were far-ranging and often intense, but according to the House Report, the section of the bill dealing with "the reproduction of music by mechanical means has been the subject of more discussion and has taken more of the time of the committee than any other provision in the bill."[33] The Report went on to discuss the international situation, noting "several leading countries of the world have

---

29. White-Smith Music Pub. Co. v. Apollo Co., 139 F. 427; 1905 U.S. App. LEXIS 4695 (S.D.N.Y. 1905).
30. White-Smith Music Pub. Co. v. Apollo Co., 147 F. 226; 1906 U.S. App. LEXIS 4231 (2d Cir. 1906).
31. H.R. REP. 1 on the Copyright Act of 1909, at 1, quoting statements of Samuel J. Elder of the Boston bar. [Appendix 8–13 to NIMMER ON COPYRIGHT]
32. *Id.*
33. *Id.* at 3.

provided by law that anyone may with perfect freedom and without any compensation to the composer reproduce by mechanical means copyrighted music." Germany had a modest legislative restriction on specific types of reproduction, and an Italian court had found mechanical use to be an infringement, but historically the international community had treated "machine made" music as outside the confines of copyright. The tide was beginning to turn, as iterations of the Berne Copyright Convention recommended granting composers an exclusive right of reproduction by mechanical means; each country was left to devise its own implementation, however, and, in any event, the United States was not a member.[34]

Against this backdrop, the panel became convinced that the United States should move forward on its own. "Your committee have felt that justice and fair dealing, however, required that when the copyrighted music of a composer was appropriated for mechanical reproduction the composer should have same [sic] compensation for its use and that the composer should have the further right of forbidding, if he so desired, the rendition of his music by the mechanical reproducers."[35] But an additional quandary faced the committee: "How to protect [composers] in these rights without establishing a great music monopoly was the practical question the committee had to deal with." A "great music monopoly"? Who could exert such control over the business of music?

The "mechanical rights" issue went to the heart of copyright policy. "In enacting a copyright law," the Report declared, "Congress must consider . . . two questions: First, how much will the legislation stimulate the producer and so benefit the public; and, second, how much will the monopoly granted be detrimental to the public. The granting of such exclusive rights, under the proper terms and conditions, confers a benefit upon the public that outweighs the evils of the temporary monopoly."[36] Based on the testimony of popular composers, Victor Herbert and John Philip Sousa among them, the committee was at first inclined to give composers the unfettered right to "do what they pleased" with regard to mechanical reproduction, "but the hearings disclosed that the probable effect of this would be the establishment of a mechanical-music trust," detrimental to the public interest. "This danger [lay] in the possibility that some one company might secure, by purchase or otherwise, a large number of copyrights of the most popular music, and by controlling these copyrights monopolize the business of manufacturing [and] selling music machines, otherwise free to the world."[37]

A jolt had been delivered in the early hearings on the bill by engineer George Howlett Davis, who warned of a "complete monopolistic octopus," in which (his former employer) "the Aeolian Company forms the head and brains, and the Music

---

34. The United States did not join the 1886 Berne Copyright Convention until 1989.
35. H.R. Rep. 1 on the Copyright Act of 1909, at 4.
36. *Id.* at 5.
37. *Id.*

Publishers' Association the body, the independent publishers the writhing arms, and the composers the suckers and baiters."[38] More specifically, he referred to a plan hatched by Aeolian executives to dominate the piano roll market by entering into contracts with some eighty leading publishing houses. The contracts, eventually examined by the committee, showed that Aeolian had acquired the exclusive rights for mechanical reproduction of all the compositions controlled by each publisher for a period of thirty-five years, with a royalty of 10 percent on each roll sold.[39] In return for exclusive, long-term access to the publishing catalogs, Aeolian agreed to finance a test case, including appeals up to the Supreme Court if necessary, seeking to extend the publishers' copyrights to include mechanical reproductions. A successful result in court would trigger the contracts. Although White-Smith was the plaintiff in name, Aeolian's deep pockets financed the litigation against Apollo (its fellow manufacturer) on behalf of the entire music publishing community.

The Supreme Court's decision came on February 24, 1908, in an opinion authored by Justice William Rufus Day, a Roosevelt appointee in 1903, who had served as Secretary of State and on the U.S. Circuit Court of Appeals.[40] During his two decades on the court, Justice Day developed a reputation for voting for the dissolution of trusts, a strong undercurrent in the case at hand.

Since the facts, lower court decisions, and earlier precedent were all squarely against it, White-Smith turned to policy, arguing that the primary purpose of the copyright law was to protect the "author"[41] against "every form of piracy without distinction," including "perforated music." Thus, a broad interpretation of the statute (and its constitutional mandate) was required, one that covered all manner of music reproductions made possible by emerging technologies, whether "read" by the human eye or a mechanical device. White-Smith asserted that music was pure intellectual property, "the order of notes in the author's composition," which by Apollo's admission had been copied in making piano rolls. For support White-Smith looked to the 1897 copyright revisions, which prohibited the public performance of a musical work. If an ephemeral public performance of "Little Cotton Dolly," played back on a player piano, was prohibited by the statute, so too should be the act of copying the same notes in the process of manufacturing the roll itself. Getting to the heart of the appellate court's ruling against it, White-Smith argued that it was "impossible to say" that the ordering of notes on a roll was "the mere adjunct of a valve mechanism, because the valve mechanism would work in whatever order. It is not the machine that puts or requires the perforations in this order, but [Apollo]."

---

38. SANJEK, *supra* note 11, at 398.

39. *Id.*

40. White-Smith Music Pub. Co. v. Apollo Co., 209 U.S. 1; 28 S. Ct. 319; 52 L. Ed. 655; 1908 U.S. LEXIS 1766 (February 24, 1908).

41. Corporate copyright owners often cloak themselves in the rhetoric of "authors" and "creators" to position themselves sympathetically in public debate. Adam Geibel, the true "author" of the two compositions in issue, would benefit only indirectly, by contract, if White-Smith were to prevail.

The arguments had the force of logic, and a strong dose of author-friendly public policy, but were quickly defused by Apollo's predictable focus on the language of the statute. "Copyright in this country is the creature of statute pure and simple," argued Apollo, and "[t]he statutes creating and covering copyright must be strictly construed in all respects." Apollo insisted that it was not the judiciary's place to "enter the domain of legislation" by reinterpreting the statute to address technologies unknown at the time of drafting: "All arguments directed to the supposed reasonableness of treating copyright as covering automatic means of audible reproduction of speech and music are utterly irrelevant and beside the question." Apollo presented a contrasting view of music copyright, arguing that the musical compositions in issue were the "tangible and legible embodiments of the intellectual product of the musician, and not the intangible intellectual product itself." Therefore, the statute prohibited only the selling of tangible, human-readable "copies," consistent with the earlier *Rosey* and *McTammany* decisions, decided on similar facts.

After summarizing the parties' contentions, the substance of Justice Day's opinion began with a discussion of the new technology and its wide acceptance by the public. The factual record disclosed that nearly 75,000 player pianos were in use in the United States in 1902, a year in which more than 1 million piano rolls were produced.[42] Thus, the legal question was one of "very considerable importance, involving large property interests, and closely touching the rights of composers and music publishers." The Court then explained the methods used for translating sheet music notes into perforated rolls, and the manner in which they functioned to render a musical performance, before addressing the crux of the matter. It offered an evaluation of the "opposing theories as to the nature and extent of the copyright given by statutory laws." Did copyright protect the pure "intellectual conception" of a song, or only its "tangible results"?

Apollo invoked the judicial doctrine of stare decisis (the policy of courts to abide by, or adhere to, prior decisions on similar facts), pointing, of course, to the *McTammany*[43] and *Rosey* cases. It also cited to the English court decision in *Boosey v. Whight* (1901), which found that piano rolls did not infringe under British law. The cases were strong precedent, and certainly informed the court's deliberations. However, an English opinion was not binding on a U.S. court, and *McTammany* and *Rosey* were lower court decisions on similar, but not on identical facts, so legally the issue was not entirely foreclosed.

The Court considered it significant that Congress had not overturned the prior cases through legislation, despite opportunities to do so. *McTammany* was twenty-year-old precedent in 1908, and Congress would have been aware of it when it

---

42. The numbers were significantly larger in 1908, but the trial court record was developed in 1904–1905, explaining why more current industry statistics were not referenced.

43. The opinion notes that the *McTammany* case had in fact been appealed to the Supreme Court, making it the first music copyright case to arrive there, only to be dismissed "for failure to print the record."

amended the copyright statute in 1891 and again in 1897. The fact that Congress made no revisions with respect to mechanical reproductions implied its acceptance of the earlier decisions as proper interpretations of the statute. Similarly, although the U.S. was not a party to the 1886 Berne Copyright Convention, Congress was aware of its terms, including the explicit understanding among signatory countries that "the manufacture and sale of instruments serving to reproduce mechanically the airs of music borrowed from the private domain are not considered as constituting musical infringement." Thus, interpreting the U.S. statute as covering mechanical reproductions could have given foreign composers more generous rights than American authors enjoyed overseas, which Congress would not have intended.

However, as the lower court opinions had stressed, "in the last analysis [the] case turn[ed] upon the construction of a statute"—specifically, the meaning of "copy," a term not defined in the act itself. Considering the statutory language as a whole, the court reasoned that "[t]hroughout the act it is apparent that Congress has dealt with the concrete and not with an abstract right of property in ideas or mental conceptions." Put another way, "[t]he statute has not provided for the protection of the intellectual conception apart from the thing produced." Consistent with this analysis, the Court adopted the definition of "copy" offered by Apollo's expert: "a written or printed record . . . in intelligible notation." As perforated rolls were not readable by the human eye, they were not "copies within the meaning of the copyright act." Rather, the Court said, echoing earlier decisions, they were "part of a machine."

White-Smith had lost its gambit, and the opinion of Justice Day, the trust-busting Roosevelt appointee, appeared to frustrate Aeolian's monopolistic intentions. But his opinion also acknowledged a perceived unfairness, allowing manufacturers to "enjoy the use of musical compositions for which they pay no value." Nevertheless, "such considerations properly address themselves to the legislative and not to the judicial branch of the Government." In a concurring opinion, Justice Oliver Wendell Holmes went further, urging Congress to act. Like Justice Day, Holmes was a Roosevelt appointee, in 1902, who in his thirty years on the bench became one of America's most celebrated and widely cited jurists, known for his pithy, quotable opinions on a wide variety of topics. The scope of composers' rights would return to Holmes' docket in a decade's time, in a landmark case involving the right of public performance, but *White-Smith* presented his first opportunity to opine on the nature of copyright. Holmes agreed with the court's reasoning, but the result, he believed, gave copyright "less scope than its rational significance." For Holmes, the notion of property started with a "tangible object," but in copyright "reached a more abstract expression." In an oft-quoted passage that gave solace to the composing and publishing community, Holmes defined a musical composition as a "rational collocation of sounds . . . reduced to a tangible expression from which the collocation can be reproduced either with or without continuous human intervention." "On principle," he added, "anything that mechanically reproduces that collocation of sounds ought to be held a copy, or if the statute is too narrow ought to be made so by a further act, except so far as some extraneous consideration of policy may oppose."

Holmes drew a distinction between traditional, tangible property, and "tangible expression"—*intellectual* property, which in the case of music was a collocation of sounds that could be "copied" in a variety of forms, as sheet music, for example, as a recorded cylinder or platter, or in the perforations of a piano roll. The existing statute did not accommodate this expansive notion of music as intellectual property and thus, according to Holmes, it required revision.

13. 1909

Final hearings on copyright revision commenced within a month of the Supreme Court's decision in *White-Smith*. As we have seen, based on several years of fact gathering and testimony, the responsible committees were inclined to grant composers an exclusive right to mechanical reproduction, as urged by Justice Holmes. But even Holmes' opinion acknowledged that public policy should be considered, and Aeolian's attempted monopoly remained on legislators' minds. The *White-Smith* decision had avoided the intended "music trust," but as the committees soon discovered, Aeolian had hedged its bets further, entering into a second set of publishing contracts giving it the same exclusive rights, this time premised on Congress passing mechanical rights legislation.[44]

Aeolian's competitors, including Apollo (fresh from its hard-fought victory in court), lashed out at the potential monopoly, as did phonograph, record, and cylinder manufacturers, whose businesses would also be constrained by a mechanical music trust. The recording companies also played the promotional card, insisting that phonograph records were sought-after marketing tools for popular songs. As evidence, they submitted "countless letters" from publishers to the Big Three labels—Columbia, Edison, and Victor—pleading for recordings to be made of a particular new song.[45] These claims were supported by the continued growth of the sheet music business, which had escalated from $2.2 million in wholesale value in 1900, to $4.1 million in 1904, and an estimated $6 million in 1906, a period in which the sale of phonographs, discs, and cylinders also grew significantly.[46] As far as manufacturers were concerned, there was no "unfairness" in the fact that mechanical

---

44. H.R. Rep. 1 on the Copyright Act of 1909, at 5. [Appendix 8–13 to Nimmer on Copyright]. The report also expressed concern over similar attempts to corner the mechanical music markets in Italy and Germany.

45. Sanjek, *supra* note 11, at 399.

46. *Id.*

reproductions did not require royalty payments to publishers. For them, the evidence confirmed their instincts—that *manufacturers* were the ones providing value in the equation. According to their logic, perhaps publishers should be paying *them* for the service of popularizing songs (and thus promoting the sale of sheet music) through the medium of new recordings.

Naturally, publishers held a different worldview, but their interests did not always perfectly align.[47] On certain issues, entrepreneurial song publishers, like the Witmarks, found themselves at odds with old-line publishers of classical music, as well as the leadership of the Music Publishers Association, whose president, James Bowers, was an executive of Lyon & Healy in Chicago, Midwest representative of none other than Aeolian. As the copyright hearings progressed, the Witmarks, with the help of rising entertainment attorney Nathan Burkan, formed a splinter group called the New York Publishers Association, which they used as a platform to present their specific agenda in Washington.[48]

In his business memoir, *From Ragtime to Swingtime*, Isadore Witmark recalled his induction into the ways of Washington, squaring off against the better-organized manufacturing lobby.[49] Realizing that he represented no sizable constituency, he created one by convincing 6,000 would-be composers that their prospects would greatly improve by the passage of mechanical rights legislation. The result was an avalanche of letters to Congress from across the country, which prompted legislators to take publishers' concerns more seriously. Witmark, and his close comrades Burkan and Victor Herbert, were constantly present in Washington in the critical weeks and months in which copyright reform took its final turns. Particularly effective, according to Witmark, were sessions in the "Inner Sanctum," the only place in the Capitol building where liquor was served.[50]

Manufacturers and publishers remained at loggerheads, but with the legislative session ending, both sides realized that a negotiated resolution was preferable to taking their chances with Congress. Finally, a Victor representative reintroduced the radical notion of creating a compulsory license for mechanical reproductions, in return for a mandated, statutory royalty.[51] It was an extreme idea, but attractive in that it could resolve the logjam and also, importantly, defuse Aeolian's second attempt to establish a "mechanical trust." After concluding that such a provision would survive constitutional scrutiny, the committee, along with representatives from both sides, settled on language granting the owner of a musical composition

---

47. Manufacturer/labels were also entering the publishing business themselves, complicating matters further. By 1906 Victor had spent $35,000 acquiring song copyrights to be recorded by its own artists. Sanjek, *supra* note 11, at 397.

48. *Id.* at 399.

49. Witmark & Isaac Goldberg, *supra* note 23.

50. *Id.*

51. Sanjek, *supra* note 11, at 399. The concept is said to have been first introduced by Representative Currier, inspired perhaps by a similar provisions once discussed, but not implemented, with respect to book publishing. Charney, *supra* note 28, at 45.

the exclusive right "to make any arrangement or setting of it or of the melody of it in any system of notation or any form of record in which the thought of an author may be recorded and from which it may be read or reproduced."[52] Justice Holmes was undoubtedly pleased with the expansive language, as were Witmark and his fellow publishers.

The language continued, however, stating specifically that "as a condition of extending the copyright control to such mechanical reproductions . . . whenever the owner of a musical copyright has used or permitted . . . the use of the copyrighted work upon the parts of instruments serving to reproduce mechanically the musical work, any other person may make similar use of the copyrighted work upon the payment to the copyright proprietor of a royalty of 2 cents on each such part manufactured."[53] Now the manufacturers had reason to rejoice. Whenever a publisher allowed a party to mechanically reproduce a composition, the compulsory license would be triggered, and any other manufacturer could do the same, simply by paying the statutory fee. And because the license was compulsory, neither Aeolian nor any other manufacturer could corner the market for mechanical music.

The royalty amount was a battleground in and of itself. The 2-cent rate proposal was based on the average sheet music royalty of one and a half cents per copy, rounded up.[54] After much haggling, the parties agreed to the proposed amount, and Congress approved the legislation and rushed it to the White House for signature. With just five minutes remaining in his term, Theodore Roosevelt carried out his last official act as president, signing the Copyright Act of 1909 into law on March 4, 1909.[55]

As in all compromises, both sides were dissatisfied. Manufacturers remained hostile to the notion of paying for what they considered free promotion of songs through their recordings, while publishers were disappointed with the fact that they could be compelled to license their copyrights for use in the burgeoning market for mechanical music, and for only 2 cents a copy. But it was done, and its longevity suggests that the mutual compromises made practical sense. The compulsory license put in place in the 1909 Copyright Act has stayed in place for more than a century, surviving later copyright revisions, accommodating all manner of new formats enabled by technology—piano rolls; cylinders and discs; long-playing records; cassettes, eight-track and digital tapes; compact discs; and finally, the format with no tangible form at all, digital downloads. The current Section 115 of the Copyright Act allows any person to "make and distribute" copies of a musical work by paying the statutory fee (now 9.1 cents per copy). In turn, copies are defined as "phonorecords"—"objects in which sounds . . . are fixed by any method now

---

52. Copyright Act of 1909, Section 1(e); Public Law 60–349 (Mar. 4, 1909), 35 Stat. 1075.
53. *Id.*
54. SANJEK, *supra* note 11, at 399.
55. The Act had an effective date of July 1, 1909.

known or later developed, and from which the sounds can be perceived, reproduced, or otherwise communicated, either directly or with the aid of a machine or
device."[56] "Machine"-made music thus persists in the statute, and in the common,
colloquial reference to "mechanical licenses," a term that harkens back to the first
days of "mechanical music" more than a century ago.[57]

14. Prelude to Public Performance

The Copyright Act of 1909 was an omnibus piece of legislation that updated and
recast copyright for the new century. Among its features were added protection for
pictorial, graphic, and sculptural works; a simplified registration process; strengthened remedies for infringement; and, notably, an extended copyright term of up to
fifty-six years (including a twenty-eight-year renewal period), twice the duration
as in the original statute in 1790.

For the music business, the focal point of the new regime was the compulsory
mechanical licensing provision implemented in the wake of the Supreme Court's
White-Smith decision, which ensured a flow of income to publishers when their
works were reproduced as part of the physical objects of music consumption—
rolls, cylinders, and discs. In the years to follow, however, the act's "public performance" provisions would also have a profound impact on the business of music.
As we have seen, the exclusive right of public performance had been granted to the
owners of musical compositions in an 1897 amendment, a by-product of the dramatists' legislative victory.[58] The 1909 Act made two important changes in this
realm. First, with respect to musical compositions in particular, the law restricted
the exclusive right to "for profit" performances only. As we will explore in Part III,
the process of defining this term in the context of early twentieth century technology and culture would generate a battleground of litigation, including two trips to
the Supreme Court by 1931.

The 1909 Act also exempted one new technology from the payment of public
performance fees. The so-called jukebox exemption applied to all "coin-operated
machines," unless a direct admission fee was charged "for admission to the place
where such reproduction or rendition occurs."[59] As we have seen, the early jukebox
was the first viable commercial use of the phonograph, before it became a staple of

---

56. 17 U.S.C. §§ 101, 115.

57. Mechanical licenses can be obtained by compliance with the statute, but are more often extended
either directly by publishers, or on their behalf through the Harry Fox Agency, established by publishers
as a clearinghouse for mechanical licensing and royalty collection.

58. *See* Chapter 8.

59. 17 U.S.C. § 1 (1909).

home entertainment. By 1909, a nascent industry was beginning to flourish, as jukeboxes became common amusements in a variety of public places. Typically, no admission was charged for entry to the parlors and arcades where jukeboxes were placed—the only "fee" was the coin deposited to operate the machine itself. Alarmed by the new costs to be imposed in the form of a performance royalty, juke operators (and the manufacturers supplying them with records) deftly side-stepped the new law by making their case as music promoters.

The proposed jukebox exemption appeared "for the first time in a bill introduced approximately 6 weeks prior to the final enactment of the bill in March 1909," but its short legislative history says much about the tensions created by the growing industry.[60] Apart from the interest of jukebox operators, publishers and recording companies were at odds on the issue, an early example of the "two sides" of the music business having divergent interests. Labels wished to protect their sales to an important and growing network of juke operators. Publishers, on the other hand, sought to maximize their exclusive right of public performance. These issues were brought into focus by Columbia vice president Paul Cromelin, in testimony before a joint House and Senate committee on patents. Cromelin referred to letters in which publishers, including Jerome H. Remick & Co., ordered hundreds of copies of phonorecords, for the purpose of giving them away to arcade owners for use in coin-operated machines.[61] He then asked, "Why does the Jerome H. Remick & Co. . . . , who claim that we are stealing the product of the composers' brains, use the Columbia Phonograph Company to the extent of ordering from us and paying for 250 to 300 records of every song as soon as they publish it? For the purpose of selling the records? No—absolutely not—but to give them away to the owners of penny arcades in consideration of their putting them on their automatic graphophones, so that the public will become acquainted with the tune and buy the sheet music."[62] Cromelin also introduced a 1906 letter from Roth & Engelhardt, a manufacturer of player pianos, which read: "If we recollect rightly the Automatic Vaudeville Company in Fourteenth Street, who run the Penny Arcade there, are being paid by certain music publishers for displaying ads of certain compositions over the automatic piano or piano player which is used to attract the public. It seems to us that this would amply demonstrate the fact that publishers and composers consider the piano player an advantageous medium to increase the sale of their compositions. If this could be proven it might be a useful point."[63]

---

60. 5 George S. Grossman, Omnibus Copyright Revision Legislative History 33 (2001).

61. 4 Legislative History of the 1909 Copyright Act 321–30 (E. Fulton Brylawski & Abe Goldman, eds., 1976).

62. *Id.* at 326.

63. *Id.* at 325.

Cromelin found it hypocritical (or at least, greedy) for publishers to oppose a jukebox exemption, when they were in fact paying *for* advertising space in connection with the "new media" of player pianos and jukeboxes. Fatigued by the long legislative process leading to the 1909 Act, and having achieved the primary goal of protecting their works against uncompensated mechanical reproduction, publishers conceded the issue, acknowledging that "the so-called 'penny parlor' [was of] first assistance as an advertising medium."[64]

The 1909 Act represented a significant step forward for music publishers, but the "power of promotion" had won the day for jukebox operators. As the jukebox trade flourished, the exemption became a major source of contention, as publishers perceived millions passing them by in foregone performance royalties.

15. 1909 Epilogue
—*Leeds & Catlin v. Victor*

Developments in the spring of 1909 had a profound impact on the music industry. In addition to the legislative changes ushered in with the new copyright act, the Supreme Court issued its decision in *Leeds & Catlin Company v. Victor Talking Machine Company*[65] on April 19, 1909, even before the new law took effect on July 1. The lawsuit was not concerned with copyright principles, and did not impact publishing interests directly. Rather, *Leeds* involved the closely related field of patent law, specifically the right to manufacture discs using the technologies invented by Emile Berliner in the 1890s.

The equivalent of what we would now call an "independent" label, New York-based Leeds and Catlin recorded, manufactured, and distributed discs only, not phonographs. The company had been a pioneer in cylinder manufacturing, then turned to selling disc records around 1900, primarily under the "Imperial" label. Leeds' fortunes were tied directly to the exploding popularity of the disc format; by early 1907, its Middletown, Connecticut plant was pressing 100,000 discs a day. In contrast, Victor was one the Big Three manufacturers of phonographs and recorded music, along with Columbia and Edison. Victor had acquired the patents relating to Emile Berliner's early phonograph inventions, particularly patent No. 534,543, issued in 1895, which made claims bearing on the phonograph apparatus itself, and also the methods of recording and reproducing discs, that is, creating recorded musical content. Columbia and Edison maintained their own patent

---

64. S. Rep. No. 1108, at 6 (1909).
65. Leeds & Catlin Co. v. Victor Talking Machine Co., 213 U.S. 301 (1909).

portfolios, which, beginning in the 1890s, were pooled and shared in varying combinations, in furtherance of their oligopoly.[66]

More than 27 million phonograph records and cylinders were manufactured in 1909, having a wholesale value of around $12 million.[67] Such figures were small in comparison to the value of the phonograph equipment business, but nevertheless represented a marketplace worth protecting. The same manufacturers who had cried out against Aeolian's attempts to monopolize the publishing side of the music industry were singing a different tune when it came to recordings: Victor sued Leeds for patent infringement, as part of a broader campaign to keep "record pirates" from infiltrating the business.

The district court quickly found in favor of Victor, issuing a preliminary injunction, which had the crippling effect of barring Leeds from selling discs while the case was pending.[68] The appellate court affirmed, leaving the Supreme Court as Leeds' last chance.[69] Leeds raised multiple defenses in a gallant attempt to void the patent, but Victor had a track record of enforcing the invention on at least five earlier occasions. The merits raised highly technical questions as to the scope of Berliner's invention, but ultimately it was no contest. Finding no abuse of discretion in the lower courts' actions, the Supreme Court affirmed the injunction.

In essence, the decision meant that Victor's patents included phonographs *and* the process of recording and reproducing discs—independent companies such as Leeds could not produce records playable on Victor's phonographs. As David Suisman explains, this was "the cultural equivalent of the absolute authority that railroads initially claimed over both the physical rails and the means of conveyance—who and what traveled on its lines, and on what terms—and it was not until key phonograph patents expired in the second half of the 1910s that independent cultural producers—in this case, record companies that were not also phonograph manufacturers—could operate in the business with any kind of reliable legal foundation."[70]

In July 1909, Victor president Eldridge Johnson boasted to its dealers: "There is no longer a great profit to be made for a small effort in the talking machine business . . . It now requires large capital, large manufacturing plants and most of all a well-chosen and well-organized army of experts."[71] This was no exaggeration with respect to Leeds and Catlin, which had declared bankruptcy in June.

---

66. SUISMAN, *supra* note 12, at 153.

67. RUSSELL SANJEK & DAVID SANJEK, AMERICAN POPULAR MUSIC BUSINESS IN THE 20TH CENTURY (1991).

68. 146 Fed. Rep. 534.

69. 148 Fed Rep. 1022.

70. SUISMAN, *supra* note 12, at 154.

71. SUISMAN, *supra* note 12, at 154, quoting Eldridge R. Johnson, *The Recent Supreme Court Decision; Its Effect; and the Future of the Talking Machine Business*, 4 VOICE OF VICTOR 5 (July 1909).

PART III

Public Performance for Profit—From Lüchow's to the La Salle Hotel

Composing legend Victor Herbert
(1859-1924) helped establish the country's first
performing rights organization, ASCAP, in 1913, and
took "public performance" issues to the U.S. Supreme
Court in 1917 (*Herbert v. Shanley*).
Author's collection

16. Dinner at Lüchow's

Upon his passing in 1936 at the age of fifty-six, the *New York Times* hailed Nathan Burkan as a "theatrical attorney," in reference not to his style but to his A-list clientele of entertainers and personalities, which had included Charlie Chaplin, Florenz Ziegfeld, Mae West, Al Jolson, and Gloria Morgan Vanderbilt, for whom he appeared in the sensational (and for her, unsuccessful) litigation over the custody of her daughter. The *Times* obituary also noted that Burkan had been prominent in Tammany Hall, the Democratic Party machine that played a major role in New York City politics for almost 200 years, serving as a member of the New York State Constitutional Convention in 1915, and later as chairman of the Triborough Bridge Authority. At the time of his death he was a legal and political tour de force, whose offices occupied an entire floor of the Continental Building, at Broadway and 41st Street in the heart of Times Square.[1]

Though these vast successes awaited him in the future, in 1906 Burkan was a newly minted attorney, enamored with the entertainment business and in search of his first significant client. He found him in Victor Herbert, the Irish-born and German-raised composer who, at the age of forty-seven and almost twenty years Burkan's senior, was a seasoned music professional, in need of a creative and energetic advocate to assist him in navigating the copyright revisions percolating in Congress. The two struck up a close professional and personal relationship that lasted until Herbert's death in 1924, and which produced both landmark legislation and legal precedents defining composers' rights in the twentieth century.

Beginning in 1906 Burkan accompanied Herbert on numerous trips to Washington, where they took part in the hearings and negotiations that led to the Copyright Act of 1909, including its seminal provisions calling for compulsory mechanical licensing of musical works. Also included in the new act was a revised provision regarding public performance, a right first extended to musical compositions in 1897.[2] The new law confirmed that the owner of a music copyright had the exclusive right to perform the work publicly, but only if the performance was "for

---

1. *See generally Nathan Burkan, 56, Attorney, Is Dead*, N.Y. Times, June 7, 1936.

2. Only three infringement suits were brought with respect to musical performance rights between 1897 and 1909, all dealing with use of music in dramatic, theatrical productions, as opposed to nondramatic performances. Russell Sanjek, American Popular Music and Its Business, The First Four Hundred Years, Vol. II, From 1900 to 1984, 37 (1988).

profit."[3] With assistance from his friend and client Victor Herbert, Nathan Burkan would make his reputation as a music lawyer by turning the revised performance clause into the biggest "for profit" bonanza composers and publishers had ever seen.

Victor Herbert was a fixture at Lüchow's, the famous New York eatery located on East 14th Street, on the edge of Tin Pan Alley. A regular patron whose table was known as "Victor Herbert Corner," beginning in 1901 Herbert persuaded founder August Lüchow to engage musicians to play during lunch and dinner, adding ambiance to the fine food and surroundings. Over the years it became a musical enclave, a comfortable place to compose and perform music, and to commune with like-minded artists and publishers. Nathan Burkan was a regular as well, and in October 1913 he and Herbert, along with Jay Witmark (another Burkan client), songwriter Raymond Hubbell, and George Maxwell (a representative for the Italian publisher G. Ricordi and Co.), called for a meeting of their colleagues at Lüchow's, for the purpose of discussing performance rights.[4] Heavy rains, and perhaps a misunderstanding of the meeting's purpose, kept most of the thirty-six invitees away; just nine attended—the five organizers, Glenn MacDonough (a Herbert collaborator), and the composers Gustave Kerker, Silvio Hein, and Louis Hirsch.[5] Some suggested canceling, but Herbert urged them on with the promise of a good meal. "What more do you want?" he asked. "Come on, let's eat!" He turned to Burkan to start things off: "Nathan—tell us about this society! Let's start it!"[6]

Burkan of course had a working knowledge of the performance right as stated in the 1909 Act. Moreover, he and Maxwell had traveled in Europe, where performance rights had been recognized for many years, and composers and publishers were collecting royalties through performing rights societies established for such purpose. The earliest and best known of the collecting societies was France's SACEM (Societe des Auteurs, Compositeurs et Editeurs de Musique), formed in the wake of the defiant acts of composer Ernest Bourget. In 1847, Bourget was sipping sugared water at the fashionable Paris café, Les Ambassadeurs, when he heard the establishment's musicians perform a rendition of one of his compositors, "Bluettes." At the time French copyright law had included a performance right for the composer for fifty years, but this was simply ignored. Bourget took a stand, refusing to pay for his water until he was paid for the use of his music. "How come," he cried, "you charge me two francs for your glass of water and for listen-

3. The "for profit" limitation was reportedly implemented at the suggestion of the American Bar Association. RUSSELL SANJEK, AMERICAN POPULAR MUSIC AND ITS BUSINESS, THE FIRST FOUR HUNDRED YEARS, VOL. II, FROM 1790 TO 1909, 399 (1988).

4. Lucia S. Schultz, *Performing-Right Societies in the United States*, 35 NOTES 513 (1978–1979).

5. *Id.*

6. Stanley Adams, *The ASCAP Story*, BILLBOARD, February 29, 1964, at 7, quoting from EDWARD N. WALTERS, VICTOR HERBERT: A LIFE IN MUSIC (1955). A second Herbert biography indicates the meeting began at the Lambs club, and continued later at Lüchow's. *See* NEIL GOULD, VICTOR HERBERT: A THEATRICAL LIFE 319 (2008).

ing to my own song?"[7] The issue wound up in the French courts, which ruled for Bourget in 1849, ordering the café to pay performance royalties, and leading ultimately to the formation of SACEM in 1851.

Indeed, SACEM had opened a New York office in 1911, seeking to collect from concert promoters and theater producers when French compositions registered in the U.S. were performed in public, and even signing a few American composers, including the rising star, Irving Berlin.[8] The notion of a French society collecting American composers' royalties under a U.S. law struck a nerve with Nathan Burkan. On cue from Herbert, Burkan presented those gathered at Lüchow's with what was essentially a duplicate of SACEM's articles of association, including the stipulation that, regardless of copyright ownership, all performance royalties collected would be split evenly between writers and publishers (giving birth to the so-called writer's share that persists to this day). He described an organization that would achieve strength by pooling the music copyrights of thousands of rights holders; together, they would offer their works en masse pursuant to a blanket license, in return for a set monthly fee, depending on the size and nature of the business. Unlike any individual songwriter or publisher, the group would have the resources to police and enforce the public performance right and, equally important, to collect and disburse royalty revenue to its members, according to an agreed formula.

There being no downside to such a venture for publishers or composers, the idea for an American performance rights society spread quickly among the music community in the following months. By the time a second meeting was called on February 14, 1914, this time at the Hotel Claridge in Times Square, over one hundred attended. The group made quick work of the organizational necessities, and (after switching the usual order of referring to "authors" and "composers" for the sake of a better acronym), agreed to call the society ASCAP—the American Society of Composers, Authors and Publishers.

With its first offices established in the Fulton Theater Building, all the fledgling group needed was willing buyers. Rector's Restaurant and Lüchow's have each been reported to be the first licensee,[9] the latter undoubtedly persuaded with some gentle arm-twisting by its famous customer, Victor Herbert.[10] In any event, by the end of 1914 ASCAP had signed around eighty-five licensees, who paid between five and fifteen dollars a month—a respectable start, but not enough to cover expenses (even with its officers and general counsel, Burkan, working for free), let

---

7. David Sinacore-Guinn. Collective Administration of Copyrights and Neighboring Rights 2 (1993).

8. *See* Schultz, *supra* note 4, at 512; Sanjek, *supra* note 2, at 37–38.

9. *Happy 94th Birthday, ASCAP*, ASCAP, posted at http://www.ascap.com/press/2008/0213_birthday .aspx.

10. Paul Goldstein, Copyright's Highway: From Gutenberg to the Celestial Jukebox 55 (2003).

alone distribute royalties to its members. Indeed, most establishments scoffed at the idea of paying to perform music, especially the restaurants and hotels that, as opposed to offering concerts or shows, employed performers only to provide background music. Through their own trade group, the New York Hotel and Restaurant Association, they insisted that their use of music was not "for profit"; ASCAP fees were simply a musical "tax" they had no intention of paying.[11] Soon it became clear that, as in France, a definitive legal precedent would be necessary to give meaning, and teeth, to the public performance provisions of the 1909 Act.

17. "From Maine to Oregon" (By Way of Manhattan)

Completed in 1913, the twenty-two-story Vanderbilt Hotel on Park Avenue was one of New York's most exclusive establishments, a terra cotta showcase "worth crossing a continent to see."[12] Its namesake financier, Alfred Gwynne Vanderbilt, took up residence on the top two floors, ensconced in the lap of luxury. Vanderbilt only enjoyed his new home for a short time, however; in May 1915 he died a hero's death after surrendering his life jacket to a woman on the ill-fated *Lusitania*, which sank after being hit by a German torpedo off the coast of Ireland.[13] An architectural focus on the large number of permanent residences at the Vanderbilt eliminated the need for a grand ballroom; instead, the entire first floor served as a large lounge, dining, and entertainment area, where live musicians would frequently perform.

John Philip Sousa was not among ASCAP's founders, but he became a charter member of the society early in its existence, along with his primary publisher, John Church & Co. Like the Vanderbilt Hotel itself, Sousa's latest march, "From Maine to Oregon," was unveiled in 1913, as part of his operetta *The American Maid*. Sousa's latest work was well-suited to the posh hotel: following the operetta's debut in Rochester, "From Maine to Oregon" made its way down to Manhattan, and onto the playlist of the Vanderbilt Hotel's orchestra. Although the proprietor, Hilliard Hotel Co., spared no expense in operating the opulent hotel, the company had respectfully declined an ASCAP license. Ever vigilant with regard to his copyrights, Sousa (through his publisher, John Church Co.) filed suit against the hotel.

---

11. Sanjek, *supra* note 2, at 39. For the latest reference to performance royalties as a "music tax," *see* Chapter 45.

12. Christopher Gray, *Streetscapes/Vanderbilt Hotel*, N.Y. Times, reprinted at http://www.nyc-architecture.com/MID/MID026.htm.

13. *Id.* Notably, the renowned tenor and Victor recording artist, Enrico Caruso, took over the penthouse suite in 1920, where he lived until his death the following year.

There was no disputing that the Vanderbilt band had played the song—the only question was whether the performance was "for profit," and therefore infringing. The district court made quick work of the issue, deciding that the performance was in furtherance of the hotel's general "for profit" operations, and taking the extraordinary step of entering a preliminary injunction barring the Vanderbilt, "and the leader of the orchestra," from further performances while the case was pending.

The hotel promptly appealed to the Second Circuit Court of Appeals, which, in a devastating blow to ASCAP's interests, reversed the decision on February 9, 1915.[14] The appellate court reached its conclusion in a roundabout way, considering each of the three different uses of the "for profit" terminology in the statute— the provision extending the exclusive right to public performance, and also the sections defining copyright infringement and penalties generally, including the language imposing criminal liability in the case of "any person who [infringes] willfully and for profit," making that person subject to fines and imprisonment for up to one year. Considering these various provisions "together," the court reasoned, "Congress seems to have meant by the words 'for profit' a direct pecuniary charge for the performance, such as an admission fee."[15] A decision in the publisher's favor, said the court, could subject a church "together with the organist and every member of the choir" to fines and imprisonment when copyrighted anthems were played in religious services, since "there is an expectation that the congregation will be increased by making the service more attractive." Refusing to believe that Congress intended such a result, the Second Circuit declared that the hotel orchestra's performance of "From Maine to Oregon" was not "for profit," and vacated the injunction.

The case returned to the trial court for further proceedings, where it percolated for many months, but the practical effects of the Second Circuit's ruling were immediate. It was impossible for ASCAP to recruit new customers, and some existing licensees ceased payments, claiming that the decision voided their contracts. Burkan worked feverishly to stem the tide, successfully enforcing some existing restaurant licenses on purely contractual grounds, even though the establishments charged no admission fee for music.[16] At best, these efforts were a finger in the dike. Immediate additional legal action would be necessary if ASCAP's charter was to be saved.

---

14. John Church Co. v. Hilliard Hotel Co., 221 F. 229 (2d Cir. 1915).
15. *Id.*
16. *See* ASCAP v. Faust Co., Inc., 90 Misc. 702 (N.Y. Sup. Ct. 1915).

18. A Pleasant Dinner at Shanley's, Gone Bad

A robust figure with a healthy appetite, Victor Herbert frequented restaurants other than Lüchow's, which had been ASCAP's incubator. Among his other haunts was Shanley's, the popular Times Square restaurant that served as a tourist destination and community hub for entertainers, politicians, judges, journalists, and merchants alike. Herbert had completed his latest comic operetta, *Sweethearts*, in 1913, and the original Broadway production ran for 136 performances at the New Amsterdam and Liberty Theatres, ending in January 1914. Some of the individual songs from the show, including the title number, were popular enough to support sheet music releases, and lived on as staples of live music showcases, like those provided in Manhattan restaurants, hotels, and other public venues, including Shanley's.

As the legend goes, Victor Herbert was enjoying a pleasant dinner at Shanley's, but when the band struck up its version of "Sweethearts," his "Irish temper boiled over," and he demanded payment from the proprietor.[17] Herbert may have been there, but at a minimum his reaction was embellished for dramatic effect.[18] A seasoned music man, he could hardly have been surprised by the entirely common practice of hearing live musicians performing background music, or to hear one of his recent show tunes in the mix. And the incident occurred on April 1, 1915, well after ASCAP was formed and Herbert was serving as its first vice president, and less than two months after the devastating ruling in the *Church* case, with which he was only too familiar.[19] Moreover, Herbert's version of events bears a striking resemblance to the story of Ernest Bourget and the founding of SACEM, sixty years earlier. In all likelihood, Herbert simply wished to paint himself in a similar heroic light, and why not? The feigned indignation might serve him well in the litigation he and Nathan Burkan were planning to unleash.

After confirming the sequence of events, Burkan completed and filed a complaint on behalf of Herbert and his publisher, G. Schirmer, Inc., alleging that Shanley's had infringed two separate copyrights—the first in the *Sweethearts* operetta, a "dramatico-musical composition," and the second in the individual title

---

17. Brendan Charney in *Congress and the Culture Industry: Copyright Law and the Development of the American Popular Music Business, 1890–1940*, p. 5 (Apr. 10, 2008) (Senior Thesis, History Department, Columbia University, quoting Leonard Allen, *The Battle of Tin Pan Alley*, HARPER'S MAG., June 1940, at 514.

18. One source credits John Leffler, a theater manager, as the individual who testified to hearing the performance. *See* Schultz, *supra* note 4, at 514.

19. 19. SANJEK, *supra* note 2, at 39; Schultz, *supra* note 4, at 513.

song, a straight "musical composition." The approach was ingenious; the statute did not include the "for profit" limitation on performances of dramatico-musical compositions, thus presenting what appeared to be a fail-safe approach.[20] Burkan requested an immediate injunction against further performances.

The case was assigned to judge Billings Learned Hand, the brilliant jurist appointed by William Howard Taft in 1909 at the age of thirty-seven, who would later serve as Senior Circuit Judge on the prestigious Second Circuit Court of Appeals. Hand was known for his analytical precision, and for opinions that amounted to legal literature. He rendered his decision *Herbert v. Shanley* on May 1, 1915, just two weeks after Victor Herbert's dinner was so rudely interrupted. "That the opera was a dramatico-musical composition seems to me of no question," he wrote, "a performance need not, therefore, be 'for profit' to infringe."[21] "Furthermore," he reasoned, "a performance in words and music alone infringed the dramatico-musical copyright . . . So far the case is all with the plaintiffs." Burkan's stomach surely churned when he reached this point in the opinion, knowing that Judge Hand was about to change course. "However," the court continued, "the authors took out a copyright upon the song separately as a musical composition, and in so doing they necessarily gave into the public domain all musical rights, except as they were covered by the resulting copyright." "Singing the words to the music, accompanied by the orchestra, is therefore within the musical rights so dedicated." Citing to the *Church* ruling that was barely three months old, Hand concluded that Shanley's performance "did not infringe." The request for an injunction was denied. Burkan's dual infringement theory had failed. As Judge Hand saw it, Herbert "was really trying to eat [his] cake and have it." The court would not allow for "double protection"—Herbert would have to live by the more restrictive public performance right attached to the song. In four short paragraphs, Judge Hand dealt a second, crippling blow to Herbert, ASCAP, and the music publishing community. Burkan lodged an appeal to the Second Circuit.

The Second Circuit's decision, issued in January 1916, was a foregone conclusion. There was no reason for the court to depart from the reasoning it had expressed in the *Church* matter less than a year earlier. In addition, the court agreed with Judge Hand's analysis on the issue of double protection. The court of appeals reached two definitive conclusions: First, Herbert could not rely on the dramatic-musical copyright, since he had taken out a separate copyright in the musical composition alone; and second, confirming the *Church* decision, the musical composition, "Sweethearts," was "not infringed by its being rendered in a public

---

20. With this detail having fallen so nicely into place, one wonders whether in the bowels of history there may have been an anonymous request for "Sweethearts" that evening. Or perhaps Herbert simply made himself known, and the band favored him with one of his own tunes, taking the bait set by his presence.

21. Herbert v. Shanley Co., 222 F. 344 (S.D.N.Y. 1915).

restaurant where no admission fee is charged."[22] For the second time in a year, music publishers were rebuffed by the influential Court of Appeals for the Second Circuit. There was no turning back. ASCAP's survival would hinge upon music's next trip to the U.S. Supreme Court.

19. Justice Holmes

The *Church v. Hilliard* litigation remained pending as *Herbert v. Shanley* made its way to the court of appeals. As both cases presented the same issues, they were jointly appealed to the Supreme Court. With the briefs submitted,[23] thirty-seven-year-old Nathan Burkan and his counterparts presented arguments to the Supreme Court on January 10, 1917. Surely he directed his points to Justice Holmes, whose opinions, including his concurrence in *White-Smith v. Apollo* in 1908, displayed an expansive view of copyright.[24] When the decision came down on January 22, Burkan and his clients were heartened to see that Justice Holmes had written for the court.[25]

After setting forth the essential facts of both matters, Holmes declared that it would "not be necessary to discuss" the questions raised by the plaintiffs' ownership of separate copyrights in an operetta and a musical composition. The cases would turn solely on the issue of whether the performances were "for profit." He dispatched with this question, and reversed the rulings in both cases, in a single, oft-quoted paragraph: "If the rights under the copyright are infringed only by a performance where money is taken at the door they are very imperfectly protected. Performances not different in kind from those of the defendants could be given that might compete with and even destroy the success of the monopoly that the law intends the plaintiffs to have. It is enough to say that there is no need to construe the statute so narrowly. The defendants' performances are not eleemosynary [for charity]. They are part of a total for which the public pays, and the fact that the price of the whole is attributed to a particular item which those present are expected to order, is not important. It is true that the music is not the sole ob-

---

22. Herbert v. Shanley Co., 229 F. 340 (2d Cir. 1916). On its first conclusion, the court noted in addition that the sheet music for "Sweethearts" did not refer to the earlier copyright in the operetta. The question of whether "if [plaintiffs] had inserted a notice of the previous copyright, they could have retained the advantage of it as to the republished song" was not considered.

23. If Herbert's "Irish temper" hadn't truly boiled over at the Shanley's performance, it surely did upon reading the defendant's contention that "[w]hile the purpose [of the performance] was to amuse and attract guests, whether it was actually accomplished is a matter of pure conjecture; the song 'Sweethearts' may have driven more patrons from the dining-room than it lured in."

24. There is a fine narrative of Holmes' copyright opinions in GOLDSTEIN, *supra* note 10, at 48–61.

25. *Herbert*; John Church Co. v. Hilliard Hotel Co., 242 U.S. 591 (1917).

ject, but neither is the food, which probably could be got cheaper elsewhere. The object is a repast in surroundings that to people having limited powers of conversation or disliking the rival noise give a luxurious pleasure not to be had from eating a silent meal. If music did not pay it would be given up. If it pays it pays out of the public's pocket. Whether it pays or not the purpose of employing it is profit and that is enough."

Learned Hand had sucked the life from ASCAP in four short paragraphs; Justice Holmes' resuscitation required only three. ASCAP was back in business.

There was much to be read between the lines of Holmes' short opinion. In his *White-Smith* concurrence, Holmes was compelled to agree with the court's narrow interpretation of "copy," based on considerable earlier precedent. It took an act of Congress—the 1909 Act—to bring mechanical copies within the purview of copyright. Here, on the other hand, the "for profit" provisions in the statute were new, with little or no legislative history demonstrating congressional intent. Thus, there was "no need to construe the statute so narrowly" as to require "money . . . taken at the door." With this judicial freedom, Holmes could evaluate the performances in their commercial and cultural context.

Long recognized as an effective method for promoting the sale of sheet music, by 1917 musical performance was becoming something quite different. Music, particularly in urban areas, was everywhere—in dining rooms, dance halls, and ballrooms, along with department stores, hotels, and all manner of open spaces. Music "consumption" was moving from the private parlor into public spaces, a cultural shift that created the possibility that performances might actually "replace" sheet music, instead of promoting its sale. In Holmes' words, the kind of public performances taking place at Shanley's and the Vanderbilt Hotel "might compete with and even destroy the success of the monopoly that the law intends the plaintiffs to have." In the court's view, the new copyright act was intended to accommodate these fundamental changes in social habits and industry dynamics by granting additional rights that in turn created new streams of revenue. Consumers were paying for music not only as sheets, rolls, cylinders, and records, but also in the ephemeral form of public performances; a portion of the money paid for live performances would now flow through to creators and publishers.

♪♪ ♫♫ ♪♪

The Supreme Court decisions in *White-Smith* and *Shanley* were fitting bookends for the 1909 Act; together, these legislative and judicial developments ushered in a new era in music copyright. *White-Smith* exposed the need for updated legislation to accommodate the explosion of new methods for reproducing music brought on by the Industrial Revolution. The imperfect but satisfactory solution, still in place today, was the compulsory mechanical license. On the other hand, and with some irony, the *Shanley* decision dragged the oldest "technology" of all—the live performance—into a new statutory scheme that defined music copyright in a more expansive way, accommodating changes in social habits that gave performances greater commercial value.

The initial decisions interpreting the 1909 Act signaled a broader conception of copyright. Instead of the narrow "right" to make a material "copy," copyright was treated as "intellectual property"—a "bundle" of different rights that could be exploited in various ways. In the words of David Suisman, these developments "transformed the music publisher from primarily a seller of sheet music to primarily a manager of copyrights."[26] That is, the business of music became predominantly a licensing business. As World War I came to a close and the Roaring Twenties got underway, publishers were still selling sheet music, to be sure, but increasingly, they were managing the licensed use of their music copyrights in piano rolls, disc recordings, and as an element of performances given in public spaces of every kind. Still, groundbreaking technologies waited in the wings to test the new, broader conception of music copyright.

20. ASCAP Goes to the Movies

As motion picture productions grew more sophisticated, music became a vital part of the moviegoing experience: Theaters hired individual organists, small ensembles, and sometimes full orchestras to provide live musical accompaniment for silent films.[27] Large orchestras accompanied the 1915 release of the silent film *Birth of a Nation*, for example, performing songs from a commissioned score, as well as popular numbers compiled by director D.W. Griffith and Joseph Carl Breil, ranging from Stephen Foster's "Swanee River," to standards such as "Dixie," "Turkey in the Straw," and "O Tannenbaum"; classical pieces like Tchaikovsky's Fifth Symphony and Wagner's "Ride of the Valkyries"; and the patriotic "My Country 'Tis of Thee" and "The Star-Spangled Banner."[28] Music was particularly important in deluxe, first-run theaters, where shows often started with an overture, which could last as long as ten minutes, followed by a musical soloist, then a newsreel and comedy short (both accompanied by music), and finally, the feature film.[29] Hiring musicians to perform multiple shows daily became a significant expense for theater owners. Movie music remained a "live" concept well into the 1920s. With the exception of a few experimental uses of sound on film, or recordings synchro-

---

26. DAVID SUISMAN, SELLING SOUNDS: THE COMMERCIAL REVOLUTION IN AMERICAN MUSIC 176 (2009).
27. DOUGLAS GOMERY, THE COMING OF SOUND 18 (2005).
28. *Id.* Indeed, theater musicians played as many as fifty different "scores" for *Birth of a Nation*, depending on where the film was being shown.
29. *See* GOMERY, *supra* note 27, at 19.

nized with projection, film music was performed by live musicians, conducted in synchronization with onscreen projections.

Invigorated by its court victory in *Shanley*, a nascent ASCAP aggressively targeted movie theaters as licensees. Theater owners resisted, noting the significant fees paid to performing musicians, as well as the costs of purchasing sheet music for use in theaters. These tensions first came to a head in April 1918, when the Motion Pictures Exhibitors League of America organized a lawsuit challenging ASCAP's right to collect license fees from movie houses.[30] The named plaintiff, a theater located on 174th Street in Manhattan, brought suit in New York state court, seeking an order restraining ASCAP from demanding performance fees. Rather than basing the suit on copyright principles, the theater alleged that ASCAP's tactics amounted to improper "coercion," contrary to "an understanding between authors, publishers, and composers prior to the formation of [ASCAP] that the purchase of copies of the printed music entitled them to be rendered in the place of business of the plaintiff or others similarly situated without further cost or expense."[31] In other words, because the theater purchased sheet copies of the music it used to accompany pictures, it did not want to pay ASCAP for performing the same music. Referencing what was becoming a familiar "promotion" defense, the theater argued further that it spent thousands of dollars *advertising* the music that its orchestra performed, thereby promoting sheet music sales, to the benefit of ASCAP publishers.

The suit went nowhere. Since ASCAP had been formed for a "lawful purpose," the court found "no exercise of any coercion," noting that the "institution of legal actions by individual members of the association for violation of copyright is justified for the protection of income from their music."[32] Further, the court not only rejected the promotion argument, but turned it against the plaintiff, finding that "[t]he fact that the music of the authors who are members of the association is popular and in demand presents just so much more reason why it should be protected."[33]

Their legal strategy had failed, but many theater owners continued to refuse ASCAP's overtures. In due course, it became apparent that legal action would again be necessary to test the scope of the performance right as applied to theaters. The new test case, brought in federal district court in Pennsylvania in 1922, was *Harms v. Cohen*.[34] In *Harms* the plaintiff publisher sued the owner of the Model Theater in Philadelphia, alleging that the theater organist had unlawfully performed portions of the copyrighted composition, "Tulip Time," a song from the 1919 version of the *Ziegfeld Follies*, in synchronization with the silent films exhibited there. Following the Supreme Court's reasoning in *Shanley*, the court found

---

30. *See id.*
31. 174 St. & St. Nicholas Amusement Co. v. Maxwell, 169 N.Y.S. 895, 896 (N.Y. Sup. Ct. 1918).
32. *Id.*
33. *Id.*
34. Harms v. Cohen, 279 F. 276 (E.D. Penn. 1922).

infringement, noting that "the furnishing of music was an attraction which added to the enjoyment of persons viewing the motion pictures," and was therefore "for profit," despite there being no "direct" charge for music, apart from the price of a movie ticket.

With two more court victories in hand, ASCAP used its leverage to set performance license rates for theaters. In 1923, following lengthy negotiations with the national Motion Picture Theater Owners of America, fees were standardized at ten cents per seat, per year, for every movie theater in the country.[35] Movie theaters were firmly within the ASCAP hold, at least for the time being. Despite its unblemished court record, ASCAP could not rest. Yet another new technology had appeared on the scene, one that would redefine public performance in more profound ways, turning the music industry on its head—radio.

21. "L. Bamberger & Co., One of America's Great Stores"

With over 200 manufacturers flooding the business, 1921 was a peak year for talking machine sales. Revenues reached $106 million at retail, a figure that would not be exceeded for twenty-five years.[36] As Americans turned toward the newer format, record sales outpaced sheet music purchases the following year.[37] Music publishers were well-positioned for the change in music consumption, as the two-cent mechanical license royalty flowed into their coffers with every record sold. And publishers were earning revenue from public performances as well; 1921 was also the first year ASCAP's collections exceeded expenses, allowing for initial royalty distributions to its affiliated publishers and writers.[38]

Radio was a miracle of science and sound. The notion of receiving wireless transmissions broadcast from distant locations in the comfort of one's own home was nothing short of revolutionary, as was the warmth and quality of sound generated by vacuum tubes and amplified speakers. The ability to receive information and entertainment in this way transformed American life, from the farm to the city and at all points in between. Radio technology had been bubbling since the turn of the century, when the first wireless experiments were conducted in Europe and, a few years later, the United States. By 1910 regular transmissions were being made to small audiences, and by the middle of the decade, ideas were hatched to

---

35. *See* GOMERY, *supra* note 27, at 19.

36. SANJEK, *supra* note 2, at 62.

37. Charney, *supra* note 17, at 54.

38. As reported in Schultz, *supra* note 4, at 515, out of $236,723 collected, $81,883 was distributed, half to publishers and writers respectively; *see also* Adams, *supra* note 6, at 7.

make radio a "household utility."[39] World War I intervened however, slowing the commercial development of radio technology, as the government took control of various radio patents, and stations were either closed or turned over to the armed forces. When hostilities ceased and the technology moved back into private hands, sales of radio equipment began to boom, reaching $8 million in 1919, the year the Radio Corporation of America (RCA) was incorporated.

Station KDKA in Pittsburgh is said to have made the first regularly scheduled commercial broadcast on November 6, 1920, announcing, between musical numbers, the election of Warren G. Harding as President.[40] In 1922, the number of active commercial radio stations jumped from 28 to 670, and music (live and recorded) became a mainstay of radio programming.[41] Among the newly licensed broadcasters was station WOR in Newark, New Jersey, transmitting from the sixth floor of the city's "gigantic department store," L. Bamberger & Co.[42] Founded in 1893, like many department stores, Bamberger's had been in the music business for years, first selling sheet music, and later phonograph equipment, to its legions of customers. As phonograph and record sales were peaking, store management perceived demand shifting to radio receivers. Accordingly, Bamberger's began to stock the newfangled equipment and, to bring attention to its new offerings, launched radio station WOR in February 1922, featuring "vocal and instrumental concerts and other entertainment and information." Naturally, each program began and ended with the on-air mention of the store's familiar slogan: "L. Bamberger & Co., One of America's Great Stores, Newark, N.J."[43]

By 1922 the Witmark brothers were an established Tin Pan Alley publishing house, founding members of ASCAP with a growing catalog that included the copyright in the popular "Mother Machree," a sentimental tribute to an Irish mother's love, written in 1910 by Rida Johnson Young, set to music by Chauncey Olcott and Witmark staff writer Ernest R. Ball.[44] "Mother Machree" was recorded by numerous artists, and remained popular into the 1920s and beyond, making it a natural number for inclusion in WOR's early programming.

The Witmarks were vigilant in protecting their copyrights, and ASCAP, having failed to convince broadcasters in private negotiations, was searching for another test case, hoping to confirm that publishers were entitled to fees for radio broadcast performances. The suit was put in place. As with the earlier public performance cases, the facts of *Witmark v. Bamberger* were not in dispute—only the

---

39. SANJEK, *supra* note 2, at 75–76.
40. MARK COLEMAN, PLAYBACK: FROM THE VICTROLA TO MP3, 100 YEARS OF MUSIC, MACHINES, AND MONEY 33 (2003); SANJEK, *supra* note 2, at 77.
41. Charney, *supra* note 17, at 58.
42. M. Witmark & Sons v. L. Bamberger & Co., 291 F. 776 (D.N.J. 1923).
43. *Id.*
44. Ball collaborated with Young again in 1912 on the classic, "When Irish Eyes Are Smiling," solidifying his position as a composer of Irish ballads.

proper application of law. WOR had indeed broadcast "Mother Machree" "by means of singing," but contended that the performance was not "for profit" "because everything it broadcasts . . . is without charge or cost to radio listeners." With facts closely analogous to those addressed by Justice Holmes in the *Shanley* matter less than five years before, the result seemed inevitable, but Bamberger's mounted a vigorous defense, arguing "strenuously" that Shanley's made a "direct" charge for music, in the form of higher-priced food. The court disagreed, reasoning that *Shanley* involved an "*indirect* way of collecting the charge for musical entertainment." In reaching this conclusion, the court found "quite helpful," the opinion rendered one year before in *Harms v. Cohen.*[45]

With the *Shanley* and *Harms* decisions as recent guidance, the court found "the problem now presented for solution not so difficult." Bamberger's made no "direct" charge to its radio listeners, but was "the broadcasting done for an indirect profit"? To make the determination, the court looked to the underlying reason for broadcasting. Adopting Justice Holmes' language, the court noted that Bamberger's was not an "eleemosynary institution," but rather a "department store . . . conducted for profit, which leads us to the very significant fact that the cost of broadcasting was charged against the general expenses of the business. It was made part of a business system." And although the store's programming did not advertise specific products and prices, each broadcast included its slogan, for the purpose of promoting the enterprise and, indirectly, increasing its profits. Considering all the facts and circumstances, Bamberger's broadcasts were deemed "for profit" within the meaning of the law.

A deeper look at the *Bamberger* decision reveals a significant extension of the law, not merely the affirmation of the existing precedents in *Shanley* and *Harms.* In the earlier cases, courts analyzed situations where a monetary charge, though not *directly* related to music, was made more or less simultaneously with the musical performance. The expenses incurred in providing music were built into the costs of the specific goods being sold—food and movie tickets, respectively. In contrast, WOR's performance of "Mother Machree" was not connected to the sale of any particular product or service; it served only an *advertising* function, intended to raise the store's profile and increase the prospects for making profits on future sales. Music expenses were incurred by the business only at the most general level, but they were still incurred in furtherance of a profit-making venture, and that was enough.[46] The decision was another significant win for the music

---

45. Harms v. Cohen, 279 F. 276 (E.D. Penn. 1922).

46. The Court of Appeals for the Sixth Circuit drew this distinction two years later, in Jerome H. Remick & Co. v. American Automobile Accessories Co., 5 F.2d 411 (6th Cir. 1925), concluding: "It is immaterial, in our judgment, whether that commercial use [of music] be such as to secure direct payment for the performance . . . or indirect payment, as by a hat-checking charge, when no admission fee is required, or a general commercial advantage, as by advertising one's name in the expectation and hope of making profits through the sale of one's products, be they radio or other goods."

publishing community. After *Bamberger*, it appeared that the public performance of music in connection with the operation of any commercial enterprise was likely to be deemed "for profit" and therefore infringing, unless licensed by ASCAP.[47]

Before leaving *Bamberger* and *Harms*, it is worth observing that in both cases the familiar "promotion" argument was again raised, and rejected, as a defense. In *Bamberger* the store argued that the publisher should not complain of radio broadcasts "because of the great advertising service thereby accorded the copyrighted number." Indeed, the court's "own opinion of the possibilities of advertising by radio le[d] . . . to the belief that the broadcasting of a newly copyrighted musical composition would greatly enhance the sales of the printed sheet." However, determining the best methods for song promotion was "the privilege of the owner," who "has the exclusive right to publish and vend, as well as to perform," so the promotion argument was deemed "immaterial." Similarly, the defendant movie theater in *Harms* argued that the plaintiff publisher had given the sheet music in question to the theater's organist, encouraging that it be played, and thus had benefited from, instead of being damaged by, the performance. But distributing "professional copies" did not create a performance license, making the promotion argument, in the court's view, "clearly immaterial."

22. 1931: *Buck v. Jewell-La Salle* and the Birth of Background Music

The *Bamberger* decision did not mark the end of ASCAP's efforts to solidify the scope of the performance right. The ongoing struggle would require music's fourth trip to the U.S. Supreme Court in 1931, in *Buck v. Jewell-La Salle Realty*.[48] The case involved multiple complaints filed by Gene Buck as president of ASCAP against the owners of two Kansas City businesses—radio station KWKC and the La Salle Hotel, on Linwood Boulevard.

As was becoming a common practice, the La Salle had a "master radio receiving set," connected "by means of wires" to the hotel's public spaces and 200 guest rooms. In this fashion, programming received on the master set, including transmissions from station KWKC, were "simultaneously heard throughout the hotel."[49] Anticipating today's more sophisticated systems, the La Salle provided incidental background music for its patrons' pleasure. Both the station and hotel ignored

---

47. *See* Jerome H. Remick, 5 F.2d 411; Jerome H. Remick & Co. v. General Electric Co., 16 F.2d 829 (S.D.N.Y. 1926).

48. Buck et al. v. Jewell-La Salle Realty Co., 283 U.S. 191 and 283 U.S. 202 (1931).

49. Buck v. Jewell-La Salle Realty Co., 32 F.2d 366 (W.D. Mo. 1929).

initial license proposals, so on May 29, 1928, ASCAP sent a formal warning that "unless and until [a] license was obtained . . . [they] should strictly avoid the rendition or performance . . . of any musical compositions copyrighted by any member of said society, under any circumstances."[50] The demand was ignored, and in October the society confirmed that the hotel continued making KWKC's broadcasts available to guests, including "Just Imagine," a popular number owned by ASCAP publisher DeSylva, Brown and Henderson, Inc.

Litigation commenced against both offenders, and when the station failed to appear, a default was entered and the case proceeded against the hotel alone. ASCAP brought the full force of its growing legal resources to bear on the matter, retaining attorneys from New York (including Nathan Burkan), Los Angeles, Chicago and Kansas City. ASCAP focused on its string of victories, from the Supreme Court decision in *Shanley* to the most recent opinion in *Bamberger*, confirming that radio broadcasting qualified as public performance for profit. But the broadcaster defendant had defaulted and, as the La Salle's attorneys pointed out, the specific way in which the hotel was using music had not been addressed in earlier cases.

District court judge Merrel E. Otis rendered his decision on April 18, 1929, noting that the case was "one of first impression" and citing "no authorities because there is none." Having sidestepped earlier precedent, the court raised a series of hypothetical situations, opining on which might involve a musical "performance." "If I throw open a window so that I can hear the music of a band passing by, am I producing that music?" he asked. "Am I then the performer or participating in the performance? If I lift a telephone receiver and hear the voice of a friend, am I producing that voice? Is it my speech or his? If in perfect analogy to these illustrations, by mechanical means, I receive as music what has been produced elsewhere in such a way that it penetrates my house, I am not the performer who has produced that music." By focusing on the hotel's "receiving" broadcasts, as opposed to the affirmative acts involved in making them available to guests, Judge Otis concluded that "the defendant did not perform these musical compositions in the sense the word 'perform' is used in the act." Regardless of whether the hotel's activities were "for profit," there had been no "performance" at all, and therefore no infringement.

Shocked by the turn of events, ASCAP appealed to the Court of Appeals for the Eighth Circuit.[51] "[B]eing in doubt on the question of 'performance,'" the appellate court passed (the) *Buck* on to the Supreme Court by "certifying" a specific

---

50. Buck v. Jewell-La Salle Realty Co., 51 F.2d 726 (8th Cir. 1931).

51. There were additional aspects of the case that became the subject of a separate appeal. The hotel's orchestra had also performed ASCAP songs live without a license; infringement was found and the $250 in damages awarded under the statute. The amount was questioned on appeal and this issue, too, was ultimately reviewed by the Supreme Court, which found that the district court's award was appropriate. *See Buck*, 51 F.2d 730.

question for the high court. It would be up to Justice Holmes (in his final year on the bench at age ninety) and his brethren to decide whether "the acts of a hotel proprietor, in making available to his guests, through the instrumentality of a radio receiving set and loud speakers installed in his hotel and under his control and for the entertainment of his guests, the hearing of a copyrighted composition which has been broadcast from a radio transmitting station, constitute a performance of such composition."

With assistance from the newly formed radio lobby, the National Association of Broadcasters, which had inserted itself by filing an amicus (friend of the court) brief, the hotel advanced three lines of reasoning. First, as Judge Otis had concluded, the hotel insisted it was merely receiving, not performing, and that to find otherwise would grant every copyright owner "autocratic power to exact tribute from every person operating a receiving set in public." For the hotel, any radio broadcast involved only one "performance," occurring at the broadcast source. Revealing the NAB's influence, and showing how deeply radio had penetrated everyday life, the hotel urged that a "multiple performance theory" would reduce the overall radio audience by "making hazardous the operation of radio sets in hotel lobbies and hotel rooms, restaurants retail radio stores, railroad club cars, dance halls, theaters, moving picture houses, hospitals and other public places."[52] The Supreme Court characterized the hotel's second argument as being "based on an elaborate discussion of the theory of radio transmission and reception. Defendant's hypothesis is that the energy which actuates the receiving apparatus—that is, which varies the currents in the receiver to produce audible sound—is part of the original energy exerted upon the air by the performer. Hence it is urged that the radio receiving set is no more that a mechanical or electrical ear-trumpet for the better audition of a distant performance."[53] Finally, the hotel argued (in the face of considerable precedent) that any performances were not "for profit."

Justice Louis Brandeis, another of the high court's most esteemed jurists, authored the Supreme Court opinion dated April 13, 1931. Brandeis wrote that "[n]othing in the Act circumscribes the meaning attributed to the term 'performance,' or prevents a single rendition of a copyrighted selection from resulting in more than one public performance for profit." Reflecting on the new technology giving rise to the issue, he noted that "[w]hile this may not have been possible before the development of radio broadcasting, the novelty of the means used does not lessen the duty of the courts to give full protection to the monopoly of public performance for profit which Congress has secured to the composer."

As to the second, more metaphysical argument, the court was "satisfied that the reception of a radio broadcast and its translation into audible sound is not a mere audition of the original program." Rather, guests' ability to hear the broadcasts

---

52. Buck v. Jewell-La Salle Realty Co., 283 U.S. 191 (1931).
53. *Id.* n. 7.

was brought about "by the acts of the hotel in (1) installing, (2) supplying electric current to, and (3) operating the radio receiving set and loudspeakers." Instead of merely "receiving," the hotel was, in essence, "rebroadcasting" music to its patrons. In the end, the La Salle's use of music was deemed the legal equivalent of the live orchestra that had performed "From Maine to Oregon" at the Vanderbilt Hotel in New York: "There is no difference in substance between the case where a hotel engages an orchestra to furnish the music and that where, by means of the radio set and loud-speakers here employed, it furnishes the same music for the same purpose. In each the music is produced by instrumentalities under its control." "The question certified is answered Yes," said the court, referring the matter back to the court of appeals for further disposition, including a decision on the third, "for profit" argument, which had not been properly placed before the Supreme Court. On July 23, 1931, the Eighth Circuit rendered its opinion, citing *Shanley* in holding that "the performance was a public one and was for profit."[54]

ASCAP was again vindicated by the nation's highest court, and its legal efforts were seemingly complete, having established that any use of music by a commercial establishment—from traditional live venues, to movie houses, or through the miracle of radio broadcasting—was within the scope of the publishers' exclusive right of public performance.

23. Reshaping an Industry—Radio, Movies, and Music

Lack of success in the courtroom did not diminish broadcasters' resistance to paying performance fees. In the wake of the *Bamberger* decision in 1923, the radio industry formed its own trade group, the National Association of Broadcasters, which began lobbying activities on a variety of issues. One of the NAB's first efforts was teaming with the motion picture lobby in pursuing the so-called Dill Bill in 1924, intended to eliminate the public performance right. In response, Nathan Burkan and Victor Herbert led a contingent of the nation's leading composers to Washington, helping defeat the legislation.[55] The NAB probed in other ways, too, convincing the Justice Department to investigate ASCAP's alleged "monopoly on music," only to see the matter dropped, largely because of the demonstrated impossibility of individual copyright owners enforcing rights on their own.[56] These initial squabbles between music producers and users established patterns that continue to this day, a time when public performance issues are again at the fore-

---

54. *Buck*, 51 F.2d 726.
55. Suisman, *supra* note 26, at 174; Sanjek, *supra* note 2, at 81.
56. Schultz, *supra* note 4, at 516.

front of music copyright policy debates.[57] As music-formatted radio programming grew in popularity, bringing advertising revenue to broadcasters, radio became a more significant royalty stream for composers and publishers, accounting for 35 percent of ASCAP's 1929 revenues of $5 million.[58] The two industries needed one another, but they were wary partners whose mutual dependence was part of an increasingly complex web of untested commercial and cultural interactions.

As radio's fortunes grew, ASCAP sought a larger share of the profits, which it justified with propaganda pieces purporting to show radio's *negative* effects on publishers. ASCAP's 1933 pamphlet, "The Murder of Music," attributed declines in sheet music and record sales to radio's influence. Broadcasters maintained that radio in fact promoted music, but according to another ASCAP publication, the peculiar nature of radio airplay had the opposite effect, by reducing the life cycle of popular songs. "It is particularly significant that radio 'kills' music," said the pamphlet. "There is such insistent demand by the public for music that the constant and frequent repetition of a song over the radio has reduced its life from a term of years to a period of a few months."[59] In 1935, the *Motion Picture Herald* published statistics tending to support ASCAP's claims, based on analysis of 40,000 programs broadcast on the NBC and CBS networks. Of the nearly 24,000 compositions aired overall, only 85 songs were broadcast more than 10,000 times. The most-performed song was "Love in Bloom," penned by Leo Robin and Ralph Grainger for the film *She Loves Me Not*, which had received 24,374 plays. The song sold 500,000 sheets—a respectable number, but far less, ASCAP maintained, than a hit song enjoyed in the pre-broadcast era.[60] The conclusion was that radio's insatiable demand for new content shortened the selling window for sheet music from sixteen months (when stage performers and concert artists would keep the same songs in their productions for over a year) to just three, reducing average sales to around 230,000 copies.[61] On the strength of such analyses, in 1935 ASCAP set performance fees at 5 percent of station revenue. Broadcasters were unable to resist the increase, but did convince the Justice Department to bring suit against ASCAP for antitrust violations. Hearings began in June 1935, but fizzled a short time later, and the case lay dormant for years.

In the meantime, ASCAP's membership was shifting, as Hollywood film producers began investing in music copyrights. In early 1925, Sam Warner of Warner Bros. met Western Electric salesman Nathan Levinson, who pitched his company's new system for recording and reproducing sounds for motion pictures. Warner perceived enormous commercial potential for the process, and on June 25, 1925, the companies entered into an agreement to adapt the technology

---

57. *See* Chapter 45.
58. Suisman, *supra* note 26, at 251; Sanjek, *supra* note 2, at 39.
59. Schultz, *supra* note 4, at 517.
60. *Id.*
61. *Id.*

into a workable system for use in movie theaters.[62] The "Vitaphone prelude" debuted the following year, intended to replace the overtures and film shorts that preceded feature films.[63] Then, in 1927, Warner Bros. used Vitaphone technology in its first sound feature, *The Jazz Singer*, starring Al Jolson.[64] The film included Jolson's renditions of popular songs like "Give My Regards to Broadway," Jewish cantorial music, and an orchestral score combining excerpts from Debussy, Tchaikovsky, and Rimsky-Korsakov.[65] After the film became an international hit, Warner Bros. followed up in 1928 by featuring Jolson in an even larger blockbuster, *The Singing Fool*, which garnered more than $5 million at the box office.[66] In addition, the film's seven featured songs became extremely popular. The composers and publishers of "Sonny Boy," "It All Depends on You," "I'm Sittin' on Top of the World," "There's a Rainbow on My Shoulder," "The Spaniard Who Blighted My Life," "Golden Gate," and "Keep Smilin' at Life," reaped significant royalties from the sale of sheet and recorded music as a consequence of their songs' inclusion in *The Singing Fool*. Publishers were already compensating Jolson handsomely for including their songs in his live shows. Now his cinematic performances had the same effect, multiplied by the hundreds of theaters showing his films nationwide.

The advent of sound-on-film technology, which enabled "talkies" and "musicals," brought the motion picture and music industries into a closer relationship. In an effort to reap the promotional benefits provided by movie exhibition, studios began purchasing song catalogs and entire publishing houses. Warner led the way, acquiring M. Witmark and Sons for $1 million in 1929, followed by Harms Music Publishing Company, Remick Music Corporation, and an interest in DeSylva, Brown and Henderson, whose principals had penned songs for *The Singing Fool*.[67] From the studios' standpoint, successful films would generate publishing income from the sale of sheet music and recordings, as well as royalties (through ASCAP) for the public performance of songs in theaters and elsewhere.[68] In addition, song ownership eliminated so-called sync license costs—the fees paid to publishers for permission to "synchronize" songs in relation to a motion picture in the production process. As songs became more integral to moviemaking, it only made sense that film studios "bought up Tin Pan Alley and moved it to the West Coast."[69] By 1935 four major Hollywood producers—Warner Brothers, Metro-Goldwyn-

62. *Id.* at 37.

63. *Id.* at 38.

64. *Id.* at 43. Theaters not equipped with Vitaphone technology presented the film accompanied by phonograph records.

65. *Id.* at 186–87.

66. *See* GOMERY, *supra* note 27, at 56.

67. *Id.*

68. Warner no doubt experienced ironic pleasure in its acquisition of T.B. Harms in particular, the very publisher whose landmark legal action extended the public performance right to movie theaters.

69. Charney, *supra* note 17, at 58; *see also* SUISMAN, *supra* note 26, at 263.

Mayer, Paramount and 20th Century Fox—controlled more than half the music licensed by ASCAP.[70]

♪♪ ♫♫ ♪♪

The growth of radio broadcasting deeply impacted music publishers, but its effects on the *recorded* music business were even more profound. As the initial phonograph and record-making patents expired in the 1910s, a flood of newcomers entered the market—competing phonograph manufacturers, as well as the first wave of so-called independent labels, who served niche, but growing audiences for "race," "blues," "jazz," and "hillbilly" recordings.[71] The new competition for both phonograph hardware and recorded content, along with the introduction of radio-receiving equipment, which also vied for the same home entertainment dollar, hit the Big Three manufacturers hard.

Moreover, there was the practice of radio broadcasting itself, which record companies also considered as competing with their recordings. Why would consumers spend money on discs, when radio provided music (and other entertainment) free of charge? Victor's initial reaction to the quandary was apathy, turning to outright denial, as "employees, even executives, were said to have been warned upon their entrance to employment not to mention radio nor indicate that they owned one."[72] There was great uncertainty and confusion as to whether it made business sense to provide records for radio programming, or to make contracted recording artists available for broadcast performances.[73] Music publishers' court victories assured they would share in radio's success, by collecting performance royalties through ASCAP. But there was no corresponding right for *recordings*—no direct, guaranteed income that would flow to manufacturers (or artists) from the broadcast of records. Phonograph manufacturers held out hope that radio would be a passing fad, but reality proved different.

Despite a surge following the death of its tenor superstar, Enrico Caruso, in 1921, Victor's record sales decreased by half between 1921 and 1925, attributed largely to competition from radio.[74] Following a disastrous holiday selling season in 1924, Victor formulated a new strategy, forging an experimental alliance with AT&T, owner of one of the first nationwide broadcast networks, to begin using AT&T's Western Electric "electrical" recording technology[75] and, equally important, to

---

70. Schutz, *supra* note 4, at 520.

71. SANJEK, *supra* note 2, at 63–65.

72. Michael J. Biel, The Making and Use of Recordings in Broadcasting Before 1936, pp. 232–33 (1977) (Ph.D. dissertation, Mass Communications, Northwestern University).

73. Adding to the conundrum, the federal agencies regulating radio discouraged, and in some cases, forbade, the broadcasting of prerecorded content, which they deemed unauthentic and inappropriate for use on a limited spectrum. Nevertheless, the practice of broadcasting records grew steadily.

74. SUISMAN, *supra* note 26, at 231–33.

75. The same technology Western Electric would use as the basis for the Vitaphone process used by Warner Bros. in its Al Jolson musicals.

allow Victor recording artists to perform on the network.[76] On December 31, 1924, Victor's *New York Times* advertisement announced that performances by Victor opera stars Lucrezia Bori and John McCormack would be broadcast on New Year's Day, heralding "a new era in radio broadcasting." The broadcast, with references to the artists' availability on Victor records, reached an audience of 8 million. Sixty thousand listeners responded with letters to Victor, and sales of the featured artists spiked in the wake of the show, leading a *New York Times* analyst to conclude: "Who will pay for records when the music can be intercepted from the ether? John McCormack sang five selections in his radio debut before the microphone. It is not likely that the other 170 records in Mr. McCormack's repertoire will be criss-crossed through space. Just a 'taste' will be sent through the air and the rest of the songs will be heard by revolving the black discs on phonographs. The same will be true of all other famous stars and orchestras. Those who tuned in on Lucrezia Bori singing 'LaPaloma' and liked it to the extent they want to hear it sung by her again will have to seek the phonograph record. Thus the advertising is likely to do more good than harm to the phonograph industry."[77]

For the initial broadcast series, Victor provided its artists' services without charge, while AT&T waived its customary broadcast fees to gain Victor's participation: it was the beginning of what is still referred to as the "symbiotic" relationship between record companies and broadcasters—free music in exchange for free promotion.

Victor's broadcast alliances continued. Scarcely two months after the first series concluded, Victor signed an agreement with another growing broadcasting enterprise, the Radio Corporation of America (RCA), to install radio receivers in Victrola brand phonographs, and to broadcast Victor artist performances over the RCA network. When RCA formed the National Broadcast Company, Inc. (NBC), the ties were strengthened.[78] Through these arrangements, Victor preserved its position as an industry leader, enabling its sale to investment bankers in 1926 for the princely sum of $30 million, and leading to the ultimate radio "alliance" in 1929, when RCA acquired the company, officially fusing the recording and broadcast industries by bringing them under the same corporate roof.[79]

The 1920s were not as kind to the other members of the original Big Three. For its part, Columbia had been overextended by Wall Street speculators controlling the business, and fell into insolvency.[80] The company remained intact, however, and in ensuing years became part of the American Record Corporation, which in turn sold the label to another broadcaster, the Columbia Broadcasting System

---

76. Biel, *supra* note 72, at 323.
77. N.Y. Times, January 11, 1925, sec. 8. p. 13, quoted in Biel, *supra* note 72, at 327.
78. Biel, *supra* note 72, at 343.
79. *Id.* at 343–44; Suisman, *supra* note 26, at 268.
80. Sanjek, *supra* note 2, at 62–64.

(CBS).[81] As one observer has said, "[t]he broadcast industry had triumphed over their arch rivals in the home entertainment industry, Victor and Columbia, but also saved them from extinction."[82] Thomas Edison's company was the lone hold-out, which sealed its fate as far as music was concerned. On November 1, 1929, less than a week after the stock market crashed, Edison announced it would cease manufacturing phonographs and records altogether.[83]

♪♪ ♫♫ ♪♪

The rise of the recording and phonograph industries in the early decades of the twentieth century transformed Americans' relationship to music. In the sheet music era, the musical experience was defined by a live performance, usually the individual's own rendition of a favorite tune, played on the piano in the parlor. With the advent of mechanical devices that could render music from perforated rolls, followed by true "recorded" music (cylinders and rolls), actual playing was no longer required to enjoy music. As a result, the everyday musical experience moved from participation (playing) to consumption—from artistic to cultural expression. Technology gave the average American an opportunity to express taste and style through *consumption* of music, in the same way as fashion and other symbols of status and cultural refinement. Recorded music was the perfect mass commodity for manufacturers and consumers alike. Producers could "manufacture" an endless supply of new recordings, and consumers could refresh their preferences with new purchases, keeping themselves on the cutting edge of cultural fashion.

The player piano and pianola set this trend, creating a hybrid situation in which music consumers could maintain the appearance of performing. But in time this artifice faded, ultimately supplanted by taste expressed solely through purchasing, as opposed to playing. The popularity of disc recordings completed the transition from "participation" to "appreciation," creating new, highly commercial relationships based on the general public's fascination with those who could do what they could not—sing and play. Admiration and envy inspired further consumption—the next best thing to having musical talent was the ability to recognize and own it, in the form of the latest disc. In time, amateur musicians were replaced by music *fans*.

The transformation was essentially complete by the onset of the Great Depression. In 1929, "the phonograph industry in the United States pressed more than 105 million records and manufactured more than 750,000 phonographs, together valued at nearly $100 million. Meanwhile, the popularity of recordings sent the

---

81. Biel, *supra* note 72, at 346–47; Suisman, *supra* note 26, at 269. CBS owned Columbia until 1988, when it sold the label to Sony.

82. Biel, *supra* note 72, at 347.

83. Suisman, *supra* note 26, at 267.

American piano business into terminal decline. By the late 1920s, the popularity of player-pianos had faded, and at the end of the decade only eighty-one piano manufacturers remained in the United States, down from a peak of nearly three hundred in 1909. By 1933 that number dropped to thirty six." Sales of player pianos, the technology that had driven copyright revision in the early 1900s, dropped even more precipitously, from 170,000 in 1927 to only 2,700 instruments in 1932.[84]

The music industry survived the Depression, but emerged as a changed business. Radio conglomerates owned record labels, and movie studios had become major publishers, creating shifting allegiances, greater complexity, and more nuanced relationships among industry participants. But the music business was anything but dead. As David Suisman has concluded, "Hollywood musicals, radios, and the proliferation of jukeboxes sustained and reinforced the place of the music industry in American life" in ensuing years, allowing the industry to flourish.[85]

24. ASCAP Meets the Competition

The dual effects of technology and the Depression rearranged the music business, but the basic tension between publishers and broadcasters on the issue of performance royalty rates remained an industry flashpoint. Broadcasters gained strength and influence as the 1930s progressed, but even the powerful NAB could not resist ASCAP fee increases, as there was no other source for music.[86]

As noted, ASCAP unilaterally hiked its fees to 5 percent of station revenue in 1935, eliciting outrage from broadcasters, along with an ill-fated maneuver to pass state legislation restricting ASCAP collections. Such laws were implemented in seven states, but could not withstand judicial scrutiny, although Montana's version went out with a flourish when the governor issued "extortion" arrest warrants for ASCAP president Gene Buck. New York Mayor Fiorello LaGuardia stepped in to quash the first warrant, but a second was served on Buck while vacationing in Arizona. Having made his point, but recognizing the futility of challenging federal copyright law at the state level, the governor decided against seeking extradition, and the matter fizzled.[87] If nothing else, the state law initiative demonstrated

---

84. *Id.* at 281

85. *Id.*

86. A second "performing rights organization," the Society of European Stage Authors and Composers (SESAC) formed in 1931, but until sometime later, it represented only a small catalog of European works in the United States. Schultz, *supra* note 4, at 516.

87. *Id.* at 520–21. ASCAP sued officials in various states to enjoin enforcement of the statutes, and four cases made their way to the U.S. Supreme Court on jurisdictional and constitutional questions. *See* Buck v. Gallagher, 307 U.S. 95 (1939) and Gibbs v. Buck, 307 U.S. 95 (1939) (ASCAP suits to enjoin enforcement of Washington and Florida statutes allowed to proceed, injunction upheld in Florida); *but see*

the NAB's national presence. As those who contended with the group now realized, there was a "broadcaster in every congressional district."

The NAB denied involvement in the Montana histrionics, but had been busy laying its own plans to break ASCAP's hegemony. Anticipating another rate increase when current contracts expired at the end of 1940, the NAB prepared a new attack on ASCAP, using the marketplace as its battlefront, instead of a courtroom. Likening ASCAP to the rampaging Hitler, who had invaded Poland one month earlier, the NAB's October 1, 1939, editorial declared: "War is hell, whether its purpose is to preserve democracy in Europe against a madcap dictator or to preserve it in radio against an arbitrary totalitarian ASCAP."[88] It was the official announcement of the formation of Broadcast Music, Inc. (BMI), a new performing rights organization funded entirely by NAB members, designed to compete directly with ASCAP as a source for radio music. There was much at stake. In 1939 ASCAP collected over $6.5 million, nearly two-thirds of which—over $4 million—came from radio. On the other hand, radio industry revenues had grown from $25 million to over $170 million during the 1930s, giving broadcasters the resources to pay for the music content that was integral to their programming.[89]

ASCAP ignored the challenge and, as anticipated, announced its new pricing structures in March 1940. The NAB immediately rejected the terms, and in April, BMI began licensing its own catalog in competition with ASCAP. The war was on. BMI continued purchasing publishing catalogs and signing young composers to its service with the lure of cash advances, building a song repertoire much more efficiently than ASCAP imagined. With no new agreement in place at the end of the year, NAB members commenced a "ban" on ASCAP music, which essentially vanished from the nation's airwaves as of New Year's Day 1941. ASCAP had been counting on a public backlash against the ban, confident that their repertoire was superior to BMI's offerings, but it never materialized. Complicating things further, the U.S. government was about to make its presence known.

At the NAB's urging, the Justice Department had investigated ASCAP's business and structure at various times since the mid-1920s, even bringing suit in 1935. But it was the events leading up to the ASCAP ban that got the government's attention in earnest. On December 26, 1940, the Justice Department escalated the music war, filing suit not only against ASCAP, but also its new competitor, BMI, and both national radio networks, NBC and CBS. The suit alleged eight different violations of the Sherman Antitrust Act, the 1890 legislation design to limit cartels, monopolies, price-fixing, and other restraints on trade. The government contended that, in varying combinations, the organizations had unlawfully colluded

---

also Watson v. Buck, 313 U.S. 387 (1941) and Marsh v. Buck, 313 U.S. 406 (1941) (Florida and Nebraska statutes survive challenge).

88. Schultz, *supra* note 4, at 521.

89. *Id.* at 521–22.

to pool copyrights, monopolize the supply of music, discriminate against unaffiliated composers and music users, fix prices, and engage in boycotts designed to monopolize the source of music.

Using the excuse that, out of necessity, it was doing what ASCAP had done for years, BMI immediately settled by signing a consent decree on January 27, 1941. The agreement included the caveat that it would be revised to incorporate any more favorable terms later agreed to with ASCAP. By late February ASCAP, too, came into the fold, signing a consent decree mandating changes in its board structure and certain methods of licensing, and addressing government concerns with respect to both composers and users of music. The organizations had survived their first encounter with the Sherman Act, but now operated under the consent decrees that were to become a way of life in the decades to come.

The government's issues were addressed, but the private war remained: As the months of 1940 wore on, ASCAP continued to lose credibility, not to mention $100,000 a week in foregone royalties. After eight months of radio silence, ASCAP surrendered in August, agreeing to fees of just under 3 percent of broadcasters' revenues, two-thirds less than originally proposed. It was a stinging rebuke, but ASCAP recovered quickly. Despite reduced rates, the presence of a formidable new competitor in BMI, and the changes mandated by its consent decree, ASCAP's collections rose swiftly past pre-ban levels. By the end of 1945, the society was collecting nearly $9 million annually, trending up.[90]

25. ASCAP Goes to the Movies, The Sequel

As with radio, the motion picture industry enjoyed robust growth in the 1930s, again presenting opportunities for ASCAP. Theaters' obligation to pay performance fees had been confirmed in *Harms v. Cohen* in 1922,[91] and, again like radio, ASCAP was the only source for theater music. Following one-sided negotiations in 1933 and 1934, ASCAP established a per-seat annual license fee equating to around $100 a year for an average neighborhood theater.[92] Between 1937 and 1947, ASCAP collected $3 million to $7 million annually from 17,000 movie theater licensees.[93]

The system worked, but only as long ASCAP's fees remained reasonable. In the early 1940s, pricing issues reached a boiling point, and in April 1942, scarcely six

---

90. Schultz, *supra* note 4, at 526.

91. *See* Chapter 20.

92. Alden-Rochelle, Inc. v. Am. Soc'y of Composers, Authors and Publishers, 80 F. Supp. 888, 893 (S.D.N.Y. 1948).

93. *Id.*

months after resolution of the radio music war, a group of 164 theater owners filed an antitrust complaint against ASCAP in New York federal court.[94] Pursuant to the Sherman Act's provisions allowing for private enforcement, the owners sought an injunction against what they maintained were monopolistic practices in motion picture licensing, and "treble damages" caused by the alleged infractions.[95] The case lay dormant for several years, and may have remained that way if not for ASCAP's attempt, in 1947, to impose dramatic theater rate increases of up to 1,500 percent.[96] In response, theater owners reactivated the litigation, leading to pretrial hearings in the fall of 1947, followed by a trial before judge Vincent L. Leibell in early March 1948.[97] The extensive hearings and trial shined a light on every aspect of the increasingly complex business of licensing music for use in motion pictures, a system involving not only public performance, but also the "synchronization" of music with films themselves, a practice enabled by the sound-on-film ("talkie") technologies coming into use in the late 1920s.

The opinion discussed the short history of movie music, from the days of silent film (and "live" music), to the development of talkies, for which "the speech of the actors, the music and sound effects, were recorded on the 'sound track' of the film, which paralleled the pictures, so that when the pictures were projected on the screen the sound was heard by the audience." The court also noted that after the introduction of sound on film, motion picture producers began acquiring the catalogs of music publishers, many of whom were members of ASCAP. Based on these developments, certain licensing arrangements had evolved. First, upon request, an ASCAP member would license a producer to record—that is, "synchronize"—a musical composition "on the film," but (as required by the member's arrangement with ASCAP) the license would specifically exclude the right to publicly perform the composition in theaters.[98] (In contrast, publishers not affiliated with ASCAP routinely granted both synchronization and public performance rights in one license.) Second, producers then rented motion pictures to theater owners for exhibition, with contract provisions requiring that the films be shown only in theaters licensed by ASCAP.

Based on these facts, the court reached the heart-stopping conclusion that "[a]lmost every part of the ASCAP structure, almost all of ASCAP's activities in licensing motion picture theatres, involve a violation of the anti-trust laws."[99] The facts "clearly established" that ASCAP was a monopoly, which Judge Leibell found to have abused its power in at least two ways. The arrangement among the members of ASCAP in transferring all their performance rights to the organization

---

94. *Id.*
95. *Id.* at 890.
96. *Id.* at 895.
97. *Id.* at 893.
98. "Synch" license fees ranged from a few hundred dollars to as much as $25,000.
99. Alden-Rochelle, 80 F. Supp. 888.

was itself a "combination in restraint of interstate trade and commerce," supplemented by second unlawful combination—the agreement between ASCAP and the film producers to limit distribution to theaters holding an ASCAP license. By these methods, ASCAP and film producers "thus combine the monopoly of the copyright of the motion picture with the monopoly of the copyright of the musical compositions, which constitutes an unlawful extension of the statutory monopoly of each and violates the anti-trust laws, as a combination in restraint of trade."[100] Together, the court reasoned, these arrangements "have given ASCAP the power to fix the prices at which the performing rights are sold to the exhibitors," in a manner that had "all the evils of 'block booking'" films, which had been "analyzed and condemned" by the Supreme Court just two months earlier, in the Justice Department's antitrust action against Paramount Pictures.[101]

The plaintiff theater owners had not shown any "actual damages" flowing from ASCAP's actions, but they were entitled to an injunction against future violations. Accordingly, Judge Leibell's order barred ASCAP from "obtaining the right of public performance of any musical composition synchronized with motion picture films when such musical composition is performed publicly for profit in conjunction with the exhibition of such motion picture films."[102] In the blink of an eye, the theater licensing program ASCAP had built over three decades came crumbling down. As of July 19, 1948, ASCAP was effectively out of the movie business.[103] Since that time, no performing rights organization has collected performance royalties from U.S. movie theaters.[104]

♪♪ ♫♫ ♪♪

The copyright first extended to musical compositions in 1831 had come a long way. In its first era, music copyright provided protection against "copying" of the physical objects that embodied musical expression—initially, the printed sheet, and later, culminating in the mechanical licensing provisions of the 1909 Act, the piano rolls, cylinders, and finally, discs carrying the consumer commodity of "recorded music," brought on by phonograph technology. The 1909 Act's public performance provisions opened the door to the second era of American music copyright. In a steady stream of decisions, including two from the Supreme Court, the judiciary determined that traditional live performances (whether presented as paid concerts or mere background music) were "for profit" within the meaning of

---

100. *Id.* at 894.

101. United States v. Paramount Pictures, Inc., 334 U.S. 131 (1948).

102. Alden-Rochelle at 900.

103. The prohibitions were incorporated into ASCAP's existing consent decree. *See* United States v. The Am. Soc'y of Composers, Authors and Publishers, No. 13–95, 1950 Trade Cas. (CCH) P62,595, 1950 U.S. Dist. LEXIS 1900 (S.D.N.Y. Mar. 14, 1950).

104. While *Alden-Rochelle* applied only to ASCAP, the litigation put an end to all theater licensing as a practical matter, as neither BMI nor SESAC collects performance royalties from theaters.

the statute, as were the performances enabled by the radical new media of the 1920s—radio and motion pictures. For the first time, Judge Leibell's opinion in *Alden-Rochelle* restricted the performance right, not based on copyright principles, but because music copyrights, when pooled and licensed collectively, were powerful intellectual property rights, susceptible to abuses running afoul of antitrust laws.

Despite the setback of *Alden-Rochelle*, music copyright owners were well-positioned to profit from future performance technologies, such as television, the next broadcast miracle that would burst onto the scene in the 1950s. And yet there were those in the music business who found music copyright's progress one-sided—specifically, the recording artists who brought musical compositions to life on records, and the labels who financed their production. Their frustrations were mounting, as we will now discover.

PART IV

Recordings and Recording Artists

Friends and highly successful bandleaders Paul Whiteman (*left*) (1890-1967) and Fred Waring (1900-1984) led the charge for legal recognition of recording artists' property rights, resulting in the seminal, if frustrating, decision in *RCA v. Whiteman* (1940). Whiteman image courtesy of Penn State University Libraries and Fred Waring's America / Waring image, Author's collection

26. Notes and Lyrics, Not Sounds

We have explored the path of music copyright in its first century, including the expanded rights provided by the Copyright Act of 1909. Among other things, the statute confirmed copyright holders' right to compensation when musical compositions were "copied" in the form of phonograph records, the new medium that was transforming the industry by making *recorded* music a consumer commodity. Phonograph and recording companies resisted the change, but in the end achieved only the consolation of making the so-called mechanical license compulsory. As of 1909, music publishers succeeded in imposing their copyrights on the manufacturing side of the business, at the rate of two cents per recording.

Turn-of-the-century manufacturers were also frustrated by their inability to convince Congress that they, too, should enjoy the benefits of copyright. Record "piracy"—the unauthorized duplication, or "dubbing," of recordings—had been common since the earliest days of recorded music, but as dubbing technology improved, manufacturers sought an efficient remedy in copyright. In testimony before the Joint Committees on Patents in June 1906, Victor Talking Machine Company executive Horace Pettit argued that a recorded performance was a "picture of the voice," rendered by a "vibrating pencil" (i.e., a needle cutting through wax), and thus the legal equivalent of other "writings" protected by copyright.[1] Pettit's position implied that music copyright was developing in a lopsided way—expanding rights in musical compositions, while failing to acknowledge the equally artistic (and very expensive) works embodied in sound recordings. A representative of the Edison Manufacturing Company echoed these concerns, but a draft bill designed to confer copyright in recordings did not persuade the Committee, whose final report on the 1909 legislation said specifically that it was "not the[ir] intention . . . to extend the right of copyright to the mechanical reproductions themselves."[2]

In the wake of the 1909 Act, "compositions" remained the only form of musical expression subject to copyright. Simply put, music copyright encompassed notes

---

1. *Hearings before the Joint Committee on Patents, June 6–9, 1906*, in 4 Legislative History of the 1909 Copyright Act 26–29 (Fulton E. Brylawski & Abe Goldman eds., 1976).

2. *See* Barbara A. Ringer, *Study No. 26: The Unauthorized Duplication of Sound Recordings* (February 1957), in 2 Omnibus Copyright Revision Legislative History (George S. Grossman ed., 2001), quoting H.R. Rep. No. 2222, 60th Cong., 2d Sess. 9 (1909). In 1973, Ms. Ringer became the first woman to be appointed Register of Copyrights, and was a principal architect of the Copyright Act of 1976. Her study is an insightful and detailed discussion of legislative and judicial developments in the protection of sound recordings through 1957.

and lyrics, but not sounds. As David Suisman has noted, by "[f]etishizing the composer and the composition" in this way, "copyright law reaffirmed and materially strengthened the value of music as property, not as process."[3] The law did not recognize artistic *interpretation*, or collaborative *production*, as opposed to the original written expression of notes and lyrics that formed a composition. According to Suisman, "[i]t mattered little that this . . . flew in the face of the experience and knowledge of publishers, phonograph manufacturers, and especially consumers: that the performer, the performance, the sound and the social context mattered enormously in the valuation of a musical work. Among other things, the careers of Caruso, Al Jolson, and others signaled how performers increasingly invested songs with commercial value as much as composers did, and sometimes more. The law, therefore, protected only one dimension of the creative labor of music making. If the purpose of the law was truly to protect works of the imagination or offer incentives to those whose originality created something of economic value, then it left much to be desired."[4]

Despite the lack of copyright protection, manufacturers used other means to keep "dubbers" and "pirates" at bay. Beginning as early as 1904, courts issued injunctions based on the principles of unfair competition—the notion that unauthorized duplication was a form of "passing off," or "misappropriating" the fruits of another man's labor.[5] These remedies were far from perfect, however, so manufacturers persisted in sponsoring or supporting legislation designed to bring recordings explicitly within the copyright statute. There was a flurry of such activity beginning in 1925, when Congress considered a series of bills intended to allow U.S. adherence to the Berne Copyright Convention (the international treaty the U.S. ultimately joined in 1989). In January 1925, Representative Randolph Perkins introduced a bill, drafted by the Register of Copyrights, Thorvald Solberg, which included "phonographic records" within the ambit of copyrightable works, and specified that the manufacturer, not the artist, would be the presumptive owner.[6] The bill was reintroduced in December 1925, but no action was taken. Beginning in March 1926, Indiana Representative Albert Vestal took up the mantle with the first in a series of general revision bills that included provisions making sound recordings copyrightable. Again, no action was taken on this version, or the one he introduced in 1929. In May 1930 Vestal offered a similar bill, but the sound recording provisions were removed before the measure passed the House. In Sen-

---

3. David Suisman, Selling Sounds: The Commercial Revolution in American Music 168 (2009).
4. *Id.* at 168–69.
5. See Victor Talking Mach. Co. v. Armstrong, 132 Fed. 711 (S.D.N.Y. 1904); and Fonotipia Ltd. v. Bradley, 171 Fed. 951 (E.D.N.Y. 1909), discussed in Ringer, *supra* note 2, at 17–18. As we have seen, record manufacturers including Victor also had some success under patent law theories in enjoining competing manufacturers, but this was short-lived, as the primary phonograph patents expired by the mid-1910s. *See* Chapter 15.
6. *See* H.R. 11258 (68th Congress).

ate hearings, a representative of radio and phonograph manufacturers, Frank D. Scott, introduced an amendment that brought recordings back into the fold, which he justified in terms of investment, as opposed to art: "[W]e say we should at least be protected to the point of being able to prevent some fly-by-night fellow coming in and stealing the product we have paid for. There cannot be any objection to that."[7] Objection or no, the bill never reached the Senate floor.

Further hearings on copyright revision were convened in early 1932 by the new chairman of the House Committee on Patents, New York representative William Sirovich, a medical doctor, businessman, and successful playwright. It is said that the question of copyright in recordings became a "real issue" at this time, owing to the increased use of recorded music in radio programming.[8] Manufacturers desired not only protection against "copying," but also a right of "public performance" corresponding to the one proving so lucrative for music publishers. Between March and June 1932 Sirovich introduced five general revision bills, each defining copyrightable works broadly enough to include recordings.[9] The National Association of Broadcasters opposed vigorously, arguing that imposing a performance royalty obligation for recordings, in addition to the millions its members paid to ASCAP for airing compositions, would work an undue hardship on broadcasters, particularly small stations. Fearing its members would be forced to share performance royalties with a new class of rights holders, ASCAP also opposed, sending in cofounder and attorney Nathan Burkan to attack the legislation as an unconstitutional, illegal attempt to extend long-expired phonograph patents.[10] Once again, the measures died without reaching the floor of the House.

After 1932 there was a pause of several years in the introduction of copyright legislation, but of course, radio marched on, growing rapidly despite the Depression. Moreover, the use of recorded music was becoming a staple of radio programming, to the consternation of recording companies and, even more so, recording artists. Labels were ambivalent as to the effect broadcasting might have on record sales, but many recording artists were adamant in the belief that radio was their competition, at least when programmers used recorded music as a substitute for live musicians. Out of this confusion emerged the practice of printing legends on disc labels, declaring that the recordings were "Not Licensed for Radio Broadcast," or equivalent language purporting to restrict use to personal, noncommercial settings.[11] In terms of copyright law, such restrictions were meaningless. Recordings

---

7. Ringer, *supra* note 2, at 25. *See* Alexander S. Cummings, *From Monopoly to Intellectual Property: Music Piracy and the Remaking of American Copyright, 1909–1971*, 97 J. AM. HISTORY 659–81 (2010), discussed in Chapter 32, infra.

8. Ringer, *supra* note 2, at 25.

9. *Id.* at 25.

10. *Id.* at 26–27.

11. RUSSELL SANJEK & DAVID SANJEK, AMERICAN POPULAR MUSIC BUSINESS IN THE 20TH CENTURY 48–49 (1991). The new Big Three manufacturers—Victor, Columbia, and Brunswick—launched the practice, despite the fact that by this time both Victor and Columbia were owned by broadcasting entities.

were not subject to copyright, so there was nothing to "license" for any purpose, broadcast or otherwise. Needless to say, the warnings were ignored by the growing number of stations relying on recorded music to fill their programming days.

♩♩ ♫♫ ♩♩

Richard "Bruno" Hauptmann, the accused kidnapper of aviator Charles Lindberg's twenty-month old son, was put on trial in Flushing, New Jersey, on January 2, 1935. The crime and ensuing investigation had been radio fodder since the kidnapping on March 1, 1932. Lindbergh broadcast a message to the kidnappers on NBC radio, promising to keep confidential any arrangements necessary for the safe return of his son, but his pleas were to no avail. Despite contacts by the kidnappers, no deal was reached, and the slain infant's body was discovered seventy-two days later, half buried in the woods not far from the Lindberg home. One hundred sixty-two witnesses, including Hauptmann himself, appeared during the month-long "Trial of the Century," their testimony riveting radio audiences across the country, courtesy of, among others, New York station WNEW. As compelling as the testimony was, there was also significant downtime—caused by either lulls in the action, or technical difficulties, which WNEW announcer Martin Block filled by playing records. By the time the guilty verdict was delivered (Hauptmann was electrocuted on April 3, 1936), Block's music programming had taken on a life of its own, and continued on as the aptly titled *Make Believe Ballroom*. Block broadcast from an imaginary, crystal-chandeliered dance hall, conducting "make believe" interviews with prominent recording artists between spins of their platters. As the show gained traction, Block brought in his first sponsor, the manufacturer of "Retardo" weight-reducing pills, who paid $129.50 for six quarter-hour broadcasts per week. Block was an experienced salesman, and his smooth pitch for Retardo preyed delicately on female insecurities: "Ladies, does your husband kiss you when he comes home at night? . . . Maybe, just maybe, you've added an extra curve or two . . ." Six hundred orders poured in after the first show, convincing WNEW to raise Block's salary by five dollars, to $25 a week, which he supplemented with the sponsor's contribution of 10 percent of all mail orders for Retardo. Within four months, four million listeners were tuning in to seven hours of daily programming from the *Make Believe Ballroom*.[12] The era of the disc jockey was born.

Despite (or perhaps because of) the show's success, record executives, including Joe Kapp of the emerging Decca label, disapproved of the practice of playing records on air.[13] Recording artists maintained their objections as well, insisting that every spin of a record was a performing musician's opportunity lost. As a response, in 1934 the Society of American Recording Artists was formed in Califor-

---

12. Russell Sanjek, American Popular Music and Its Business, The First Four Hundred Years, Vol. III, From 1900 to 1984, 128–29 (1988).

13. *Id.* at 129.

nia, led by none other than Al Jolson, with Fred Astaire, Eddie Cantor, and Gene Austin among its members. SARA sent contracts to over 600 commercial broadcasters, requesting payments of five to fifteen cents for each use of recorded music, depending on the size of the station. Their requests had no force of law, and were ignored.[14] A short time later, bandleader Fred Waring (whom we will get to know shortly) organized the National Association of Performing Artists to pursue the legislative and court actions necessary to gain recognition for artists' rights in recorded performances. NAPA was involved in hearings on copyright bills introduced by Representatives Sirovich and John Daly in early 1936, which between them contained the most comprehensive and artist-friendly provisions yet considered by Congress.[15] NAPA members and other performers maintained that they were intellectual creators on par with songwriters, and that their interests could be fully protected only by copyright. Recording companies agreed that recordings should be protected, but insisted that ownership should vest in the manufacturer, not the artist. In support of their position, manufacturers again emphasized the perceived negative effects of repeated radio broadcasts on the sale of recordings.[16] Neither bill was reported out of committee.

By the close of the 1930s, the idea of copyright in sound recordings had been discussed widely, and had gained support from the likes of the American Bar Association, whose Copyright Committee approved the principle in its 1939 report, reversing its initial position taken in 1937.[17] But the decade ended with no traction where it mattered, in Congress. In explaining the omission of sound recording provisions in a 1940 revision bill, a Senate committee commented that, with respect to performers, "thought has not yet become crystallized on the subject," and that "no way could be found at the present time for reconciling the serious conflicts of interests arising in this field." Further, the committee noted that "there is considerable opposition to giving copyright in recordings for they are not commonly creations of literary or artistic works *but uses of them.*"[18]

27. Whiteman and Waring

The parallel careers of the bandleaders Paul Whiteman and Fred Waring had a profound impact not only on American music, but also on the law of music copyright, in particular the nettlesome question of whether, and to what extent, performers were entitled to property rights in their sound recordings. Paul Whiteman

---

14. *Id.* at 128.
15. Ringer, *supra* note 2, at 27–28.
16. *Id.* at 29–30.
17. *Id.* at 31–32.
18. *Id.* at 34 (emphasis added).

was born in 1890 in Denver, schooled in music from a young age by his father, a prominent musician and teacher. By age seventeen he was a violist with the Denver Symphony Orchestra, followed by stints in the same capacity with the San Francisco Symphony, and then as a Navy bandleader in World War I. But his heart lay outside the classical music mainstream, and in 1918 he quit the symphony to devote his artistic energies to the new and untamed world of jazz. By 1920 he was leading a "jazz orchestra" in New York, and released his first recording for Victor—a jazzed-up, instrumental version of "Whispering," written by bandleader Vincent Rose in collaboration with Richard Coburn and John Schonberger, that went on to sell more than two-and-a-half million copies. It was the launching pad for, quite literally, the "biggest" popular music career of the 1920s and 1930s; Whiteman dominated the sales charts with recordings, and captivated audiences across the land, leading his big bands and orchestras with an oversized baton, matched only by his outsized, 300+ pound frame.[19]

Whiteman's career reached an early zenith on February 12, 1924, when he presented newly commissioned works by Victor Herbert and George Gershwin in a grand concert at Aeolian Hall in New York City. The event was to feature "concertized" or "symphonic" jazz, an experimental attempt to appeal to both the jazz vanguard and devotees of more traditional classical fare. Amongst the many celebrity guests in the crowd was the tenor, and fellow Victor recording artist, John McCormack, whose New Year's Eve radio performance the same year would help usher in a new era in music broadcasting.[20] The more adventurous second half of the program commenced with the commissioned pieces, beginning with Herbert's first composition for a jazz orchestra, followed by Gershwin's. Seating himself at the piano, Gershwin nodded to Whiteman, who, through a stream of tears, commenced conducting the debut performance of the timeless piece of Americana that Gershwin had composed in just five weeks—"Rhapsody in Blue." Thunderous applause brought three curtain calls, followed by reviews hailing Whiteman, Gershwin, and their colleagues for proving "conclusively that the dance orchestra or the band or the jazz craze, or any of other names it has been identified with, will never die. It is part of modern American culture and an absolute necessity."[21]

Fred Waring was as American as apple pie. Born in 1900, ten years after Whiteman, and raised in small-town Tyrone, Pennsylvania, he took up the banjo and fiddle as a youngster, and was active in high school music programs, including glee club. By 1917 he was performing in musical groups with his brother, Tom, who remained his musical partner for decades. After working his way through college at Penn State, he left just shy of a diploma to pursue a career in music, maturing

---

19. The Whiteman background information is drawn largely from Thomas A. DeLong, Pops: Paul Whiteman, King of Jazz (1983).
20. *See* Chapter 23.
21. DeLong, *supra* note 19, at 8–10.

into a performer whose work encompassed nearly every aspect of show business—dance, theater, vaudeville, recording, and concerts—ultimately earning separate stars on Hollywood's Walk of Fame for contributions in radio, movies, and television.[22] (All this in addition to his perfecting and marketing the "Waring Blendor," the first home mixer appliance to find wide acceptance among consumers.)[23]

From the Boy Scout days of his youth, Fred Waring projected a wholesome, clean-cut, collegiate image, reflecting an undying love and devotion to mother, God, and country, reconfirmed at the end of each performance with a rousing rendition of his closing theme, "The Battle Hymn of the Republic." He was also a stern taskmaster with a relentless drive for perfection that made him both loved and hated among his employees and peers, and whose style was also polarizing; there were critics who decried Waring as a panderer who homogenized jazz into pablum (he admitted to "conveying corn long before Lawrence Welk could count to two"), but in terms of public acceptance he was an unmitigated success. As one of the first to introduce singers to big bands, commercialize choral music, and combine orchestral and glee club performances, Waring broke ground in ways that appealed to a wide swath of the American music audience. For all these talents, however, Waring was not a songwriter or composer; like Paul Whiteman, he was an interpreter whose performances (live and on record) were his stock-in-trade.

Upon leaving Penn State in 1921, Waring reached out to Whiteman, his musical idol, gaining an audition for Waring and his brother's act, the "Waring Banjo Orchestra." Whiteman liked what he heard and offered the pair a slot on a satellite tour of acts Whiteman sponsored and lent his name to. Waring declined, resolving instead to emulate and compete with Whiteman. Physically, the two were opposites, Waring standing just 5'6" and tipping the scales at less than 130 pounds, while "Tiny" Whiteman stood over 6' tall and weighed more than twice as much. Despite their physical differences, and a shared competitive spirit, the two became good friends, mutual supporters, and even coinvestors in a music publishing enterprise some years later.[24] They also collaborated in the trenches of litigation in their mutual pursuit of recording artists' rights.

Beginning in the early 1920s, Waring and his band, now dubbed "The Pennsylvanians," traveled incessantly, honing their unique style of "syncopated" music. Having "made a lady of jazz," Paul Whiteman had gained popular appeal, but Waring's clean and tight sound pushed even further into the pop mainstream. Early on, Waring learned his first lesson in copyright, when he and brother Tom teamed with the religious composer Adam Geibel (whose secular songs "Kentucky Babe" and "Little Cotton Dolly" were the subjects of the *White-Smith* Supreme

---

22. The Waring background information is drawn largely from Virginia Waring, Fred Waring and the Pennsylvanians 3 (1997). *See also* the Penn State online collection, "Fred Waring's America," available at https://secureapps.libraries.psu.edu/content/waring/1920s.html.

23. Waring, *supra* note 22, at 144–51.

24. *Id.* at 38, 131–32.

Court decision in 1908)[25] to compose "Sleep," which became Waring's first recording, for Victor in 1923. The copyright claims in the composition were manipulated by music publisher Sherman & Clay, and only after battling for nearly thirty years did Waring legally confirm a half-interest in the song.[26] Waring's recordings for Victor continued apace—among many others, an uptempo, jaunty version of "Collegiate" by Nat Bronx and Moe Jaffee, in 1925 (featuring the proud vocal cry, "Yes, we are collegiate!"); a version of Warren and Green's clever "Wobally Walk" in 1927; and, in 1930, Waring's take on Cole Porter's "Love for Sale," dripping with the sweet pop sheen of a female vocal trio. By the end of 1932, Waring and the Pennsylvanians had delivered nearly 300 records.[27]

As Waring's successes piled up, he continued to acknowledge Whiteman's groundbreaking efforts and influence. "Paul Whiteman plays the best jazz music in the world," he said. "Every night, every bandleader in the country ought to remember Paul Whiteman in his prayers. He was the one who started this whole business."[28] By 1932 the Pennsylvanians were commanding thousands per week in concert performance fees, but Waring began looking to the developing radio medium as a way to expand his audience and earnings. He wound up as the bandleader for an Old Gold cigarettes–sponsored show, broadcasting every Wednesday night on the CBS network (again following in the footsteps of Whiteman, whose Old Gold Saturday night show debuted in February 1929).[29] In 1934, still the heart of the Depression, Waring moved to a Ford Motor Company–sponsored show at an eye-popping $13,500 a week. The miracle of radio broadcasting had taken his career to a higher plane, but at the same time, posed a threat. For every sponsored radio appearance by the Pennsylvanians, at least one disc jockey was broadcasting Waring's Victor recordings, without compensation, in what Waring regarded as direct and damaging competition. Waring saw ethical issues in black and white, and for him the broadcasting of commercial recordings was patently unfair. By using his recordings as a substitute for the "real" Fred Waring, broadcasters unfairly avoided the substantial appearance fees the Pennsylvanians commanded. The issue simmered in Waring's gut, just as it did in the more substantial belly of his friend Paul Whiteman.

♪♪ ♫♫ ♪♪

In another apocryphal story arising from a famous New York eatery, Fred Waring is said to have been approached by a colleague while dining at Lindy's deli in the spring of 1935, who complimented him on his radio performance

---

25. *See* Chapter 12. Waring eventually recorded "Kentucky Babe" with Bing Crosby.

26. WARING, *supra* note 22, at 51–52.

27. Walter L. Pforzheimer, Yale University, *Copyright Protection for the Performing Artist in His Interpretive Rendition*, 1 COPYRIGHT L. SYMP. 9, 10 (1938).

28. WARING, *supra* note 22, at 99.

29. *Id.* at 113; DELONG, *supra* note 19, at 130.

earlier in the day.[30] As he had not been on the air that day, Waring became angered by the realization that the compliment referred to a disc-jockey program.[31] As with Victor Herbert's feigned indignance at hearing his "Sweethearts" performed at Shanley's twenty years before, it is hard to believe Waring was surprised to learn his recordings were being broadcast in 1935. Deejay programs were becoming staples by this time, and Martin Block's *Make Believe Ballroom* was ramping up in the wake of the Lindbergh trial. Indeed, Waring had refused to record at all since November 1932, as a protest of radio's unauthorized use of his recordings.[32] Nevertheless, such an event could have spurred Waring to further action. As we have seen, around this time Waring organized the National Association of Performing Artists, enlisting those—nearly 700 of them, including Paul Whiteman and Bing Crosby—who shared the view that broadcasting records violated artists' rights. With the advice of his personal attorney, Walter Socolow, and entertainment lawyer Maurice J. Speiser, Waring devised a strategy for adding "the right of interpretation" to copyright law. To this end, NAPA lobbied for legislation designed to make sound recordings subject to copyright protection, but those efforts were thus far in vain. Litigation became the only perceived alternative.

Waring blazed the litigation trail by suing Philadelphia-based WDAS Broadcasting Station, Inc. in Pennsylvania state court, alleging that by broadcasting two of his records on July 2, 1935, the station infringed his personal rights in the recorded performances.[33] The specific recordings at issue were "You're Getting To Be a Habit with Me" (1932) and "I'm Young and Healthy" (both penned by prolific Tin Pan Alley composer Harry Warren and lyricist Al Dubin), which Waring and the Pennsylvanians had made under contract to Victor in November 1932. Waring contended that he had a "property right in the product of his intellectual effort," while the station maintained that, even if the claim had substance, the sale of Waring's records was a "publication," which had the legal effect of waiving his rights.[34] The issues were based in "common law copyright," the concept we first explored in connection with the dramatic musical works of Gilbert & Sullivan.[35] In simple terms, the theory holds that the creator of an intellectual work reserves to himself whatever rights are not specifically provided for by statute.

---

30. At this point in our narrative we have visited Delmonico's, Luchow's and Shanley's, not to mention the opulent dining hall of the Vanderbilt Hotel. Lindy's was opened by Leo "Lindy" Lindermann in 1921 on Broadway just north of Times Square, and became known for its cheesecake and as a gathering spot for entertainers.

31. Waring, *supra* note 22, at 138.

32. *Id.* at 142.

33. *See* Pforzheimer, *supra* note 27, at 9.

34. Waring v. WDAS Broadcasting Station, Inc., 27 Pa. D. & C 297 (Court of Common Pleas of Pennsylvania, Philadelphia County, Jan. 16, 1936).

35. *See* Chapter 14. Gilbert & Sullivan's efforts helped give rise in 1897 to the right of public performance in musical compositions.

Such rights are extinguished, however, if the creative work is made generally available to the public.[36]

Following a full trial in which various music industry professionals vouched for Waring's artistic achievements (and monetary success), trial court justice Chancellor P.J. McDevitt delivered his opinion on January 16, 1936. His perspective was clear from the outset, when he declared that "where legislation has not kept abreast with the advance of science, invention and the tangible or intangible product of intellectual effort, equity has always proven the bulwark of protection to conserve property rights and to prevent illegal exploitation of the efforts, ability and production of the discoverer, producer, scholar or inventor." "As the inventor is a benefactor of mankind," he continued, "so the performing artist is a creator and disseminator of the beauties of nature, of the aesthetic efforts of mankind, and, because of the benefits derived by the latter, must be aided, encouraged and protected." McDevitt then reflected on the rise of radio, which in a decade's time had developed from merely "a hope" into a miracle medium that "destroyed all . . . boundaries between states and nations . . . outdistanced time . . . and bridged the watery chasm between continents," becoming an essential public service that employed "a vast number of performing artists, interpreters and commentators, all of whom bring amusement, education or culture into the homes of its users." Protecting such artists was of paramount importance as a matter of public policy. Until legislation caught up with technology, it was the role of courts of equity to "keep free the channels of barter and trade, as well as protect the cultural and educational side of human endeavor and activity, for it has been well said, 'Man does not live by bread alone.'" "In the discussion to follow," said the court, "the chancellor will consider the disastrous effects that will follow illegal, unlawful and inequitable invasion of the intangible rights of the performing artist, with respect to his reputation, his financial rewards, the rights of the public and the sphere or scope of the contractual relationship of the respective contracting parties." Prominent composers, producers, agents, managers, and musicians had testified that broadcasting Waring's records was "very harmful both to his commercial worth and his artistic reputation," but what legal theory could give substance to these lay conclusions? Chancellor McDevitt roamed the globe for applicable precedent,

---

36. Common law copyright had percolated all the way to the Supreme Court in 1934, in George v. Victor Talking Mach. Co., 293 U.S. 377 (December 17, 1934). George claimed common law rights in the lyrics to a massive hit sung by Vernon Dalhart, the light opera singer who had "gone country" with "The Wreck of the Old '97," a true life tale of a 1903 train disaster outside Danville, Virginia. George prevailed in the trial court. The decision was reversed by the Third Circuit, but on further review, the Supreme Court found that the Court of Appeals had no jurisdiction to consider the question because the first appeal had not been timely. The case went back to the district court, which awarded George $65,000 (Victor's profits on the record), only to be reversed again by the Third Circuit on the merits of the authorship claim. Three courts, five decisions, and six years later, George had lost. In addition to the Supreme Court decision, see George v. Victor, 1933 WL 25060 (D.N.J. Mar. 10, 1933); 69 F.2d 871 (3d Cir. 1934); 1938 WL 28226 (D.N.J. July 6, 1938); and 105 F.2d 697 (3d Cir. 1939).

using British, Italian, and American cases; contemporary treatises; and legislative history dating back to Representative Ellsworth's 1830 report to Congress, all to support the general proposition that "every new and innocent product of mental labor must be protected."[37] In the case at hand, the testimony had shown that Waring's "interpretive performances [were] specifically recognizable as his own," and thus appropriate for protection as personal property.

With Waring's exclusive rights established, the court turned to WDAS' defense: had the act of selling records divested his rights through "publication"? This was where the stated restriction, "Not licensed for radio broadcast," had its relevance. Chancellor McDevitt explored the notion of a "limited publication"—one made "under conditions expressly or impliedly precluding its dedication to the public," and thus not operating as a general waiver. Before completing the analysis, however, his opinion shifted away from common law copyright to the principles of "unfair competition." As confirmed by his Ford sponsorship, Waring's services were worth the princely sum of $13,500 for a single radio appearance. Permitting a broadcaster to duplicate the radio performance by "expending a trifling sum of 45 or 75 cents for the purchase of a record" would place the performer "in competition with himself." It was "perfectly obvious" that if more stations produced concert simulations using Waring's records, his "popularity w[ould] wane, the demand for his services by the public w[ould] soon diminish, and his commercial worth decrease accordingly," as "[t]oo much of anything becomes tiresome." The decision was not a model of clarity, but based on wide-ranging examples of unfair competition, Chancellor McDevitt arrived at a bottom line: Waring had "established a property right in his talents, efforts and interpretations" (i.e., his recordings), and "unauthorized and unlimited exploitation and appropriation of his creations would constitute an unlawful infringement of his legal and definable rights." Further, the court held that "[t]he making of a record is not a publication of same," thus Waring's rights were preserved, allowing him to enforce the stated restriction prohibiting radio broadcasts. And so the decree issued, enjoining WDAS from broadcasting not only the two recordings specifically in issue, but "any" Fred Waring record. It was as though Waring's common law copyright had been "infringed" by acts of unfair competition.

WDAS appealed to the Pennsylvania Supreme Court, where Judge Horace Stern delivered an affirming opinion some nineteen months later, on October 8, 1937.[38] The decision followed essentially the same pattern established by Chancellor McDevitt in the trial court, with Judge Stern setting the stage with a lengthy introduction conveying the groundbreaking nature of the case, and hinting strongly at the outcome. "The problems involved in this case have never before been presented to an American or an English court," he said. "They challenge the vaunted

---

37. *See* Chapter 2. Ellsworth's report led in 1831 to copyright recognition for musical compositions.
38. Waring v. WDAS Broadcasting Station, Inc., 327 Pa. 433 (1937).

genius of the law to adapt itself to new social and industrial conditions and to the progress of science and invention. For the first time in history human action can be photographed and visually re-portrayed by the motion picture. Sound can now be mechanically captured and reproduced not only by means of the phonograph for an audience physically present, but, through broadcasting, for practically all the world as simultaneous auditors. Just as the birth of the printing press made it necessary for equity to inaugurate a protection for literary and intellectual property, so these latter-day inventions make demands upon the creative and ever-evolving energy of equity to extend that protection so as adequately to do justice under current conditions of life."

After recounting Fred Waring's rise from dance halls and vaudeville stages, to Ford's lucrative sponsorship of the Pennsylvanians' weekly broadcasts, Judge Stern provided more detail on the recordings in suit, pointing out that Waring had earned just $250 for each session, and that, fearing that the records would be used by broadcasters, he had insisted that Victor include the restrictive legend. Judge Stern acknowledged that Waring had no rights "under existing copyright laws," noting that an earlier attempt to register a copyright in his "personal interpretation" (i.e., recording) of a song had been rejected by the U.S. Copyright Office. Thus, the question on appeal was two-fold: did Waring in fact enjoy common law rights in his recorded performances, and, if so, were they terminated by sales of the records themselves? Judge Stern seemed to take great pleasure in answering the first question in the affirmative, waxing eloquent on the artistic nature of musical performance and recording in general, and as to Waring's talent in particular. "A musical composition in itself is an incomplete work," he wrote, "the written page evidences only one of the creative acts which are necessary for its employment; it is the performer who must consummate the work by transforming it into sound. If, in so doing, he contributes by his interpretation something of novel intellectual or artistic value, he has undoubtedly participated in the creation of a product in which he is entitled to a right of property, which in no way overlaps or duplicates that of the author in the musical composition." Under Stern's analysis, all he needed to decide was that "such a property right inheres in the case of those artists who elevate interpretations to the realm of independent works of art." "In the present case," he concluded, reflecting on the various witnesses who had testified as to Waring's talents, "the evidence is uncontradicted that plaintiff's orchestra measured up to this standard." Having affirmed Waring's "common-law property rights," the court turned to the question of "publication." With regard to the restrictive legend prohibiting broadcast use, the court asked, "[w]here public policy or some other determinative consideration is not involved, why should the law adopt an immutable principle that no restrictions, reservations or limitations can ever be allowed to accompany the sale of an article of personal property?" The restriction was not unreasonable, did not restrain trade, and guarded against "the disadvantages and losses [recording artists] would inevitably suffer from the use of their records for broadcasting." Since the restriction "work[ed] for the encouragement of art and artists," there was "no logical or practical reason" it should not be enforced.

Although these conclusions were sufficient to affirm the case for Waring, Judge Stern followed the lower court's lead in exploring an "additional ground" for relief—the notion that broadcasting records amounted to "unfair competition." In this regard, the court drew analogies to *International News Service v. Associated Press*, the seminal Supreme Court decision establishing a "sweat of the brow" principle—in essence, that the fruit of a man's earnest labor (the gathering and reporting of news in that case) should be protected against competitors who would misappropriate it for profit.[39] Noting that WDAS and Waring were competitors in "furnish[ing] entertainment to the public over the radio," the court articulated the unfairness of broadcasting Waring's recordings. WDAS realized greater profits by not having to pay "live talent," and in turn, Waring's live performances became less valuable if they could be replaced by records. Indeed, the trial testimony had established that between 350 and 450 stations used records almost exclusively, which "diminished the commercial value" of the Pennsylvanians' live performances. Judge Stern therefore concluded that "on the ground of unfair competition, apart from any other theory of equitable relief, plaintiff is entitled to the injunction which the court below awarded." The decision was grounded in a hybrid of legal principles, made more complex by the concurring opinion of Judge George W. Maxey, who agreed with the result, but saw no need to require a "novel and artistic creation" to establish common law rights. For Maxey, it was clear that "*any* interpreter of a musical . . . composition," no matter how routine, had "an interest in his interpretation to which the law accords the status of a right and which it will protect." As opposed to a common law property right, or a strain of unfair competition, Maxey equated unauthorized broadcasting to an invasion of an artist's "right to privacy."

In the end the decision rested on an admixture of theories, which reduced to the narrow proposition that a recording artist could enforce broadcast restrictions printed on record labels. More than any particular legal principle, the decision reflected the conventional wisdom of the time—that radio had caused a tremendous decline in the sale of records, harming both labels and artists in the process. As one commentator put it in 1938, "[d]isc making was once a good business both for the phonograph industry and the performing artists whose renditions were recorded. This prosperity ended when radio came into the foreground . . . These stations flooded the homes of potential record purchasers from morning until night with refrains from the latest records. Sales of manufacturers fell sharply. In 1921 the manufacturers' receipts from records sold in the United States were over $47,000,000. In 1935 this figure had been reduced to $3,628,016."[40] Overlooking

---

39. Int'l News Ser. v. Associated Press, 248 U.S. 215 (1918).

40. Pforzheimer, *supra* note 27, at 13–14, quoting Rudolph Littauer, *The Present Legal Status of Artists, Recorders, and Broadcasters in America*, 3 Geistiges Eigentum 218 (1938).

the effects of the Depression, the comment continued, stating that "[f]or the per-forming artists the situation was at least as disastrous. Not only did their income from records decrease, but the records became an instrument of displacement of themselves and their fellows . . . This whole picture represents one of the recent aspects of the march of technical progress and its consequences for older indus-tries and labor. In this case, however, those who are to be replaced by the new machine are themselves needed for the creation of the tools of their destruction, and are therefore in a position to combat the development."[41]

It was "perfectly obvious" to Chancellor McDevitt that broadcasting records was damaging to recording artists. On appeal, Judge Stern deemed such damage "inevitable," in terms of both personal and economic harm. In a twist that seems particularly counterintuitive in these days of the "golden oldie," the court rea-soned that the use of five-year-old recordings could damage Waring's reputation, if "the public were led to judge the ability of the orchestra by work rendered at a time when it probably had not attained its present high degree of excellence."[42] In this way, the *Waring* decision turned conventional wisdom into a matter of law; it had been proven that radio airplay was detrimental to artists' interests. The con-trary position, the notion that broadcasting might have a *positive* effect on an art-ist's reputation and livelihood, appears to have been absent from the proceeding.

The decision represented a huge victory for Waring and his fellow NAPA members, the first judicial recognition of an artist's property right in recordings. On the other hand, it was only a state court victory whose geographic scope was limited to Pennsylvania, and it had no effect on the hundreds of other stations broadcasting the same recordings across the country. Thus, NAPA's next initiative was to raise the stakes by pursuing the same theories in federal court, where an injunction would have broader effect, and a favorable decision would carry the imprimatur of the law of the land. The strategy was implemented in *Waring v. Dunlea*,[43] in which Waring persuaded the federal court in Wilmington, North Carolina, to issue an injunction against local station WMFD, prohibiting its broad-casting of certain recordings made for use exclusively in connection with Waring's Ford Motor Company program.[44] Parroting the reasoning of the state court deci-sions, Judge Isaac Meekins found that Waring had a "distinct and separable prop-erty right" in his recordings, and that the station's unauthorized use was an "unfair trade practice."[45]

---

41. *Id.*

42. Waring v. WDAS Broad. Station, Inc., 327 Pa. 433 (1937).

43. Waring v. Dunlea, 26 F. Supp. 338 (E.D.N.C. 1939).

44. As opposed to commercial records, the case involved "electrical transcriptions"—custom-made recordings bearing a notice restricting use to only those stations in the program network, which WMFD was not.

45. Later in 1939, the North Carolina legislature effectively overruled the decision by enacting a state law specifically intended "to abolish any common-law rights attaching to phonograph records and electrical transcriptions." *See* Liberty/UA, Inc. v. E. Tape Corp., 11 N.C. App. 20; 180 S.E.2d 414; 1971

With their first federal court decision in place, Waring and NAPA looked to expand the favorable precedent to a more influential jurisdiction. A high-profile plaintiff was needed to carry the banner further. It was a job for Paul Whiteman. According to Waring, "we had planned for Paul Whiteman to be [NAPA's] banner suit in that he was the most important musical artist of the day . . . We felt there was no way we could lose that key battle."[46] But another interested party was waiting in the wings. Having watched Waring confirm his personal "proprietary rights" in recordings it had paid to produce and distribute, RCA Manufacturing Company, Inc. (owner of the Victor label since 1929) had a different plan.

28. *Whiteman v. WBO Broadcasting Company (RCA v. Whiteman)*

Paul Whiteman brought his claims in New York's federal court, the most influential jurisdiction in the country. Hundreds of stations were broadcasting his records, but Whiteman filed his complaint against the highest-profile defendant he (NAPA) could find—WBO Broadcasting Company, owner of station WNEW, host of the biggest deejay show in the land, Martin Block's *Make Believe Ballroom*.[47] For good measure, he added Elin, Inc., a refrigerator manufacturer and WNEW sponsor, as a party defendant. Whiteman demanded an injunction against the broadcasting of nine records made (under three different contracts) for RCA Victor between 1924 and 1934, asserting a common law property right in the recordings and, taking a cue from the *Waring* decision, various forms of unfair competition. As the case got underway, RCA sprang into action, filing an ancillary complaint against the same defendants, as well as Whiteman himself, due to its "deep interest" in the litigation, and a position "antagonistic" to Whiteman's. RCA asked for the same injunction against broadcasting records, and for a judgment declaring that Whiteman had no legal interest in his recordings because of his contracts with the label. In time, Whiteman withdrew his complaint, as all the necessary issues could be resolved by addressing RCA's claims. At trial, WBO and Elin declined to defend, making Whiteman the sole active defendant in a case he had initiated as plaintiff. The ironies continued as RCA, the recording arm of the *Radio* Corporation of America, advanced the position that broadcasting records violated the label's rights and was detrimental to its business. Whiteman agreed that broadcasting amounted to infringement, but argued, of course, that the property rights were his

---

N.C. App. LEXIS 1445; 170 U.S.P.Q. 351 (1971). At least two additional states enacted such laws in the wake of the *Waring* decisions. Ringer, *supra* note 2, at 15.

46. WARING, *supra* note 22, at 141.

47. RCA Mfg. Co., Inc. v. Whiteman, 28 F. Supp. 787 (1939).

to assert. In his decision rendered July 24, 1939, trial court judge Vincent L. Leibell[48] grappled with the question of whether Whiteman, RCA, or perhaps both, might have the right to enjoin unauthorized broadcasts of their recordings.

RCA conceded that Whiteman had a common law property right in his recorded interpretations, and the court readily found as much, citing to Judge Stern's reasoning in the recent *Waring* decision. But the story was far from over; RCA set out to prove that it had similar rights, and thus "[o]ne of the most controverted issues" became "whether or not the part played by RCA Victor Company in the recording of Whiteman's interpretation and renditions constituted such intellectual and artistic contributions as to vest in RCA a common law property right in what went on the record." This was perhaps the single most important issue on RCA's agenda, an opportunity to prove that its recording techniques rendered a "picture of the voice," worthy of copyright recognition, as it had urged in congressional hearings dating back to 1906.[49] Accordingly, RCA devoted extensive trial testimony to the details of its role in the recording process: its musical directors advised on the placement of musicians and the volume of their instruments; acoustic experts were brought in to produce "a clear and well balanced rendition;" and engineers and technicians "operated the mechanical devices in the actual recording on the matrix." It was an impressive showing that nevertheless did not persuade the court. "All these [elements] were important and necessary in producing a perfect recording of the performance," said Judge Leibell, "but the performance was Whiteman's." Elaborating, Leibell reasoned that none of the label's efforts was directed toward perfecting Whiteman's rendition, as opposed to merely "capturing" the musical performance in a technically precise way. The quality of RCA's recording techniques was undeniably excellent, but not unique. "The well known manufacturers of phonograph records use the same apparatus and methods," he wrote, and "the average person could not tell by listening" which company had made the record or supervised the recording. Production techniques did not rise to the level of creative interpretation. The process of recording a musical performance was not an artistic performance in and of itself. RCA had not established a common law property right in the recordings produced with Whiteman.

The tide seemed to be turning for Whiteman, but another factual twist made the resolution unclear—the differing terms of his three contracts with RCA, under which the nine recordings in the suit were made.[50] Revealing the increased bargaining power Whiteman enjoyed as his reputation grew, in the first two agree-

---

48. Judge Leibell would put an end to ASCAP's movie theater licensing program with his decision in the *Alden-Rochelle* case in 1948. *See* Chapter 25.

49. *See* Chapter 13.

50. The titles were "San," "O So Blue" and "Whiteman Stomp," recorded under the first contract; "By the Sycamore Tree," " You Excite Me," "Cuban Love Song" and "There's Nothing Else to Do," recorded under the second agreement; and "Singing a Happy Song" and "A Waltz Was Born in Vienna," recorded under the third.

ments he had granted the label the right to "transmit" the recordings, but in the third, in 1934, RCA acknowledged that it had not acquired the right to use the records for broadcasting. Further, the broadcasting restriction itself was used only on Whiteman's records issued after 1932, meaning, logically, that only he would have the ability to enforce the prohibition placed on recordings made under the third contract. Unexpectedly, the court went much further, finding that, even without any notice at all, broadcasting records still amounted to "unfair competition." The court found it "manifest" that WBO's broadcasting of phonograph records was unfair to Whiteman, and that he was entitled to protection of his interests. However, Whiteman did not have complete authority—he could not, "acting alone," permit any broadcaster to play records made by RCA. The conclusion was logical as it pertained to records made before 1934, but Judge Leibell reached the same result even with regard to the third agreement, in which the artist kept broadcast rights to himself. As a basis for such an outcome, the court concluded that the broadcaster, WBO, was also competing unfairly with the *label*, RCA, "in the business of public entertainment." Thus, under the principles set forth by the Supreme Court in *International News v. Associated Press*, RCA was entitled to protection of its "civil right of a pecuniary nature." Given the court's methodical consideration, and rejection, of RCA's claim to common law copyright, the result was surprising. But there it was: regardless of the terms of Whiteman's contracts, RCA's permission was necessary to authorize broadcasts of the records it produced.

Judge Leibell's opinion seems to reflect a desire to please the litigants before him (both of whom, after all, had sought essentially the same relief against a broadcaster, WBO, who chose not to defend). But in fact the result pleased no one. Whiteman and NAPA had received confirmation of their common law proprietary rights in recordings, but they could not, "acting alone," enforce broadcast restrictions. In effect, Whiteman had lost his rights to RCA, as the label had claimed from the beginning. For its part, RCA had been granted the desired injunction, but only on the basis of a nebulous "civil right of a pecuniary nature"; its attempt to establish a common law copyright of its own was flatly rejected. Both Whiteman and RCA appealed, as did WBO, against whom the injunction had been entered.[51]

The case moved to the Second Circuit Court of Appeals, where it was addressed by a three-judge panel that included Learned Hand, the celebrated jurist who had dealt so harshly with music interests back in 1916, rejecting Victor Herbert's claim that a rendition of "Sweethearts" by the Shanley's restaurant band violated his right of public performance (and ruined his dinner), by ruling that the performance was not "for profit."[52] Justice Holmes and the Supreme Court rode to Herbert's rescue on that occasion, but Paul Whiteman and his counsel would have

---

51. Only Elin, Inc., the refrigerator maker who had sponsored WBO programming, did not appeal.
52. *See* Chapters 18 and 19.

been none too pleased to have Judge Hand on their panel, or to receive the opinion he authored for the court on July 25, 1940.[53]

Learned Hand was not inclined toward the flowery language of the *Waring* decisions (and Judge Leibell's trial court opinion) suggesting that it was the judiciary's responsibility to protect artists with respect to new uses of their creative products enabled by advancing technology. He wrote in more pragmatic terms of the technology that enabled "reproductions" of performances. "Of late," he said, "the power to reproduce the exact quality and sequence of sounds ha[s] become possible, and the right to do so, exceedingly valuable; people easily distinguish, or think they distinguish, the rendition of the score . . . by their favorite [artists], and they will pay large sums to hear them. Hence this action." Hand was willing to assume that the common law property right "covers the performances of an orchestra conductor, and—what is far more doubtful—the skill and art by which a phonographic record maker makes possible the proper recording of those performances on a disc." He also assumed that radio broadcasting did not forfeit performance rights by "publication." But these issues were beside the point, given his blunt conclusion that "the 'common-law property' in these performances ended with the sale of the records." "Restrictions upon the use of chattels once absolutely sold" were presumptively invalid, and could be imposed only for an "exceptional reason." Judge Hand drew a strained analogy between rights in recordings as compared to "musical scores," then concluded that even if the parties enjoyed "a 'common-law property' which performance does not end, it is immaterial, unless the right to *copy* the rendition from the records was preserved through the notice of the restriction." The court's analysis remained focused on *copying*, as opposed to public performance, the right actually in issue, and which Judge Hand had analyzed in detail twenty-five years earlier in the *Shanley* decision. "Copyright in any form, whether statutory or at common-law, is a monopoly; it consists only in the power to prevent others from *reproducing* the copyrighted work." WBO had not "*copied* [Whiteman's] performances at all; they . . . merely used those copies which he and the RCA Manufacturing Company, Inc. made and distributed." Behind the technical language on "servitudes" and "restrictions on chattels," the issue for Judge Hand reduced to the troubling notion of extending a perpetual "common-law right" (the consistent use of quotes showed his disdain for the concept) in a recording, when works given copyright protection under the federal statute enjoyed only limited terms. In the end, he wrote, "[a]ny relief which justice demands must be found in extending statutory copyright to [recordings], not in recognizing perpetual monopolies, however limited in their scope."

In concluding that neither RCA nor Whiteman could enforce broadcast restrictions, the result was squarely at odds with the Pennsylvania Supreme Court's decision in *Waring*. "We have of course given the most respectful consideration to

---

53. RCA Mfg. Co., Inc. v. Whiteman, 114 F.2d 86 (2d Cir. 1940).

the conclusions of that great court," Hand said, "but with much regret we find ourselves unconvinced for the reasons we have tried to state." The court politely fenced in the *Waring* decision, concluding that "in our judgment the act [of broadcasting records] is unlawful only in Pennsylvania."

In addition to "common-law copyright," Whiteman and RCA had made claims based on the theory of "unfair competition," and indeed both the *Waring* decision and Judge Leibell's opinion in the trial court were grounded in part on the principles set forth in *International News Service v. Associated Press*. Judge Hand limited the case to its specific facts. "That much discussed decision really held no more than that a western newspaper might not take advantage of the fact that it was published some hours later than papers in the east, to copy the news which the plaintiff had collected at its own expense. In spite of some general language it must be confined to that situation." Appealing to a general sense of fairness and equity, Whiteman and RCA pressed the previously successful argument that "courts must adjust themselves to new conditions, and that in the case at bar justice clearly points the way to some relief." But Judge Hand refused to use "unfair competition" as a catchall theory. The issue was for Congress, and the marketplace, to determine. "We cannot agree," he wrote. "[N]o doubt we should be jealous to execute all reasonable implications of established doctrines; but we should be equally jealous not to undertake the composition of substantial conflicts of interest, between which neither the common law, nor the statute, has given any clue to its preference. We cannot know how Congress would solve this issue." "If the talents of conductors of orchestras are denied that compensation which is necessary to evoke their efforts because they get too little for phonographic records, we have no means of knowing it, or any right to assume it; and it is idle to invoke the deus ex machina of a 'progress' which is probably spurious, and would not be for us to realize, if it were genuine."[54] "It follows that the complaint must be dismissed," Hand concluded, "and for reasons which make it unnecessary to determine how far Whiteman's contracts with RCA Manufacturing Company, Inc. preserved any common-law copyrights he might have had, if they had survived the sale of the records."

Many accounts of the decision, including Fred Waring's,[55] wrongly suggest that the case turned on the language of Whiteman's contracts, but in the end they made no difference: neither Whiteman nor RCA could prevent broadcasting of their records.[56] The parties appealed, but when the Supreme Court refused to hear the case on December 16, 1940, it became official—Judge Hand's opinion was the last word on the legality of broadcasting sound recordings.

---

54. To complete the process, Hand dismissed the privacy theory raised by Judge Maxey's concurrence in the *Waring* decision, noting in derogatory fashion that "[i]t scarcely seems necessary to discuss the strange assertion that to broadcast the records in some way invades somebody's 'right of privacy' . . ." *Id.* at 14–15.

55. *See* WARING, *supra* note 22, at 141.

56. 311 U.S. 712, 61 S. Ct. 394, 85 L. Ed. 463 (1940).

Despite the devastating loss, NAPA pressed on with one more complaint. Returning to Pennsylvania state court, the scene of its sole victory, the group sued Philadelphia broadcaster Wm. Penn Broadcasting Company and various of its sponsors, seeking an injunction consistent with the *Waring* decision, which, as Judge Hand had confirmed, was still good law in the state of Pennsylvania. Using a procedural maneuver, the broadcaster deftly moved the case to federal court, where the *Whiteman* precedent held sway. NAPA's litigation campaign was over.[57]

29. After *Whiteman*

News of the *Whiteman* result reached Fred Waring as he was leading a "trainload of artists" to a copyright hearing in Washington, DC. "A bill was being sponsored in our favor," he said, "but our lobbying suffered greatly after the debacle . . . We were doomed for failure." Some years later, Waring recalled the hollow nature of his victory against WDAS, saying it motivated his "enemies," including "broadcasting stations, the disc jockeys, the publishers, the record companies, and even ASCAP," to pressure NAPA members into curtailing their demands.[58] Attorney Socolow recalled: "As the radio broadcasters united in bitter opposition, progress through the courts became increasingly difficult, slow, and tremendously costly."[59] Waring was more blunt, referring to his fellow artists as "the rats [who] left the ship and left me holding the bag."[60] Socolow remembered how Waring "suffered substantially" due to NAPA's failures. Waring had spent "thousands of dollars and hours of his precious time" pursuing the cause, and had "lost a fortune" by refusing to record for a full decade between November 1932 and January 1942, while the primary efforts were underway.[61]

Waring made efforts to bury the hatchet, signing a new contract with Decca early in 1942 (again following Whiteman, who had done so in 1938), for whom the Pennsylvanians would turn out some seventy sides within a few months.[62] But the bitterness remained, even beyond his passing in 1984, into the next generation. Fred Waring, Jr., who followed in his father's footsteps as a bandleader, felt the ramifications of NAPA's efforts years later. "One day I was in Howard Johnson's sitting near a jukebox when a man was changing records on the machine," he

---

57. Nat'l Ass'n of Performing Artists v. Wm. Penn Broad. Co., 49 U.S.P.Q. 563 (E.D. Pa. Apr. 25, 1941).
58. WARING, *supra* note 22, at 140.
59. *Id.* at 141.
60. *Id.*
61. *Id.* at 142.
62. *Id.*

recalled. "I asked him if he ever used any Fred Waring records." "No," was the reply, "the son-of-a-bitch is trying to wreck my job."[63] Later in life, Waring lamented that "we gained nothing except for the precedent and the long-winded testimony in law books."[64] He was technically correct, but Waring's efforts were not in vain. The case bearing his name is still "good law," at least in Pennsylvania, and was referenced as recently as 2011 in Copyright Office proceedings involving sound recording copyrights.[65] Moreover, he inspired subsequent generations of artists—Tommy Dorsey, Stan Kenton, Tony Bennett and Frank Sinatra among them—to carry the torch of performers' rights in connection with the public performance of their recordings.[66] As we will see, their efforts have borne fruit in recent years, but remain one of the most contentious issues in the twenty-first-century music industry.

Although performers' advocacy for sound recording rights "suffered greatly" in the wake of the *Whiteman* decision, they did not grind to a complete halt. Rather, taking a cue from Judge Hand, performers refocused their efforts from the courts to Congress. No fewer than six bills were introduced between 1942 and 1951; they were designed to bring recordings under the copyright statute.[67] Four bills introduced during the war years saw no legislative action, but gave rise to a report from the American Bar Association's Committee on Copyrights, which, after analyzing the policy considerations in some detail, concluded only that it lacked the facts necessary to make a recommendation.[68] In January 1947, Representative Hugh D. Scott, Jr. (not coincidentally, from Fred Waring's home state of Pennsylvania), introduced an essentially identical bill, holding hearings in which recording artists, including Waring, renewed their arguments as to the creative nature of recorded performances and the inadequacy of common law protection. Artists should be permitted to obtain an individual copyright on records, Waring insisted, "in such a way we can control the playing for profit of our recordings."[69] Responding to inquiries on common law protection, NAPA attorney Maurice Speiser said that such a state-by-state effort "would take at least two lifetimes," adding in sarcastic reference to Judge Hand's opinion "the judge ruled that when an artist makes a recording, he is 'dedicating a monument to the public.'"[70] Consistent

---

63. *Id.* NAPA's efforts to curb the public performance of recordings also extended to jukebox operators, even though they were exempt from paying even *publishers'* performance royalties under the terms of the 1909 Copyright Act.

64. *Id.*

65. *See* "Comments of SoundExchange, Inc.," *In re* Fed. Copyright Protection of Sound Recordings Fixed Before February 15, 1972, Docket No. 2010–4, Before the U.S. Copyright Office, Library of Congress.

66. Kenton, Bennett, and others formed the National Committee for the Recording Artists in 1967.

67. *See* Ringer, *supra* note 2, at 34–37.

68. *Id.* at 35.

69. Billboard, May 31, 1947, at 21.

70. *Id.*

with RCA's position in *Whiteman,* record labels opposed the measure on the ground that any copyright should vest with them, not performers.[71] Broadcasters also joined the opposition, arguing that the law would unfairly penalize radio stations, since broadcasting was "the principal factor in making a record popular."[72] Interestingly, the "promotion" issue had not surfaced in *Waring* or *Whiteman.* To the contrary, it was proven as fact that radio airplay was detrimental to both artists and labels, having caused a significant decline in record sales by providing the same content over the air, free of charge. In any event, as *Billboard* magazine reported, the Scott Bill was "roundly denounced" by every branch of the music business other than artists, and went nowhere; when the same measure was reintroduced in 1951, it received no attention at all.[73]

The failure of the Scott Bills at the turn of the decade marked a paradigm shift in the music business, one reflected in the activities of Paul Whiteman. Whiteman had cooperated in NAPA's efforts, acting as plaintiff in the flagship litigation intended to solidify artists' rights in their recordings, but his views were never as strident as Waring's, and he took the defeat much differently. Despite the legal uncertainties surrounding his recorded output, Whiteman continued making recordings during NAPA's most active period, signing with Decca in 1938, and working his way further into the radio business as a performer and executive. By the early 1940s he was director of music for the ABC radio network, and rose to a vice presidency after the war. Early in 1947, ABC program director Charles Barry was considering ideas for a Saturday morning program for flagship station WJZ in New York that could be expanded to key markets across the country. When Campbell Soup expressed interest as a sponsor, Barry approached, but was turned down by a number of music, stage, and film personalities for the host position. So when a certain ABC colleague walked into his office, Barry had nothing to lose in popping the question: "Whiteman, how would you like to be a disc jockey?" "Don't be crazy," was the stunned response, but Barry succeeded in getting the star into the studio for a test program, which went well enough to pique Whiteman's interest. Whiteman gained confidence in the format during a trial run of shows in the spring of 1947, and on June 30, *The Paul Whiteman Club* made its debut as the first coast-to-coast disc jockey program, broadcasting each weekday afternoon over 228 stations. Capitalizing on the public's immediate acceptance, ABC brought in Camel Cigarettes, Premium Crackers, Wesson Salad Oil, and Nescafe Instant Coffee, who paid a collective $6 million as annual sponsors, the largest time sale in the history of radio.[74] At the age of fifty-seven, Paul Whiteman entered a new chapter in a storied musical career, pitching housewives on coffee and tobacco

---

71. Ringer, *supra* note 2, at 36.
72. *Id.* at 36.
73. *Id.* at 37; BILLBOARD, *supra* note 69, at 18.
74. DELONG, *supra* note 19, at 276.

while spinning records along with the occasional behind-the-scenes yarns of a bandleader who had performed live in virtually every market he now reached without leaving the comfort of ABC studios.

In its favorable review, trade paper *Variety* noted that the new program put the deejay "into long pants," backing up "ABC's conviction that integration of disc jockeyism and personality can add up to entertainment and box office at the corner store." On July 14, 1947, a nattily dressed Whiteman appeared on the cover of *Newsweek* magazine, photographed at the ABC microphone holding up a prized shiny platter. The article, "Jazz King to Disc Jockey," described the rise of the deejay from "the cocoon of the local station to become the rich butterfly of the networks." The transformation was indeed complete: as the first nationwide network disc jockey, Paul Whiteman legitimized the same practice he had sued to enjoin less than a decade earlier. As it happened, however, *The Paul Whiteman Show* was short-lived. Once the novelty of a celebrity deejay wore off, audiences grew tired of what some said was a stilted, arrogant manner that lacked warmth or sincerity. "No man of his caliber could really believe what he was saying about Nescafe," wrote one listener.[75] After 250 hours of broadcasting, the show finished its one-year run in mid-1948.

In court, the *Whiteman* ruling "put the disk-jockey for the first time on secure legal footing."[76] On the air, Whiteman helped raise the deejay's profile to that of a performer in his own right. At the same time, however, Whiteman's experience showed that, to achieve lasting success, a disc jockey needed certain talents—the gift of gab, sincerity, and an unbridled enthusiasm for *recorded* music. Martin Block, whose folksy patter in the *Make Believe Ballroom* was still wooing the ladies after a dozen years on the air, embodied these qualities, and as a result, was very well compensated. Paul Whiteman had earned a respectable $800 per show during his short-lived program, but Block was in another league. Fred Waring's stomach surely churned as he read *Billboard* magazine's coverage of the music industry for the week of May 31, 1947. The very same issue that reported Waring's testimony on the failed Scott Bill also made note of Martin Block's network deal with the Mutual Broadcasting System, which brought his potential earnings to an astounding $14,000 per week, more than Waring himself had earned during his rich Ford sponsorship.[77] In the smug tone of a victor, Block added, "It amuses me to recall that when we first started spinning disks on the air the record companies were almost unanimous in their opposition to this new medium of entertainment."[78] In the course of a decade, the deejay had gone from "sued to wooed."[79] By the close of

---

75. *Id.* at 280.

76. Erik Barnouw, The Golden Web: A History of Broadcasting in the United States (1968).

77. Billboard, *supra* note 69, at 7.

78. Albin J. Zak III, I Don't Sound Like Nobody: Remaking Music in 1950s America 9 (2010).

79. Matthew Lasar, *What Would Paul Whiteman Say About the Performance Rights Act?* Radio Survivor Blog, June 24, 2009, http://www.radiosurvivor.com/2009/06/24/what-would-paul-whiteman-say-about-the-performance-rights-act/.

the 1940s, the restrictive legend, "Not licensed for radio broadcast," disappeared from record labels altogether, and the notion that broadcasting had a negative impact on record sales, or a recording artist's career, was fast becoming a quaint relic of an earlier era.[80]

30. After the War

The end of the war released a pent-up demand for consumer products, including music. In 1946 record sales doubled from the prior year, the vast majority released by the three major labels—Columbia,[81] RCA Victor, and Decca—but with a significant contribution from a fast-growing upstart out of Los Angeles called Capitol Records. Capitol was founded in 1942 by Buddy DeSylva, a songwriter turned executive producer at Paramount Pictures, legendary songwriter Johnny Mercer, and Glenn Wallichs, whose Music City superstore at the corner of Sunset and Vine stocked records, sheet music, and radios, and offered on-site custom-recording facilities.[82] Through his experience as a retailer, Wallichs was familiar with the distribution business, while Mercer knew repertoire and was a pipeline to performers, and DeSylva kept a capable eye on the big picture. With this seasoned team of creators and entrepreneurs, the company accelerated quickly, acquiring its own record pressing facilities in 1944 and going public in 1946. The founders brought on James B. Conkling, who led their development of the first strategic radio promotion platform in the industry. Capitol anticipated (and promoted) the changes in musical tastes that were moving away from big band and swing toward the stylings of individual pop singers, and helped move fringe styles, particularly Country & Western and "Hillbilly," toward the mainstream. Eventually its impressive roster of pop artists would include Nat King Cole, Peggy Lee, guitar wizard Les Paul, and Frank Sinatra, among many others. The Capitol label continued to thrive following its acquisition by London-based Electric and Musical Industries Limited (EMI) in 1955, recording and distributing rock-era acts, from Gene Vincent to the Beach Boys, the Beatles, and today, the likes of Coldplay.[83]

---

80. *See* ZAK, *supra* note 78, at 30.

81. The Brunswick label had been sold to Warner Brothers Pictures in 1930, and on to CBS in 1938. The rights reverted in 1940, after which the label was transferred to Decca in 1941, which was ultimately acquired by the Music Corporation of America (MCA). For portions of this history, and that of many other early American labels, see BRIAN RUST, THE AMERICAN RECORD LABEL BOOK (1978).

82. For detailed coverage of the explosion of independent record labels from the 1940s through the 1960s, see JOHN BROVEN, RECORD MAKERS AND BREAKERS: VOICES OF THE INDEPENDENT ROCK 'N' ROLL PIONEERS (2009).

83. *See* BRIAN SOUTHALL, THE RISE & FALL OF EMI RECORDS (2009).

Another independent label that rose quickly in the ranks was Chicago's Mercury Records, formed in late 1945 by Irving Green, a "plastics expert" (whose father, Al, ran the National label in New York), his friend Ray Greenberg, and Chicago talent agent Berle Adams. From the start, Mercury had ample access to capital, taking advantage of opportunities like the bankruptcy of the Majestic label, from which it purchased nearly 2,000 masters, and the availability of Keynote Records, another early acquisition that brought producer Mitch Miller into the fold. Like Capitol, Mercury was a creative marketer, organizing promotional concert tours for its leading artists, and methodically pushing its records to both radio stations and jukebox operators.[84] Berle Adams departed the company and moved to California for health reasons in late 1947, but soon returned to the industry as an executive at MCA, running MCA Records until 1971. Mercury soldiered on without him, gaining No. 1 pop hits with Vic Damone and Frankie Laine in 1949, before striking the mother lode with Patti Paige's pop smash, "The Tennessee Waltz," which hit No. 1 in January 1951, and went on to sell an estimated 7 million discs in the early 1950s. Mercury eventually went the way of Capitol, selling to Philips of Holland in 1961. The label has continued to flourish under various conglomerate umbrellas, currently as an imprint of the largest music company in the world, Universal Music Group, a unit of France's Vivendi-Universal.

Capitol and Mercury were notable success stories, but they were only two of the hundreds of independent labels that began dotting the postwar musical landscape. In addition to Capitol, Los Angeles gave birth to Excelsior, Exclusive, Modern, Jukebox and Specialty, while New York was home to Apollo, National, Savoy, Atlantic, and dozens more. Chicago had Mercury and Vitacoustics, among others, and the list continued with a potpourri of labels from smaller cities and towns across the country—Nashville's Bullet, Cincinnati's King, and Sun Records of Memphis, founded by Sam Phillips in 1952. One of the common denominators among successful indie labels was their marketing savvy, particularly their persistence in promoting new records to jukebox operators and, more important, radio stations. As independent records started breaking through regionally, then nationally with million-selling hits, the major labels jumped on the radio bandwagon as well. Soon after Capitol's radio program was implemented, Columbia adopted a radio promotion strategy, sponsoring Martin Block's *Make Believe Ballroom*, among many other shows. The holdouts, Decca and RCA Victor, had both capitulated by 1947, when Victor became the last of the original big three labels to fully embrace radio promotion, sending free copies of its new releases to 2,800 program directors and deejays across the country. The new marketing strategy had an immediate impact on the industry's bottom line: in 1947, an estimated 375 million discs were sold, generating nearly $215 million in retail sales, exceeding

---

84. Sanjek, *supra* note 12, at 230–31.

the previous high-water mark set in 1921, when the great tenor Enrico Caruso held sway, and before commercial radio gained its presence and influence.

The industry's growth was interrupted for a year during a second recording strike organized by James Petrillo, the powerful head of the American Federation of Musicians. As he had done in 1942, Petrillo convinced union members to cease recording, as a protest against the increasing mechanization and broadcasting of music, which Petrillo insisted was costing professional musicians opportunities for employment. The first strike resulted in the creation of a union Performance Trust Fund, to which labels contributed based on each record sold. But the Taft-Hartley Act prohibited fund contributions after December 31, 1947, prompting a second strike, which lasted scarcely a year, before being settled by an agreement allowing for continued fund contributions from the labels. The twelve-month interim saw significant advances in technology, including the adoption of magnetic tape by both radio stations and recording studios. Stations used tape to prerecord shows in convenient segments, and in the studio, tape recording quickly replaced the practice of recording directly onto acetate discs. The new technology proved superior in many ways—tape could run interrupted for a full half hour, could be played back immediately, repeated indefinitely, and, most important, made editing (by splicing) a simple process. Tape allowed for unprecedented sonic experimentation, as evidenced by the echo chamber effect in Victor's million-selling single by vocalist Vaughan Monroe, "Riders in the Sky" (1949); the first multitrack experiments from Capitol's pioneering electric guitarist, Les Paul;[85] and the overdubbing techniques that became Mitch Miller's trademark in the series of pop hits he produced for Mercury Records and later Columbia.

As an accompaniment to these developments in recording techniques, music playback technology was also changing, leading to another edition of the "format wars" first waged among disc and cylinder makers in the early twentieth century. Columbia introduced a 12-inch, 33 ⅓ rpm Long Play (LP) record album at a New York press conference on June 21, 1948, boasting of its improved sound reproduction. The format achieved $3 million in sales in its first year. Rather than accepting and licensing Columbia's technology, RCA Victor responded with a new format of its own, introducing the first 45 rpm single, a 7-inch disk with a large center hole, in February 1949. "45s" provided sound quality equal to "LPs," but, as with the existing 78 rpm records, contained only four minutes of playing time—too short for classical music programs, but just right for a self-contained pop song. They were also small, lightweight, durable, and easy to carry and handle. Consumer confusion resulted from the competing formats initially, but in a matter of months both companies capitulated; RCA began making LPs, and Columbia offered 45s. The rest of the industry fell in line, releasing new records in both formats. In 1951, sales

---

85. The "Les Paul" model introduced by Gibson Guitar company in 1952 remains a best-selling instrument sixty years later.

of 45s exceeded LPs for the first time, establishing the smaller format as the cultural currency of the coming decade. Efforts to sort out the speed wars helped bring about the formation of the Recording Industry Association of America (RIAA) in late 1951, a trade association that became, and remains, the united and powerful voice of the recorded music industry. Having undergone these technological changes, the industry was poised to expand further in the new decade, and yet the legal tools available to address conflicts concerning recorded music remained the same, as evidenced by the "battle of the independents" waged between Capitol Records and its rival, Mercury.[86] Ironically, these young American labels became embroiled in a dispute over the U.S. distribution rights for old foreign recordings—specifically, World War II era "matrices" made for a German label, Telefunken, by artists including Erna Sack and the renowned Igor Stravinsky. As it moved from district to appellate court, the case gave judges Vincent Leibell and Learned Hand another opportunity to explore the question of copyright in sound recordings.

During German occupation in the early 1940s, Telefunken entered into an agreement authorizing a Czech label, Ultraphon, to use Telefunken matrices to manufacture and distribute records in Czechoslovakia. Following Germany's surrender, the Czech government seized all German property within its borders, including the matrices, which were later transferred to another Czech company, Gramophone. In 1947, Gramophone gave Keynote Recordings (Mercury) permission to manufacture and distribute records based on the matrices in the United States. The following year, 1948, Telefunken itself entered into an agreement granting Capitol the same distribution rights. When the conflict ripened, Capitol filed suit in New York federal court, seeking a declaration that it had exclusive rights in the U.S. As federal copyright did not apply to sound recordings, the question was which party had superior rights under the "common law" principles explored in the *Waring* and *Whiteman* decisions. The case was assigned to Vincent Leibell, who had decided the *Whiteman* case a dozen years earlier, only to be reversed by Learned Hand's opinion for the Second Circuit. Judge Leibell examined the competing contracts, distinguishing between the matrices themselves (physical property) and the underlying recordings—those valuable, intangible "property rights" the recording artists had assigned to Telefunken in their agreements. Leibell concluded that "[t]he confiscation of the circular metal discs, known as matrices, did not invest the Czechoslovakian government with the right to reproduce records . . . and distribute them beyond the Czechoslovakian borders." Mercury's contract rights were valid only in Czechoslovakia, consistent with Telefunken's original grant to Ultraphon. On the other hand, Telefunken had granted U.S. distribution rights to Capitol only. Thus, Mercury's U.S. sales amounted to "duplication of a competitor's phonograph records," a form of "unfair competition."

---

86. Capitol Records, Inc. v. Mercury Record Corp., 109 F. Supp 330 (S.D.N.Y. 1952).

Capitol's contract rights were superior, but Learned Hand's reasoning in *Whiteman* suggested that Telefunken (and its licensees) may have lost their common law property rights upon the first distribution, or "publication," of the records in the United States, leaving them with no rights to enforce. Judge Leibell interpreted the case narrowly, however, saying that the "meat" of the *Whiteman* decision was that "'the records themselves could not be clogged with a servitude' which limited the use of the records 'for non-commercial use on phonographs in homes.'" Since there was "no [such] servitude on an article to be sold at retail," rights in the recorded performances remained intact and enforceable.

Mercury appealed to the Second Circuit, where the case was heard by Edward Dimock, a district court judge sitting temporarily on the court of appeals, along with appellate judges Harold Medina and Learned Hand, now a veteran of music copyright matters and author of the *Whiteman* decision. But it was Judge Dimock who wrote the affirming opinion on April 12, 1955.[87] Interestingly, the court began by posing the question of whether phonograph records "are susceptible of copyright," an issue that seemed well-settled in the negative, and to which the parties had stipulated. Nevertheless, Judge Dimock surveyed a half-century's jurisprudence, beginning with the *White-Smith v. Apollo* decision and the provisions in the 1909 Act that overturned the result, allowing for the mechanical reproduction of musical compositions by any party willing to pay the statutory rate. But Congress had provided no means for copyrighting the mechanical reproductions themselves, whether piano rolls, or the modern equivalent, sound recordings. Thus there was no basis on which to apply federal law to the current conflict, leaving the court to decide the matter "on principle," under the law of New York. By the terms of the contracts, only Capitol had the right to sell records in the U.S., but "was that right lost as soon as [Capitol] sold the first records?" Judge Leibell had dodged the question with his narrow interpretation of *Whiteman*, but the appellate court addressed the issue in substance, quoting Judge Hand's conclusion that "the commonlaw property in the performances of musical artists which had been recorded ended with the sale of the records and that thereafter anyone might copy them and use them as he pleased." However, the court continued, "the quoted statement . . . is not the law of the State of New York."

The surprising conclusion was based on a reading of the New York state court's opinion in *Metropolitan Opera Association v. Wagner-Nichols Recorder Corp.*, decided in 1950, in which the defendant made and sold recordings of opera radio broadcasts. The Met had given Columbia the exclusive right to market recordings of its performances, and the label had released a number of *studio* recordings (not

---

87. Capitol Records, Inc. v. Mercury Record Corp., 221 F.2d 657 (2d Cir. 1955).

taken from broadcasts).[88] The New York Supreme Court[89] enjoined the activity based on the broad, amorphous principle that "property rights of commercial value are to be and will be protected from any form of commercial immorality." Judge Dimock viewed the *Metropolitan* decision as the definitive statement of New York law on the question of publication. "We believe the inescapable result ... is that, where the originator ... of records of performances by musical artists puts those records on public sale, his act does not constitute a dedication of the right to copy and sell the records." Perhaps deliberately, the court failed to acknowledge that Wagner-Nichols had not "copied" any recordings at all—it had made its own, off the air—and thus the question of "publication" by the sale of a previous recording was not in issue. In other words, the operative facts were different: unlike Wagner-Nichols, Mercury was copying and distributing the very same recorded performances released by Capitol, clearly raising the question of whether rights in those particular recordings had been forfeited by publication. Regardless, Judge Medina joined with Judge Dimock, forming a majority of two that affirmed the district court.

Learned Hand took exception in a thoughtful dissenting opinion that confirmed his personal belief "that the performance or rendition of a 'musical composition' is a 'Writing' under ... the Constitution separate from, and additional to, the 'composition' itself." But Congress had not yet reached the same conclusion, leaving recordings outside the scope of copyright. In light of this, Hand expressed the same concerns he had identified in *Whiteman*: the effect of following state law on the issue of publication (at least in New York) was to grant a perpetual monopoly right in sound recordings under the "subnomine" of "unfair competition," while property that was subject to copyright (musical compositions, for example) enjoyed only limited duration. In addition, the courts of various states might draw different conclusions as to publication, leading to inconsistent results in an area—copyright—where federal law was intended to foster uniformity. Indeed, this had already occurred, as illustrated by the differing results reached in the *Whiteman* and *Capitol* cases. Had he spoken for the majority, Learned Hand would have been compelled to reverse Judge Leibell (again) and dismiss Capitol's complaint, although he admittedly would not have been pleased by the harsh result. "Unhappily," he said, "we cannot deal with the situation as we should like, because the copyrightability of such 'works' is a casus omissus from the Act. That was almost certainly owing to the fact that in 1909 the practice of recording the renditions of virtuosi had not sprung up." Hand was actually wrong in this

---

88. Metropolitan Opera Ass'n v. Wagner-Nichols Recorder Corp., 199 Misc. 786, 101 N.Y.S.2d 483 (Sup. Ct. 1950); Id., 279 App. Div. 632, 107 N.Y.S.2d 795. Columbia joined as a plaintiff, as did the American Broadcasting Company, arguing successfully that the defendant's recordings also interfered with its exclusive agreement to broadcast the performances.

89. The "Supreme Court" is the trial court tribunal in New York State.

assessment (as we have seen, Victor lobbied for copyright protection in sound recordings as early as 1906), but the point was well taken. Congress chose not to
bring recordings under copyright in the 1909 Act, and despite the efforts coordinated by NAPA and its supporters, had not been persuaded otherwise in the following decades.

31. From Recordings to Records

No one has written about the cultural and technological forces that transformed
the postwar music industry with more insight and passion than Albin Zak in his
revealing book, *I Don't Sound Like Nobody: Remaking Music in 1950s America.* [90]
With a historian's eye and musician's ear, Zak chronicles the transitional period
between the end of the Swing Era and the rise and dominance of rock and roll in
popular music by the mid 1960s. As Zak relates, "[w]hile myriad events shaped the
postwar musical climate, the key catalyst was sound recording."[91] By 1950 the nationwide wave of independent label startups had fostered a new approach to the
process of recording music. Recording was no longer perceived as an effort to preserve a particular performance—it was an opportunity to shape a unique sonic
creation, reflecting the talents not only of the primary artist, but also the team of
producers and engineers who used improved recording and sound effect technology to make creative contributions of their own. Rather than merely "capturing" a
musician's rendition, as Judge Leibell had said of RCA's recordings of Paul Whiteman, these teams of alchemists collaborated in creating entirely new works in the
form of sound recordings. It was the beginning of the Production Era in music-
making, in which "capturing performances" gave way to "making records."

We might pinpoint the onset of the Production Era to the fall of 1949, when
Frankie Laine, a rising singer for the Mercury label, addressed his fans at the conclusion of a Detroit concert.[92] Would the audience like to hear his usual closing
number, or the *recorded* version of his upcoming single, "Mule Train"? When the
crowd called for the latter, Laine cued the sound booth and took a seat at the edge
of the stage, experiencing the powerful attraction of recorded sound along with his
audience. What came over the loudspeakers was new and different, Laine's driving
chant—"Mule Traaaaeeeen!"—mixed with echo-laden, ambient fiddles and sounds
of whips cracking. Even Laine's vocals were more like sound effects in their cadence,
as he imitated the sounds of the animals "clipetty, clippetty-clopping along." The
Western theme was apparent, but there wasn't much of a storyline, just repetitious

---

90. ZAK, *supra* note 78.
91. *Id.* at 2.
92. *Id.* at 52.

chants and references to the wares the mules carried—"a plug of chaw tobaccy for a rancher in Corolla; a guitar for a cowboy way out in Arizona." As the sound faded, the crowd demanded an encore "performance," boosting Laine's confidence in his upcoming single. "Mule Train" raced to No. 1, knocking Laine's prior record, "That Lucky Old Sun," from the top spot, marking the first time the same artist simultaneously held the top two chart positions. Later, "Mule Train" would be credited as the first song to utilize the kind of "aural texture" that "set the pattern for virtually the entire first decade of rock."[93]

"Mule Train" was one of three Frankie Laine recordings to reach No. 1 in the six months beginning in October 1949, having been recorded by production guru Mitch Miller for Mercury, before he was recruited to a major label, Columbia, in February 1950. Miller's early efforts established that "the interface of music and technology was now fundamental to modern record production," and his methods "brought together singer and sound effects man in a new kind of collaborative project."[94] Traditionalists lashed out at what they deemed studio trickery in the place of "real" music, but the public response to Miller's techniques was undeniable. In his first eighteen months at Columbia, the label's pop record sales increased 60 percent, and by 1953 he had crafted over fifty hit recordings for the label. Between 1950 and 1956 Miller produced records that sold an astounding 80 million copies.[95] Miller was a high-profile, mainstream success story, but he hardly had a lock on making hit records. The creative use of sound recording techniques accelerated in the latter half of the 1950s, coming from all corners of the business, major labels and independents alike. The nascent rock and roll genre was generating its first heroes in the likes of Chuck Berry, Bill Haley, and the one with the crossover appeal to carry the message to the masses, Elvis Presley. But just as Presley's music was an amalgamation of influences, the broader market was also a polyglot of styles and sounds, in which a hit could emerge from anywhere. In 1958 no fewer than seventy-two labels placed records in the top fifty, representing a breathtaking diversity of styles—from rock and roll to rhythm and blues, country, pure pop, and everything in between.[96] But regardless of source or style, "songs" were subordinate to "sounds," or, as Albin Zak puts it, "the records *were* the songs . . . As record production evolved through the fifties, the result was not only new music but a new way of making music. It was perhaps the most enduring musical concept to emerge from the postwar period: records were no longer simply aural snapshots but deliberately crafted musical texts."[97] Sales of sheet music had been in steady decline during the 1940s, as record sales increased. Now records existed unto

---

93. WILL FRIEDWALD, SINATRA! THE SONG IS YOU 174 (1997).
94. ZAK, *supra* note 78, at 69.
95. *Id.* at 49.
96. *Id.* at 211.
97. *Id.* at 191, 162.

themselves as both artistic creations and as the primary consumer product of the music business.

As techniques for making recordings changed, so did attitudes as to how to promote and sell them. As seen through the experiences of Fred Waring and Paul Whiteman, in earlier decades artists objected to their records being broadcast, based on the idea that by their nature, recordings were inferior to live music. It was fine to sell recordings for home use, where they were the only practical alternative to the "real thing," a live performance, but *broadcasting* those same recordings was another matter. Since broadcasters (and their sponsors) could afford to pay live musicians, their use of records as a cheaper, artificial substitute was considered unfair to performing musicians (whose work was being replaced), and to the listening audience, duped into thinking they were experiencing a live performance. On top of these concerns was the conventional wisdom that by saturating the market with "free" music, radio broadcasting caused a decline in record sales. But this conception of recorded music changed dramatically in postwar America, along with the fundamental relationships among music producers and the consuming public. In the Production Era, the *performance* of records was no longer a concern; indeed, the opposite was true: the "symbiotic relationship" among record labels, recording artists, and broadcasters had produced a different reality, one in which the new conventional wisdom held that radio broadcasting was the single most important driver of record sales.

♪♪ ♫♫ ♪♪

The Radio Act of 1927 mandated "sponsorship identification," requiring that all broadcast content for which "valuable consideration" was received "be announced as paid" at the time of broadcast.[98] The "disclosure requirement" was the price to be paid for the privilege of using a public resource—the radio spectrum—for commercial purposes. The law was rarely invoked in its original form, or as replaced by Section 317 of the Communications Act of 1934, since advertisers had every reason to make themselves known as broadcast sponsors.[99] This remained the case well into the 1950s, when the rapid increase in television broadcasting, and the music industry's newfound focus on recordings, made covert forms of sponsorship more prevalent, bumping up against the disclosure requirement. These tensions erupted into a full-blown scandal involving sponsors' roles in rigging television quiz shows, on which the House Special Subcommittee on Legislative Oversight convened public hearings late in 1959. Shortly after the investigation commenced, Burton Lane, president of the American Guild of Authors and Composers, wrote to the subcommittee, charging that "commercial bribery has become a prime factor in determin-

---

98. Radio Act of 1927, Pub. L. No. 69–632, 44 Stat. 1162.

99. Communications Act of 1934, ch. 652, 48 Stat. 1064 (codified as amended in various sections of 47 U.S.C.).

ing what music is played on many broadcast programs and what musical records the public is surreptitiously induced to buy."[100] With this catalyst, the practice of "pay for play" (what the subcommittee called "payola," using the term originated in a 1938 *Variety* magazine article) was suddenly swept into the national spotlight. Related investigations were initiated by federal agencies and district attorneys from a number of states, and the U.S. attorney general issued a report at President Eisenhower's request. But it was the subcommittee's hearings that created a public spectacle, featuring testimony from various industry participants, most notably the prominent deejays and show hosts, Dick Clark of *American Bandstand*, and Alan Freed, known as the "Father of Rock and Roll" to his legions of teenage fans.

Dick Clark's career began in 1952 when he became a disc jockey at radio station WFIL, outside Philadelphia, whose television affiliate broadcast *Bob Horn's Bandstand*. Upon Horn's departure in 1956, Clark became the full-time host, and the next year ABC picked up the show and renamed it *American Bandstand*. During this time, Clark began acquiring interests in a variety of music businesses, and by 1959 he was established as both a show host and entrepreneur. When called before the subcommittee, Clark acknowledged his interests in publishing houses, recording companies, distributors, and production companies, but denied taking direct payments in return for airplay. Nevertheless, under pressure from ABC, Clark agreed to divest his music business interests to avoid the appearance of impropriety. Clark's long-term interests were unaffected by the investigation, and he went on to become a major music business impresario, still active at the time of his passing in 2012.

Alan Freed met a different fate. Freed was an accidental deejay, falling into the position after subbing for the regular jockey at station WAKR in Akron, Ohio, beginning in 1945. His natural broadcast talent and growing enthusiasm for new music took him to Cleveland and ultimately to WINS in New York, where he held forth as emcee of the *Rock 'n' Roll Party* starting in 1954. His influence grew along with the fledgling rock genre, and by the late fifties he was the most influential deejay in the country. His popularity was both a blessing and curse, as Freed worked around the risky cultural fringe, promoting cutting edge shows that mixed black and white performers and audiences, always drawing attention from conservative authorities. In 1958 WINS terminated Freed's employment in the wake of a concert debacle in Boston, where fights had broken out over access to an oversold show, leaving Freed to face charges of "inciting to riot during a rock and roll show" on his own.[101] He resurfaced immediately on New York station WABC, but the

---

100. For an excellent overview of sponsorship disclosure and enforcement over the years, *see* Richard Kielbowicz and Linda Lawson, *Unmasking Hidden Commercials in Broadcasting: Origins of the Sponsorship Identification Regulations, 1927–1963*, 56 Fed. Comm. L.J. 329 (Mar. 2004); *see also* Kristen Lee Repyneck, *The Ghost of Alan Freed: An Analysis of the Merit and Purpose of Anti-Payola Laws in Today's Music Industry*, 51 Vill. L. Rev. 695 (2006).

101. For a general biography of Freed, see http://www.alanfreed.com/wp/biography/; *see also* Zak, *supra* note 79, at 37–42.

payola scandal soon exploded, again putting Freed and ABC in an uncomfortable spotlight. ABC hoped to wash its hands of the mess by having Freed sign an affidavit denying he had accepted payola. Freed could not do so in good conscience, however, which ABC used as grounds for his dismissal in November 1959. The decade was over, as was the professional career of Alan Freed.

Freed was indicted in New York in February 1960 for commercial bribery, and in April faced a grilling from the payola subcommittee. There had already been plenty of testimony confirming the payment of "consultant fees" to disc jockeys in major markets across the country, and Freed was candid in acknowledging receipt of his share. His candor won the praise of one lawmaker, who called Freed "one of the few completely truthful men we've had before us," but his admissions gave the New York district attorney's office ample reason to continue its prosecution.[102] The legal process churned away for another two years before Freed pled guilty in 1962 to commercial bribery. Although he received only a fine and suspended sentence, the damage was done: Freed tried to restart things at stations in California and Florida, but the positions were short-lived. Freed fell into an alcoholic haze and died in 1965 at the age of forty-three.

In the wake of the pay-for-play scandal, Congress added Section 508 to the "payola statute," applying a disclosure-type mandate to individual station employees as well as broadcasters. But the general disclosure requirements of the law and related regulations were essentially unchanged, penalties were minor, and with no visible "victims" there was little perceived need for ongoing vigilance. As a result, when the hoopla of the public hearings died down, it was back to business as usual in the world of music promotion. The system of exchange became more sophisticated and less direct, oftentimes including a new middleman—the independent, or "indie" promoter—who facilitated the exchange of value between labels and broadcasters in a manner that arguably avoided disclosure requirements. But payola in its various forms continued unabated, and would enjoy its heyday in the years and decades to come, regardless of periodic investigations and prosecutions of labels, broadcasters, and indie promoters.[103]

Consolidation of radio station ownership following the 1996 Telecommunications Act allowed the "indie promoter" system to flourish, until Congress and then-New York Attorney General, Eliot Spitzer, responded to mounting evidence that payola had once again reached a scale that could not be ignored. Spitzer collected information implicating the four major labels and four largest broadcast groups in an elaborate system of pay for play. In 2005, the labels paid a collective $35 million in fines, and following Spitzer's referral to the FCC, in 2007 the broadcast groups paid an additional $12.5 million in penalties, and entered into a

---

102. SANJEK, *supra* note 12, at 447.

103. For the gory details, *see* FREDRIC DANNEN, HIT MEN: POWER BROKERS AND FAST MONEY INSIDE THE MUSIC BUSINESS (1990).

consent decree designed, in part, to provide air time for artists not affiliated with major labels. A 2009 study by artist advocacy group the Future of Music Coalition found "almost no measurable change" in playlist composition," however, and concluded more generally that "radio's long-standing relationships with major labels, its status quo programming practices and the permissive regulatory structure all work together to create an environment in which songs from major label artists continue to dominate. The major labels' built-in advantage, in large part the cumulative benefit of years of payola-tainted engagement with commercial radio, combined with radio's risk-averse programming practices, means there are very few spaces left on any playlist for new entrants."[104]

The complete history of pay-for-play is beyond the arc of our story, but for present purposes, the payola scandals illustrate several points. Radio payola was only the latest incarnation of a practice that had been present in one form or another since the earliest days of the music business, long before recorded music was a reality. But as the Production Era accelerated in the fifties, it was records, not songs, that became the promoted products, and broadcast radio's unparalleled power to expose records to a mass audience guaranteed that promotional dollars would flow in its direction. Scarcely a decade before, labels and artists complained that broadcasting records was unfair and contrary to their interests, but now they were paying dearly for precious airplay, institutionalizing a sophisticated system of payola as an accepted, and costly part of their business. As a subtext to these developments, the drumbeat for copyright protection in sound recordings grew louder. Broadcasting was no longer an issue, but the unauthorized *copying* of records was a continuing and growing problem. The same kinds of technological advances that enabled advanced recording techniques also made duplicating records—"piracy"—easier than ever. Producing and bringing a record to market was an increasingly expensive proposition, and labels wanted a definitive way to protect their investments. At the dawn of the sixties, sound recordings, for all their cultural primacy, remained unprotected and unrecognized under the nation's copyright regime.

---

104. *See* Kristin Thomson, Same Old Song: An Analysis of Radio Playlists in a Post FCC-Consent Decree World (2009); executive summary and full report available at http://futureofmusic .org/article/research/same-old-song.

PART V

Revolutions
in the Air

Capitol Records advocated for
the sound recording copyright realized in
1972, and (as an EMI affiliate) has been active
in enforcing those rights in the decades since.

32. Pudding Basin Hair

The early sixties saw continued fierce competition for hit recordings among labels large and small. The majors were beginning to dominate album sales, but the singles market was wide open: in 1961, 24 labels produced the top 25 singles, with 38 labels contributing to the top 50.[1] Stylistically the field remained open as well, but by 1963 a larger concentration of "rock and roll" records was displacing other genres. Then came the Beatles, cementing both the stylistic move to rock, and the transition from written music to recordings. As Albin Zack has described the group's impact, "[t]he Beatles brought not only infectious good humor and ebullient music making to a country saddened by the recent assassination of its popular president but also a sense of tradition and the seeds of awareness that America's apparent musical meltdown of the 1950s was in fact a musical watershed, a transitional period that produced both a permanent stylistic break from the swing era and a fundamental ontological shift from written to recorded musical works."[2]

In January 1964, Capitol Records released "I Want to Hold Your Hand" (b/w "I Saw Her Standing There"); the single rocketed to No. 1, selling a million copies in three weeks. In February, the group appeared on the *Ed Sullivan Show*, and by April, Beatles singles occupied the top five chart spots and the first LP release, "With the Beatles," became the best-selling album in history. The Beatles placed eight records in the Top 40 in 1964, no fewer than five reaching No. 1.[3] Their amazing success spawned not just imitation, but direct copying. As soon as the group's sales began to surge, Nathan Shectman formed Greatest Records, Inc., whose simple if ill-fated business plan was to copy and sell Beatles recordings. In the spring of 1964 Shectman released "The Original Greatest Hits," containing identical reproductions of "I Want to Hold Your Hand," along with the first two Beatles albums in their entireties. The band's name did not appear on the album cover, which instead used shadow drawings of what a New York state judge would call the "distinctive and instantly recognizable 'pudding basin' hair style worn by the Beatles."[4] At a retail price of only $2.99, a dollar less than authorized albums, sales were healthy enough to quickly catch the attention of Capitol Records, which

1. Albin J. Zak III, I Don't Sound Like Nobody: Remaking Music in 1950s America 213 (2010).

2. *Id.* at 232. Ontology is the branch of metaphysics that studies the nature or existence of being as such.

3. *Id.* at 231; Russell Sanjek, American Popular Music and Its Business, The First Four Hundred Years, Vol. III, From 1900 to 1984, 381–82 (1988); Greil Marcus, *The Beatles*, in The Rolling Stone Illustrated History of Rock & Roll (1976).

4. Capitol Records, Inc. v. Greatest Records, Inc., 43 Misc. 2d 878, 252 N.Y.S.2d 553 (1964).

brought suit in New York state court, alleging unfair competition and seeking an immediate injunction against the "counterfeit" sales. The facts were not in dispute: Mr. Shectman had simply taped (that is, "dubbed") the recordings, made a new master, and pressed discs "just as if it was the bona fide product." Legally, such an operation seemed doomed, but like its business plan, Greatest Records' defense was simple: Capitol's sale of the recordings "constituted a dedication to the public," which "divested plaintiff of any property rights" and "rendered lawful the copying, manufacture and sale by the defendants." The position was reminiscent of Learned Hand's dissent in *Capitol v. Mercury,* but contrary to the majority decision, which held that selling recordings did not amount to a divesting "publication" for purposes of common law copyright. But the case was not as clear-cut as it seemed, for Greatest Records had a new arrow in its defensive quiver—two U.S. Supreme Court decisions rendered in March 1964, creating the so-called *Sears-Compco* doctrine.[5]

In *Sears* and *Compco,* the plaintiffs sued under state unfair competition law to prevent the copying of lighting fixtures that could not be protected under the federal patent laws, as they were not sufficiently inventive. Essentially, the cases dealt with "common law patent" rights in the same way courts had grappled with the protection of sound recordings under theories of unfair competition and common law copyright. In deciding for the defendants, Justice Hugo Black's opinion pointed out that a contrary holding would effectively extend perpetual protection under state law to articles that did not qualify for protection under federal patent law. Congress had preempted the field in passing the patent statute (giving inventors exclusive rights for only a "limited time"), so it would be inappropriate, indeed unconstitutional, for any state to grant more expansive rights in the same field, under the rubric of "unfair competition." The free market result was consistent with the views Learned Hand had expressed in *Whiteman* and *Capitol v. Mercury* (dissenting), where he was troubled by the notion of granting perpetual protection to sound recordings under a state law theory of "unfair competition," when recordings were not recognized as protected "writings" under the federal copyright statute.

But *Sears-Compco* was not enough to carry the day for Mr. Shectman and Greatest Records. On June 18, 1964, New York state justice Peter A. Quinn granted Capitol's request for an immediate injunction. Defendants' reliance on *Sears-Compco* was "ill-placed," he said, "as these cases are not applicable to the subject matter and devious conduct ... this court is presently called upon to deal with." Without articulating why Shectman's actions were more "devious" than the *Sears-Compco* defendants', the court focused on what it deemed "the only issue presented"—"whether defendants may *appropriate the performances* contained on plaintiff's phonograph records." Referring to two recent New York decisions, Justice Quinn distinguished

---

5. Sears Roebuck & Co. v Stiffel Co., 376 U.S. 225, 11 L. Ed. 2d 661, 84 S. Ct, 784 (1964), *reh'g denied,* 376 U.S. 973, 12 L. Ed. 2d 87, 84 S. Ct. 1131; Compco Corp. v Day-Brite Lighting, Inc., 376 U.S. 234, 11 L. Ed. 2d 669, 84 S. Ct. 779, *reh'g denied,* 377 U.S. 913, 12 L. Ed. 2d 183, 84 S. Ct. 1162.

Sears-Compco, concluding that, as opposed to merely copying, Shectman had appropriated "the very product itself" for his own profit. It seemed to be a distinction without a difference: Shectman had used another's intellectual property—the Beatles' artistic creations—fixed in the form of sound recordings. Similarly, the *Sears-Compco* defendants had appropriated the plaintiffs' creative designs, fixed in the form of decorative lamps. Nevertheless, the court concluded that *Sears-Compco* was not controlling. Quoting from *Capitol v. Mercury*, Justice Quinn held that "[t]he law of this [New York] is still 'that, where the originator of records of performances by musical artists puts those records on public sale, his act does not constitute a dedication of the right to copy and sell the records.'"

Greatest Records confirmed that common law copyright was alive and well in the state of New York, in the name of "unfair competition." The decision was not a model of legal reasoning, and the real story of the case seemed to lie outside Mr. Shectman's supposedly "devious" conduct. The court did not denounce Shectman for tramping on the groundbreaking art of the Beatles' recordings, and although it was their art in the grooves, and their "pudding basin" haircuts on the album cover, the Fab Four were not plaintiffs, and no personal property rights were asserted, as in the earlier *Waring* and *Whiteman* controversies. A corporation, Capitol Records, was the only plaintiff, and its efforts were focused on protecting an investment. Justice Quinn did not comment on the quality of the Beatles' performances, instead attributing the group's "unprecedented" success to "the most 'massive public relations campaign' in the history of the phonograph record industry." In truth, Capitol's promotional budget had helped break the band to a mass audience. "I Want to Hold Your Hand" was first released in the U.S. on a small R&B label, Chicago's Vee-Jay Records, to little notice. When Capitol released the same record, backed by $50,000 in promotional spending, history was made. But the "unfairness" of Shectman's conduct was couched entirely in terms of the "expenses" he avoided by dubbing—royalties to the band, and the costs of "producers, union funds and excise taxes . . . promotion [and] advertising." The justification articulated for the injunction was in protecting Capitol's investment.

33. Three Revolutions

The victory in *Greatest Records* was cold comfort to Capitol and other labels, who bristled at the notion that the legality of "dubbing"—directly copying and reselling recordings—could even be debated. Dubbers were sprouting everywhere, and there was no effective, consistent way to shut them down. Making matters worse, the "tape revolution" was underway, opening a whole new chapter in what labels called "music piracy." In 1964, William Lear, the inventor and entrepreneur behind the Lear Jet, approached Ford Motor Company with the idea for a new car audio system consisting of a continuous loop tape cartridge with four sets of paired stereo tracks. Ford bought the idea, and starting in 1966 offered "8-track" tape players as a luxury audio option. Earlier in the decade, the Philips Company introduced a "cassette tape" as part of an improved dictating machine. Philips chose not to protect its cassette as a proprietary technology, but required that all users adhere to its specifications, guaranteeing compatibility across manufacturers. As a result, the "compact cassette" was introduced for home use in the mid-1960s, and by 1968 over eighty manufacturers had sold 2.4 million players worldwide. As an affiliate of Philips, Mercury Records had a leg up on offering prerecorded music cassettes, which it introduced to the U.S. market with forty-nine titles in 1966.[6] Initially, tapes suffered from poor fidelity (cured by Dolby technology in the early 1970s), but they were portable and easy to use, and enabled individual consumers to "home tape" for the first time. Tapes were also easy and inexpensive to reproduce en masse, making them the format of choice for dubbers and pirates.

The advent of tape as a consumer format created a new sense of urgency among labels seeking an answer to the piracy problem. State legislatures, particularly those where the entertainment industries were concentrated, were the first to respond with local statutes criminalizing the practice, beginning with New York in August 1966. California updated an existing statute in 1968; Arkansas, Florida, Pennsylvania, Tennessee, and Texas followed in 1971, and by 1975 "antipiracy" laws were on the books in twenty-seven states. But just as state courts could have different standards for "unfair competition," state criminal statutes presented a patchwork approach that did not provide a complete and uniform solution to the problem.[7] A federal "anticounterfeiting" law had also been enacted in 1962, imposing criminal penalties for trafficking in sound recordings without permission of the "owner." But the law applied only to true "counterfeiting," where record label graphics and packaging were duplicated in toto and passed off as the real thing.[8] The law did not apply to those, like Nathan Shectman, who copied only recordings.

The sixties bore witness to a social revolution, driven in large part by rock music pioneers, and to a revolution in technology with the introduction of tape music formats. A third and more quiet revolution also percolated throughout the decade, one that would yield a new chapter in music copyright.

On July 10, 1961, Register of Copyrights Abraham L. Kaminstein submitted his report on general copyright revision to the Honorable Sam Rayburn, Speaker of the House. The basis for the report was Congress' request of the Copyright Office in 1955 to undertake a program of studies regarding a potential revision of the U.S. copyright law. Thirty-four studies were completed, leading to a report and

---

6. *See* ANDRE MILLARD, AMERICA ON RECORD: A HISTORY OF RECORDED SOUND 313–27 (1995).

7. *See* Alex S. Cummings, *From Monopoly to Intellectual Property: Music Piracy and the Remaking of American Copyright, 1909–1971*, 97 J. AM. HISTORY 659–81 (Dec. 2010).

8. 18 U.S.C. § 2318.

recommendations on a broad range of issues. The copyright statute, first enacted in 1790, had been through three general revisions—in 1831,[9] 1870, and 1909. The report found it "unnecessary to dwell at length upon the changes in technology during the last half century that have affected the operation of the copyright law," but pointed out that commercial radio and television were unknown in 1909 and that motion pictures and sound recordings were in a "rudimentary stage." As we have seen, a large body of judicial precedent had grown up around the then-current statute, but according to the report the law was "uncertain, inconsistent or inadequate in its application to present day conditions."

Many of the report's recommendations concerned music. First, the report called the jukebox exemption from public performance fees a "historical anomaly," which had been "placed in the law in 1909 at the last minute with virtually no discussion." At the time, coin-operated music machines were a novelty amusement of little economic consequence, but by 1961, the jukebox industry was one of the "largest commercial users of music, with an annual gross revenue of over half a billion dollars." In light of this, the report recommended that the jukebox exemption be repealed, or at least replaced by a provision requiring payment of reasonable license fees to music publishers. The report also reflected on the history of the compulsory mechanical license, finding its provisions "rather severe" for copyright owners, as it permitted "anyone indiscriminately to make records of the copyright owner's music at the 2-cent rate fixed in the statute." The report noted that the danger of a monopoly was apparently the sole reason for adopting the compulsory license in 1909, whereas in 1961 there were "hundreds of recording companies competing with one another, and the music available for recording [was] widely scattered among hundreds of competitive publishers." Songwriters and publishers urged repeal of the compulsory license as an unnecessary restriction on their rights. In contrast, recording industry representatives maintained there were other reasons for retaining the compulsory license, as it enabled the public to enjoy a variety of recordings of a particular song, and allowed smaller record companies to compete by offering different versions of hit songs. In the end, the report recommended repeal, but acknowledged the "highly controversial" nature of the issue by suggesting the alternative solution of simply increasing the two-cent rate.

Finally, the report focused on records, noting that in recent years there had been "considerable discussion" of proposals to provide protection "for performing arts and for record producers in their sound recordings." The report acknowledged that the dubbing problem had reached "serious proportions," and noted the recent court decisions protecting recordings under the principles of unfair competition. Echoing Judge Hand's concerns, the report said that the absence of federal protection for recordings "may be leading to establishment of common law rights that are unlimited in scope and duration." As a result, the report recommended

---

9. The 1831 revision extended copyright coverage to musical compositions. *See* Chapter 2.

extending federal copyright protection to sound recordings, but only "within appropriate limits" to be defined following further studies.

Congress continued its studies and fact-finding for several years, leading to the introduction of an omnibus copyright revision bill in 1965. The measure was the subject of extensive hearings before a House subcommittee—22 days of testimony over a period of three months, 16 witnesses, 2,300 pages of transcript, plus more than 150 written statements covering an additional 1,600 pages. As to music issues, the legislation proposed repeal of the jukebox exemption, an increase in the mechanical rate from two to three cents, and recognition of copyright in sound recordings, but with an exclusive right limited to copying only.

Label interests objected to increasing their mechanical royalty obligations, and were also vocal in arguing for "full" protection in sound recordings—rights extending to both copying *and* public performance. Flanked by two attorneys, Capitol Records president Alan Livingston testified at length before the subcommittee, first identifying the three major labels of the day—RCA Victor, Columbia, and his own, Capitol. He pointed out that Victor was still a division of the Radio Corp. of America (owner of NBC), while Columbia Records was affiliated with the Columbia Broadcasting System (CBS), making Capitol the only "independent company, not involved with ownership of radio and television stations." Livingston made the distinction, he said, "in order to stress the fact that Capitol speaks for the record business alone, and for the public interest with regard to the music business." From this lofty, self-appointed perspective of public guardian, Livingston testified as to what he considered the true weaknesses of the current copyright statute. First, he outlined the various sources of income in the music business, illustrating what he called a "great inequity in this division of profits very much in the favor of the songwriter and music publisher." According to Livingston, the phonograph record was "the source of almost all popular music in the United States," the vehicle through which "music is 'created,' exploited, and given its copyright value." But the record business was one of great risks, he explained, stating that "although Capitol led the industry in sales of records through retail outlets [in 1964], the company lost money on five out of six single records released, and on half the popular long playing albums released."

In light of these inequities, Livingston argued against increasing the two-cent statutory rate ("for the simple reason that the copyright owners are more than amply compensated"), and asked the subcommittee to focus on the more pressing issue of "protecting the performance rights of the vocalist, arranger and record company." Only through legislation recognizing "the rights of a performer and 'owner' of that performance, the record company, can these equities be more balanced, without in any way taking away from the writer or publisher. Look instead to the radio stations and others that use records and the performance of talented vocalists for profit without restriction or control or costs." Livingston argued that, beyond the parochial interests of labels, such legislation would further the public interest.

"If performance fees were to go to the record company and the performer," he said, "the frantic concentration on teenage rock and roll in the search for fast and large sales and quick return would stop. Sales are the only means of profit for the performer and record company right now, so all music must be designed for the mass buying market. Let us be compensated for the use of our records on the air and we can record for the benefit of the vast listening audience who want good music, but do not necessarily buy records. Allow us to make music truly for the mass audience who wants to hear everything from classical music to good ballad singers, or instrumental listening music. We as record companies cannot manufacture this music much longer under the present economic situation for we must deal only with the record buyer and the mass buyer, who today is principally the teenager."

Later, Livingston added that "if the compensation were there, we would be like music publishers, and we would be able to record for the public what the public wants to hear but may not go out and buy." Instead, the label was forced to "concentrate mostly on meeting that mass buying public of teenagers, who are buying the Beatles, who happen to be on Capitol Records, who are buying the Beach Boys, who are buying what the current hot artist is today. Next week it is another hot artist, and we move so fast and so furiously that really what the public wants to hear and use, and what is being used out of our catalog, goes forgotten, and I don't really know how long record companies, such as Capitol, Victor and Columbia can stay in business. I think we are in business by the skin of our teeth." The irony was thick, verging on hypocrisy. Livingston justified pursuing the lucrative profits from "bad music" (i.e., rock and roll) as the only way to stay in business. By his logic, extending the right of public performance to recordings was the only way labels could afford to preserve and record "good music," which had taken a back seat in the age of rock.

Even if Livingston's logic had been sound, asking radio stations to pay a new performance fee for records was a nonstarter; the National Association of Broadcasters would hear nothing of the kind. Through general counsel, Douglas Anello, the NAB made it abundantly clear that its members were not interested in paying labels or performers for broadcasting recorded music. Broadcasters were already paying $50 million a year to ASCAP and BMI in performance fees, so the idea of making additional payments to another set of rights holders was out of the question. The payola scandals had confirmed publicly the long-standing common knowledge in the industry: commercial radio was the single best method for promoting the sale of music, and labels were more than willing to pay for airtime. For broadcasters, asking *them* to pay to promote the sale of recorded music was backward and absurd.

Register of Copyrights Kaminstein spoke to the reality of the situation, testifying that "[b]y recognizing sound recordings as copyrightable works with rights of reproduction and distribution, but denying them rights of public performance, the bill reflects—accurately, I think—the present state of thinking on this subject in the United States." "I look on this, not as mere expediency, but as a necessary and conscious recognition of what will not be accepted in this country today in this evolving field." Kaminstein reiterated the government's view that "recorded performances represent the 'writings of an author' in the constitutional sense," and envisioned a time when a performance right would "eventually be recognized in the copyright law of the United States as it is now in other countries." But it was not practical to push the issue at the time. "I believe," he concluded, "that the chance now of enacting a copyright law in this country that recognizes any rights of public performance in sound recordings is so remote as to be nonexistent. You have seen no towering wave of opposition to these proposals simply because there is a general feeling that they will not get anywhere; but, if genuine fears were to be aroused on this score, I am sure you would see a wave of protest that would be likely to tear this bill apart."

Outraged that a performing right was again passing its members by, the American Federation of Musicians made its views known in a scathing report condemning every segment of the music industry.[10] The AFM report declared that the "static, rigid, and adamant opposition to performers' participation in the economic fruits of unauthorized recorded performances should be judged by its sources"—composers and songwriters who "condemn the jukebox exemption while excluding anyone but themselves form the enjoyment of creative economic opportunity"; music publishers who "press for preservation of their monopoly"; record labels, who rush free records to their own broadcast affiliates, and "assert that they, not performers, are the proper custodians of this moral right of performers"; and of course broadcasters, "who have built a vast industry on huckstering in the intervals between broadcasts of phonograph records." There was some truth to each of these allegations, but as Register Kaminstein realized, the performing musicians' philosophical pining as to "moral rights" would not carry the day under the weight of the NAB's definitive opposition.

After further delays, the omnibus copyright revision bill was reintroduced to Congress in early 1967, with provisions recognizing copyright in sound recordings, but limited to protection against copying and distribution. Performing musicians continued their objections based on the absence of a performance right, which they deemed a "moral issue" that other countries had resolved by establishing a special performer's right, sometimes called a "neighboring right," providing for the payment of public performance royalties pursuant to a compulsory license.[11] Record producers spoke to the issue as well, arguing that their talents were "responsible for the most creative and valuable elements of sound record-

---

10. *The Performing Musicians' Opposition to the 1965 Bill for General Copyright Revision* (American Federation of Musicians), available in 7 George Grossman, Omnibus Copyright Revision Legislative History 1387 (2001).

11. The Rome Convention of 1961 organized an international system of neighboring rights. The U.S. is not a member.

ings today."[12] Hit-making producer Mitch Miller led testimony for the National Committee for the Recording Artists (a NAPA successor), proposing to split performance royalties with artists. According to a House Report, "[a]lthough there was little direct response to these arguments, it was apparent that any serious effort to amend the bill to recognize even a qualified right of public performance in sound recordings would be met with concerted opposition."[13] In the end, the committee concluded that "in recognizing rights against the unauthorized duplication of sound recordings but . . . denying rights of public performance," the bill "represent[ed] the present thinking of other groups on that subject in the United States and that further expansion of the scope of protection for sound recordings is impracticable."[14] The bill was passed by the House in this form, but (again for reasons not related to music rights) bogged down in Senate. Omnibus copyright revision would wait another nine years, but the music industry (sans performing musicians) pressed forward on a more urgent timetable of its own.

As the sixties wore on, the Beatles focused their energy on recording as opposed to live performance, becoming the first "studio band" of the rock era when they stopped touring altogether in 1966.[15] Their studio focus culminated with the densely textured, dream-like, *Sgt. Pepper's Lonely Hearts Club Band*, released in June 1967, on the eve of the massive Summer of Love gatherings in San Francisco. *Sgt. Pepper's* was not only an unprecedented work of conceptual art, but a "record" in the truest sense—a work designed to be experienced only as a recording. Upon entering the studio for the sessions that yielded *Sgt. Pepper's*, the band had tired of performing. Explaining their perspective to producer George Martin, John Lennon said, "if we don't have to tour, then we can record music that we won't ever have to play live, and that means we can create something that's never been heard before: a new kind of record with new kinds of sounds."[16] The album had taken a painstaking 700 hours to record (as opposed to a mere twelve for the group's first album), and emerged as the groundbreaking studio creation the band intended. More than thirty years later, the production techniques used in the sessions are still hailed as revolutionary, yet for all the bells and whistles, the production was never at the expense of the incredible diversity of the music, which ranged in strange harmony from straight pop to psychedelia, music hall to rock and roll, the latter limited to essentially to the reprise of the title track. The popular and critical reception was as dramatic as the music, with the album spending fifteen weeks atop the Billboard 200, earning four Grammy awards in 1968, and shipping more than 11 million copies in the U.S. (32 million worldwide) and counting. In a world

---

12. H. Rep. No. 83, 90th Cong., 1st Sess. (1967).

13. *Id.*

14. *Id.*

15. *See* Zak, *supra* note 1, at 233, 238.

16. Geoff Emerick & Howard Massey, Here, There, and Everywhere: My Life Recording the Music of the Beatles 132 (2006).

of poetic justice, sound recording copyright legislation would have coincided with the release of *Sgt. Pepper's*, but it was not to be: the Beatles' masterwork arrived fully formed in 1967, but the copyright bill, still foundering in the Senate, remained a work in progress.

♪♪ ♫♫ ♪♪

Representative Robert Kastenmeier brought a hearing to order on June 9, 1971, introducing a measure designed to attack "the subject of record piracy," which had cost the music industry an estimated $100 million in lost sales in 1970.[17] After being bogged down in the Senate with the rest of the copyright reform legislation, the sound recording portion of the bill was back, presented with a sense of urgency by an industry claiming to be under siege. The measure was read into the congressional record, followed by supporting testimony from various representatives and Copyright Office officials, reiterating the extent and immediacy of the piracy problem. But Assistant Register of Copyrights Barbara Ringer became the star of the show, a "fascinating witness" whose testimony was a question-and-answer historical tour of sound recording protection in America. "The fate of the general revision bill remains uncertain," she said, "but we regard the immediate problems of unauthorized record duplication as too important and pressing to await the final outcome on the broader bill." She noted that "a number of cases have upheld rights in recordings on various principles of state common law, most recently on the ground of unfair competition," but the government's view was that "limited Federal protection under the copyright law [would be] more effective, more definite and more appropriate."[18] Ms. Ringer attributed the "enormous growth" of piracy "to the ease of tape duplication, the growing market for tape cassettes and cartridges, and the lack of clarity in both state common law, and in particular, in the Federal copyright law." These factors made piracy "an urgent enough problem to spring it out of general revision." From there, Ringer recounted the historical efforts to bring recordings within the scope of federal copyright, going back the 1909 Act, and the major cases—*Waring, Whiteman*, the "landmark" case of *Capitol Records v. Mercury Records*, and *Sears-Compco*, which together outlined the still-ambiguous parameters of sound recording property rights.

Following Ms. Ringer, representatives of the industry's major trade groups addressed the panel in support of the bill. RIAA president Stanley Gortikov highlighted the extensive (and expensive) litigation campaign waged against pirates in state courts, which was not enough to slow the growing business of piracy. "To create almost any album," he said, "a record company will expend no less that $55,000 in pre-release costs, and that is before the first record or tape is actually

---

17. Hearings before Subcommittee No. 3 of the Committee on the Judiciary, House of Representatives, 92nd Cong., 1st Session on S. 646 and H.R. 6927.

18. *Id.*

manufactured. Comparably, to reach this same pre-release stage, the pirate need only spend $300. Then, when the record company feels moderates success in its product and undertakes its manufacture, distribution, and promotion, it will have spent and risked between $180,000 to $200,000." Jack Grossman spoke as president of National Association of Record Merchandisers, noting that "[t]he problem of illegal duplication of recordings existed prior to the advent of tape," and that earlier legislation to deal with this problem had a "salutary effect."[19] With the development of tape technology, however, the problem of illegal duplication became "considerably more acute because of the greater susceptibility of tape to piracy which can be accomplished at little cost." The accused "pirates" were predictably absent, so there was no opposition voiced in the hearing. A final House Report issued on September 22, 1971, entitled *Prohibiting Piracy of Sound Recordings*, made clear that the purpose of the bill was to create a "limited right," making unlawful the unauthorized "reproduction and sale" of sound recordings.[20]

Barbara Ringer had responded to a variety of questions on the bill, including the fact that it failed to identify the sound recording copyright "owner." She reminded the panel that this was also true of other "multi-author" works, such as periodicals and motion pictures, where those involved in the creative process were left to sort out issues of authorship and ownership. The final House Report commented to the same effect, noting that "[t]he copyrightable elements in a sound recording will usually, though not always, involve 'authorship' both on the part of the performers whose performance is captured and on the part of the record producer responsible for setting up the recording session, capturing and electronically processing the sounds, and compiling and editing them to make the final sound recording . . . As in the case of motion pictures, the bill does not fix authorship, or the resulting ownership, of sound recordings, but leaves these matters to the employment relationship and bargaining among the interests involved."[21] The issue would become a major battleground between performers and labels in later years.

President Richard M. Nixon signed the amendment into law on October 15, 1971, whereupon it was promptly challenged in *Shaab v. Kleindienst*,[22] an action brought by music publisher Ronald Shaab against the U.S. Attorney General and Librarian of Congress to enjoin implementation of the new law. The complaint alleged that sound recordings did not qualify as "writings" under the Constitution, and that by failing to provide for compulsory licensing of recordings, the law unfairly discriminated against the plaintiff and other publishers, whose musical works were subject to compulsory licensing. A three-judge panel dismissed the action, finding that the requirements of authorship were satisfied by sound recording firms

---

19. 18 U.S.C. § 2318.

20. The *House Report on the Sound Recording Amendment of 1971*, H. Rep. No. 92–487, 92nd Congress, 1st Session.

21. *Id.*

22. Shaab v. Kleindienst, 345 F. Supp. 589, 174 U.S.P.Q 197 (D.D.C. 1972).

providing "the equipment and organiz[ing] the diverse talents of arrangers, performers and technicians." Moreover, the lack of a compulsory license was deemed "rational and reasonable." The compulsory scheme for compositions promoted the arts by permitting numerous artistic interpretations of a single written composition, but with respect to recordings, "[c]onsumer choices would not be broadened since identical interpretations would be supplied first by the originator and later by the licensee. Equally important," said the court, "competition and the creative aspects of the industry would be impaired since established recording firms would be discouraged from investing in new arrangements and performers, if they were compelled to license their successful interpretations to those desiring to take advantage of the originator's initiative and to add nothing themselves." Consistent with the legislative history of the amendment, the court analyzed the artistic authorship embodied in a sound recording in terms of a capital investment.

34. Back to the Future in *Goldstein v. California*

The sound recording amendment was prospective, applying only to recordings "fixed" on or after February 15, 1972. This fact has been the basis for a continuing flow of disputes involving the status and protectability of so-called pre-1972 recordings, beginning with *Goldstein v. California*, which made its way to the U.S. Supreme Court in 1973.[23] Goldstein and others were convicted of selling "pirate" versions of pre-1972 sound recordings under a California state criminal statute. Goldstein challenged the convictions by attacking the constitutionality of the state law in light of the recent amendment that brought sound recordings into the realm of federal copyright. Using a three-pronged attack, Goldstein argued that the state law granted the equivalent of a perpetual copyright, contrary to the limited-term grant allowed under the Constitution; that the *Sears-Compco* decisions showed Congress' intent to protect copyright matter under a single, uniform federal law; and third, that the recordings had been "published," and therefore could not be protected under the state statute. After an extensive discussion of the state/federal law dichotomy, reaching as far back as the principles set forth by Alexander Hamilton and James Madison in The Federalist, Chief Justice Warren Berger's majority opinion held that Congress had not totally preempted state law in passing the sound recording amendment. Thus, the amendment had no effect on pre-1972 recordings, which could be regulated under state principles moving forward.

---

23. Goldstein v. California, 412 U.S. 546, 93 S. Ct. 2303 (1973).

The decision was controversial, decided by a single vote: four of the nine justices joined in two separate dissenting opinions, generally expressing the view that the Court's decisions in *Sears-Compco* were controlling, such that the California law should be deemed unconstitutional for improperly intruding on preempted territory. Referencing Judge Learned Hand's minority view in *Capitol v. Mercury*, Justice William O. Douglas' dissent feared that upholding that statute was contrary to the broader goal of creating uniformity in copyright law. The majority opinion again couched the wrongdoing in economic terms, noting that Goldstein made no payments to artists, producers, or technicians, and avoided "the large expenses incurred in production." Justice Thurgood Marshall's dissent expressed the concern that economic interests were clouding the legal issues: "The business of piracy is not an attractive one," he admitted, but "we should not let our distaste for 'pirates' interfere with our interpretation of the copyright laws."

The tension between federal and state law with regard to sound recordings continues to the present. In its 2005 decision in *Capitol Records v. Naxos*, New York's highest state court confirmed that New York common law protects pre-1972 sound recordings, and that their public sale does not constitute "publication" that would divest the owner of rights.[24] The classical recordings in issue were made in England in the 1930s, pursuant to artist contracts that assigned all rights to EMI, Capitol's parent company. Under British law, the copyrights in the recordings expired after fifty years, prior to 1990. In 1999 the American classical label Naxos restored copies of the recordings, which it sold in competition with Capitol. Capitol sued in federal court in New York, claiming that Naxos' sales amounted to unfair competition and common law copyright infringement under New York state law. The district court decided for Naxos, primarily because the recordings had long ago entered the public domain in their country of origin, extinguishing any possible protection in New York. On appeal, the Second Circuit questioned that conclusion, and, because the issue was purely a matter of state law, used a rare procedural maneuver to "certify," or refer, the question to the New York state court for determination. The court responded with a lengthy analysis, ultimately concluding that the expiration of the copyrights in England did not terminate common law copyright; Capitol could protect its exclusive rights in the recordings under New York common law until the effective date of federal preemption—February 15, 2067.[25]

---

24. Capitol Records, Inc. v. Naxos of Am., Inc., 4 N.Y.3d 773, 825 N.E.2d 1086 (2005).

25. *See* 17 U.S.C. § 301(c). In November 2010, Congress directed the Copyright Office to study the desirability of bringing pre-1972 sound recordings immediately under federal jurisdiction. Public comments were submitted, and two days of public roundtable meetings convened in June 2011. The Copyright Office issued its report on this complex and still controversial topic in December 2011, recommending that pre-1972 recordings be brought into the federal statutory scheme. *See Federal Copyright Protection for Pre-1972 Sound Recordings: A Report of the Register of Copyrights*, Dec. 2011.

35. 1976

A "limited right" in sound recordings had come to fruition, but labels and recording artists continued their pursuit of broader rights as the general copyright revision bill made its way through Congress in the early 1970s. Music publishers pushed a separate agenda. As a result, the bill reported by the Senate Judiciary Committee in 1974 contained two highly controversial provisions, both dealing with the public performance of music: publishers proposed to eliminate the so-called jukebox exemption, in place since 1909, while labels and artists rekindled their pursuit of a sound recording performance right, which had eluded them for decades, most recently in the context of the 1971 sound recording amendment.[26]

The jukebox exemption had been in play throughout the 1965 hearings on general copyright revision. The Copyright Office favored repeal, and in testimony before a House subcommittee, George Cary, Deputy Register of Copyrights, said there was no "logical or equitable justification for the continuance of the jukebox exemption. No satisfactory explanation has been given why the circumstance of coin operation alone should exempt the performance of jukebox music, while all other commercial performances of copyrighted music remain subject to protection."[27] A Senate report put it more bluntly: "This blanket exemption has been widely and vigorously condemned as an anachronistic 'historical accident' and in terms such as 'unconscionable,' 'indefensible,' 'totally unjustified,' and 'grossly discriminatory.'" There had been various attempts to eliminate the exemption over the years, beginning with a House bill discussed in 1926, less than twenty years after the passage of the 1909 Act.[28] The bill did not get out of committee, but further attempts to end the exemption became common.[29] The House debated similar legislation in 1930, and the Senate in 1935, but a strong jukebox lobby resisted the efforts.[30] Two more bills proposed in the 80th Congress (1947–1948) met the same fate.[31]

---

26. S. 1361.

27. 5 GEORGE S. GROSSMAN, OMNIBUS COPYRIGHT REVISION LEGISLATIVE HISTORY 33 (2001). 17 U.S.C. § 1 (1909) provided that "The reproduction or rendition of a musical composition by or upon coin-operated machines shall not be deemed a public performance for profit unless a fee is charged for admission to the place where such reproduction or rendition occurs."

28. *See* Ben Atlas, *Attempts to End Copyright Exemptions Date Back to '26*, BILLBOARD, Dec. 4, 1954, at 21 (offering a synopsis of early attempts to repeal the jukebox exemption).

29. *Id.*

30. *See* ABE A. GOLDMAN, THE HISTORY OF U.S.A. COPYRIGHT LAW REVISION FROM 1901 TO 1954, 4–10 (Copyright Office of the Library of Congress 1955) (offering a detailed history of copyright revision efforts in Congress, the first in a series of studies prepared for the Committee on the Judiciary Subcommittee on Patents, Trademarks, and Copyrights as it prepared to overhaul U.S. copyright law).

31. *See* Atlas, *supra* note 28.

In 1951 Representative Joseph Bryson introduced legislation that would have imposed a two-cent royalty on each phonograph record for every week it was played in a coin-operated machine. The record industry took a strong stance in opposition. Jukeboxes had become big business: between 1934 and 1940, the number of jukeboxes in use in the United States rose from approximately 25,000 units to 400,000,[32] and in 1941, *Billboard* magazine estimated that approximately 650,000 jukeboxes were in operation.[33] In addition to generating revenue for juke operators, the nickel-play boxes spurred huge sales growth for the record industry. Record output in 1938 was estimated at 33 million discs, nearly half sold to jukebox operators.[34] In 1939, the number rose to 60 million records, 31 million of which went into jukeboxes; in 1940 the numbers were 70 million (37.4 million for jukeboxes); and by 1941, an estimated 45 percent of the 100 million records went into jukeboxes.[35] In this environment, jukebox operators and labels argued that music publishers received adequate royalties based on sales, and that forcing the jukebox industry to pay a performance royalty would amount to "double dipping." The Bryson Bill failed, but the anti-exemption rhetoric heated up again in 1953, when the Senate Judiciary Committee held hearings on a bill sponsored by Senators Pat McCarran and Everett Dirksen. Following the hearings *Variety* editor Abel Green called the Copyright Act of 1909 "as obsolete as the tandem bike," arguing that the almost $1 billion jukebox industry could afford to pay performance royalties just as Broadway theaters, concert halls, and broadcasters did.[36] The plea fell on deaf ears. Two more bills were introduced in 1955, and yet another in 1959. All failed.[37]

The jukebox exemption remained untouched in the 1960s, even as Congress moved toward comprehensive copyright reform. The jukebox industry had peaked however, as home stereos and increased radio and television programming lessened the machines' popularity. In June 1963, the House Copyright Committee approved a bill that would impose public performance royalties on jukebox operators.[38] The Judiciary Committee also approved the bill, after which a *New York Times* editorial urged an end to the exemption, calling it unfair given that radio broadcasters had long been required to pay performance royalties.[39] The bill never went to a full vote. Repeal efforts were bandied about in Congress for the next several years, and in 1967, the House passed the general revision bill, which called for a compulsory licensing rate of $8 per year per jukebox. As we have seen, omnibus

---

32. *See* Kerry Segrave, Jukeboxes: An american social history (2002), at 117.
33. *See* Walter W. Hurd, *A Busy Year*, Billboard, Sept. 27, 1941, at 84.
34. *See* Segrave, *supra* note 32, at 115.
35. *Id.*
36. Abel Green, *Time for a Change*, Variety, Nov. 4, 1953, at 43.
37. *Id.* at 265.
38. *See* Segrave, *supra* note 32, at 294.
39. *Rewarding Artistic Achievement*, N.Y. Times, Nov. 3, 1963, at E8.

legislation stalled in the Senate until the mid-seventies.[40] When the general revision bill reached its final stages, a House Committee on the Judiciary met on June 3, 1975, to hear testimony on repealing the exemption. Committee chairman Representative Robert Kastenmeier believed a compromise was inevitable. "This is a question that 10 years ago, when this subcommittee held hearings, was, as I would observe somewhat more controversial than it is today," Kastenmeier said. "Since then there have been agreements and accommodations, and while the parties are not precisely in agreement in the issue in all aspects, the differences are less grave."[41] The Committee heard comments from American composing legend Aaron Copland, popular songwriter Johnny Mercer, and big band composer/arranger Sy Oliver, who echoed one another in criticizing a system in which writers were compensated for radio performances of their compositions, but not for performances of the same songs in jukeboxes.[42]

Jukebox industry representatives also testified, with Perry Patterson, counsel for jukebox manufacturers Rock-Ola, Rowe, and Seeburg, leading the way. "I am here to reflect the manufacturers' unqualified support of the $8 [per box] annual fee," Patterson said, urging the committee to approve the royalty. His clients' philosophy had not changed, but the juke industry was no longer strong enough to keep up the fight. Only three jukebox manufacturers remained in the United States, and even Wurlitzer, one of the companies that pushed through the exemption in 1909, had recently left the business. "There are fewer jukeboxes in operation in this country . . . than there were in the years immediately succeeding World War II," he said.[43] It was a watershed moment: the jukebox industry had given up, seeking only concessions as to the frequency with which the royalty rate might be adjusted. The tide having turned, the exemption was repealed in the Copyright Act of 1976, which also created the Copyright Royalty Tribunal to collect and distribute royalties.[44] In 1978, the first year following enactment, $1.12 million in royalties were collected.[45] ASCAP received approximately $530,000 of the jukebox revenue, but it amounted to less than 1 percent of its total 1978 receipts of approximately $95 million.[46] After such a long fight, the payoff was meager. Ironically, the juke industry had been forced into paying when it was least able to do so. Fees rose over the years, but the number of registered jukeboxes declined, down from 104,391 machines in 1984 to only 96,204 in 1987. As of 1990 a new organization, the Jukebox Licensing Office, began brokering jukebox royalty rates, with the

---

40. *See* SEGRAVE, *supra* note 32, at 293–94.

41. H. REP. SUBCOMM. ON COURTS, CIVIL LIBERTIES AND THE ADMINISTRATION OF JUSTICE OF THE COMM. OF THE JUDICIARY, COPYRIGHT LAW REVISION (1975), *reprinted in* 14 GEORGE S. GROSSMAN, OMNIBUS COPYRIGHT REVISION LEGISLATIVE HISTORY, at 373 (2001).

42. *Id.* at 390–91.

43. *Id.* at 413.

44. 17 U.S.C. § 116 (2006).

45. *See* SEGRAVE, *supra* note 32, at 295.

46. *Id.*

last round of negotiations occurring in 2007. In 2010 per jukebox royalty rates averaged around \$434 per year.[47] The rates apply only to jukeboxes that play vinyl records or compact discs—not to digital jukeboxes, which since their introduction in the late 1990s have emerged to dominate the market.

The sound recording performance right was also revisited as part of the general revision bill, and remained as controversial as ever. The Copyright Office favored extending a performance right in recordings, and the Senate Judiciary Committee approved a bill in June 1974 that included provisions for payment of performance license fees by radio and television broadcasters, as well as jukebox operators. Financial data considered by the committee showed that 75 percent of the commercial time of radio stations was devoted to playing recorded music, and with 1972 broadcast revenues of nearly \$1.5 billion, broadcasters had the ability to pay. But broadcasters had the ability to pay their lobbyists as well, and remained committed to their "symbiotic relationship" with labels and artists, characterized by the unwritten contract of trading "free promotion for free music." A group of senators on the Judiciary Committee issued a minority report on the proposed bill, stating their commitment to the position that imposing a performance royalty would be "economically unwise and constitutionally unsound." "For years," they continued, "record companies have gratuitously provided records to stations in the hope of securing exposure by repeated play over the air. The financial success of recording companies and artists who contract with these companies is directly related to the volume of record sales, which, in turn, depends in great measure upon the promotion efforts of broadcasters. Radio stations and jukebox operators significantly help to popularize recordings and artists." The minority report also positioned the issue as between labels and artists. "We believe that the issue of whether performers receive adequate compensation for their work should not be determined in terms of copyright liability. Such a problem would seem more amenable to negotiation between artists and the recording companies that require their talents, rather than the stations which, since the demise of live music formats, no longer have direct dealings with performers."[48] As the bill moved into its final debates, the NAB made its presence felt, the minority position prevailed, and broadcasters again succeeded in derailing the sound recording performance right. It would take another twenty years, and another revolution in technology, for sound recording performance rights to become a reality.

The 1976 Copyright Act extended the term of protection for all copyrighted works to the author's life plus fifty years (seventy-five years in the case of works created "for hire" by a corporate entity), and codified the concept of "fair use" as a

---

47. *See* Jukebox License Office, http://www.jukeboxlicense.com/rates.htm (last visited Aug. 23, 2010) (showing the most recent rates for licensing for a jukebox that plays CDs or 45s).

48. Minority Views of Messrs. Eastland, Ervin, Burdick, Hruska, Thurmond and Gurney on the Recording Arts Performance Royalty (S. 1361).

defense to infringement, a continuing battleground in music and other contexts.[49] And yet another change relating to public performance came quietly into being when President Ford signed the omnibus copyright legislation on October 19, 1976. Justice Holmes' reasoning in *Herbert v. Shanley* (1917) came floating back, in which he held that, even in the absence of a door charge for music, the restaurant's hiring of musicians as background music satisfied the "for profit" requirement for infringement under the 1909 Act. Codifying the holding and others that had followed, the "for profit" limitation on the performance right was eliminated from the statute altogether.[50]

36. Home Taping Is Killing Music

The new copyright regime came into force on January 1, 1978, a time when the retail music market was split evenly between two playback formats: $2.1 billion in discs were sold the following year, along with $1 billion each for 8-track and cassette tapes.[51] But cassettes were a format on the move—literally—as they were compatible with the mobile music device introduced by Sony in 1979: the Walkman. Sales of personal stereos skyrocketed in the 1980s, and with them the sales of both prerecorded and blank cassettes. As vinyl sales tapered off, labels blamed the practice of home taping, and the RIAA launched an aggressive public relations campaign to convince its own customers that home taping was "killing music." The trade group also lobbied Congress for a royalty to be levied against manufacturers on each tape recorder and blank tape sold. Neither campaign saw immediate success, but the groundwork was laid for the battles soon to come.

In September 1981, the first American record rental shop opened in Providence, Rhode Island, and by 1983 there were more than 200 in operation across the country.[52] The stores were modeled after counterparts that had opened in Japan a year earlier, which had grown exponentially to over 1,600 outlets. Following the rise of record rental, the Japanese recording industry experienced its first decline in twenty-five years, and some record stores saw their sales drop by a third. In both countries the rental premise was simple and compelling, shouted in advertisements claiming that customers need "NEVER BUY ANOTHER RECORD!!"

---

49. 17 U.S.C. § 107. The issue rose to the U.S. Supreme Court in Campbell v. Acuff-Rose Music, Inc., 510 U.S. 569, 114 S. Ct. 1164 (1994) where the court found that the rap group 2 Live Crew's version of the Roy Orbison rock ballad, "Oh, Pretty Woman," was a commercial parody of the original, which qualified as a noninfringing fair use.

50. 17 U.S.C. § 106(4). *See* Chapter 19.

51. Mark Coleman, Playback: From the Victrola to MP3, 100 Years of Music, Machines, and Money 157 (2003).

52. David H. Horowitz, *The Record Rental Amendment of 1984: A Case Study in the Effort to Adapt Copyright Law to New Technology*, 12 Colum. VLA J. L & Arts 31 (1987–1988).

Record albums were made available for one-to-three-day rental at rates from $.99 to $2.50 per LP, and, conveniently, blank cassette tapes were sold in the same outlets, encouraging home taping. By this method customers could acquire a permanent home-taped copy for far less than the retail price of a new album. And renting records was perfectly legal, courtesy of the so-called first sale doctrine, a concept rooted in English common law, affirmed by American courts and first codified in the 1909 Copyright Act.[53] The first sale doctrine holds simply that a copyright owner has no right to control the distribution of a *copy* of the copyrighted work beyond its "first sale." That is, after purchasing any copyrighted work—a book, painting, or "phonorecord" (the technical term for a copy of a sound recording)—the buyer is free to resell that particular copy, or rent it out, as the market will bear. In this way, the first sale doctrine distinguishes between the copyright owner's exclusive rights in an underlying creative work and physical ownership of the material object in which it is reproduced and sold. The ink was barely dry on the new copyright act, but the major labels saw a crisis in the combination of the Walkman craze, record rentals, and the ease of home taping.

At the RIAA's urging, in October and December 1983 Representative Robert Kastenmeier convened House subcommittee hearings on the record rental phenomenon, which were reported as a recommendation to pass the Record Rental Amendment of 1984.[54] The express purpose of the legislation was to prohibit record rentals by modifying the first sale doctrine with respect to phonorecords only. After identifying the "nature of the problem," the report stated that "the direct link between the commercial rental of a phonorecord and the making of a copy of the record without the permission of the copyright owner is the economic and policy concern behind this legislation." Having heard from various industry participants— the RIAA, music publishers, and a coalition of audio recording equipment and blank tape providers—the subcommittee concluded that "the nexus of commercial record rental and duplication may directly and adversely affect the ability of copyright holders to exercise their reproduction and distribution rights under the copyright act." In other words, home taping, encouraged by record rentals, "may" kill music. The amendment became law on October 4, 1984, modifying the first sale doctrine by prohibiting the "rental, lease or lending" of records. Exceptions were made for libraries and nonprofits, but the law was intended to apply broadly to cover transactions that "common sense indicates are equivalent to rentals, but which may be disguised in an attempt to avoid liability," such as sale and buy-back schemes, or clubs where "membership fees" took the place of direct rentals.[55] The

---

53. *See* Bobbs Merrill Co. v. Straus, 210 U.S. 339 (1908); Harrison v. Maynard, Merrill & Co., 61 F. 689, 690 (2d Cir. 1894).

54. H.R. REP. No. 98–987, 1984 U.S.C.C.A.N. 2898.

55. *See* 17 U.S.C. § 109. The amendment's original sunset provisions were extended in 1988, and later became a permanent provision.

narrowly crafted legislation was designed specifically for the benefit of the recording industry.

The Record Rental Amendment freed the labels to aggressively pursue a new recorded music format called the compact disc, or "CD." The Philips company had developed a prototype CD player in 1978, which played discs much smaller than a vinyl LP, containing "digital" music. Instead of cutting sound waves into wax, digital technology reduced sound to an electric current that could be recorded, reproduced, and embedded into an object for playback in the form of a binary code of digits. Philips teamed with Sony in developing a standard disc format, and the first commercial CDs were introduced in 1982, heralded as a revolution in sound. Although many audiophiles declared their allegiance to the warmth of analog sound, the clarity and brightness of digital music made the format compelling. CDs were also highly portable, stored more data (meaning much longer playing times), and did not degrade from handling and repeated play the way vinyl did. And finally, CDs could be programmed to play specific tracks in whatever order the user preferred, allowing listeners to break away from the album format and, in a limited way, begin customizing their own playlists. Once customers showed a liking for CDs, an avalanche of both new and "reissued" catalog material poured forth in the new format. At retail prices of around $15, labels charged 50 percent more for CDs than vinyl LPs, and as disc manufacturing costs fell, margins increased dramatically.

On November 30, 1982, CBS Records' Epic label released Michael Jackson's sixth studio album, *Thriller*, marking a high point in popular music promotion and sales. Artistically, *Thriller* moved easily among pop, rock, and post-disco R&B, with songs like "Billie Jean," "Beat It," and "Wanna Be Startin' Somethin'," in addition to the epic title track, which became the subject of a choreographed film short that broke racial barriers by making its way into heavy rotation on the all-music-video cable television channel, MTV, which debuted in 1981. A combination of groundbreaking art, the sophisticated, painstaking production work of Jackson and coproducer Quincy Jones, and a strong dose of MTV airtime created a perfect promotional storm for *Thriller*, which became a massive blockbuster in three formats—cassette, LP, and compact disc.[56] *Thriller* won a record-breaking eight Grammy Awards in 1984, and became the best-selling album in history, remaining in the Billboard top ten for over a year, a full thirty-seven weeks at number one. In August 2009, two months after Jackson's untimely death, *Thriller* was certified by the RIAA as shipping at least 29 million copies in the U.S. alone. Having sold upwards of 100 million copies around the world, the album remains a classic piece of popular art, and a symbol of a time when the mainstream recorded music business was capable of producing hits of gigantic proportions.

Industry wide, 50 million CDs were sold in 1986, as compared to 350 million cassettes and 110 million LPs, but just two years later CDs were outselling cassettes,

---

56. In 1983 cassette sales outpaced LPs for the first time. *See* Horowitz, *supra* note 52, at 43, n.52.

and CD players outsold turntables by more than six to one. In 1988 the Sony organization capitalized on these trends, buying CBS Records for $2 billion, becoming a major label content supplier, as well as a leading manufacturer of home and portable playback hardware. Shortly thereafter, Sony announced a second digital music format—the digital audio tape, or "DAT," and accompanying player/recorders.[57] DAT tapes were half the size of traditional cassettes, rewound in seconds, and carried up to three hours of pristine digital sound. For consumers, they also provided a major feature that CDs did not—they could be copied. Moreover, as opposed to analog taping, there was no degradation in sound in succeeding generations of copies. For major labels, the home taping problem had suddenly gone digital. Even without the threat of a rental market, the potential for home users to make multiple, perfect digital copies on DAT tapes was perceived as a technology with the potential to "kill" music again.

After buying CBS Records, Sony walked a delicate tightrope as both electronics manufacturer and major label. It was appropriate, then, for CBS Records to propose a solution to the DAT problem—a copy-protection technology called Copycode, to be embedded in all players to prevent copying. Electronics manufacturers balked, and in response the labels refused to license their recordings for the DAT format. In later negotiations the two factions reached a tentative compromise, in which DAT players would be equipped with a "Serial Copy Management System" that allowed only a single copy of a prerecorded DAT.[58] But the labels weren't the only ones whose works were being copied—music publishers and composers had kept a watchful eye on the negotiations, and upon seeing a compromise that did not protect their interests, took matters into their own hands. Sony began importing DAT recorders in June 1990: on July 9, songwriter Sammy Cahn filed a class action suit in federal district court in Manhattan, backed by the National Music Publishers Association, accusing the manufacturer of "actively promoting the ability of DAT recorders to make perfect digital copies of compact discs." Sony was not itself engaging in any infringing acts—it merely made the technology available to those who might—so the claims were based on theories of "contributory" and "vicarious" wrongdoing. The claims of indirect infringement were no sure thing; indeed, it was not even clear that the act of "copying" by individual home tapers for private use was unlawful. In another case involving Sony technology, the Supreme Court had decided in 1984 that off-the-air home taping of television programming using a videocassette recorder was "fair use," as it amounted only to "time-shifting" broadcasting to suit the viewer's schedule.[59] Nevertheless, the Cahn litigation brought manufacturers back to the bargaining table, where they

---

57. COLEMAN, *supra* note 51, at 171–72.

58. STEVE KNOPPER, APPETITE FOR SELF-DESTRUCTION: THE SPECTACULAR CRASH OF THE RECORD INDUSTRY IN THE DIGITAL AGE 75–79 (2009).

59. Sony Corp. of Am. v. Universal City Studios (the Betamax case), 464 U.S. 417, 78 L. Ed. 2d 574, 104 S. Ct. 774 (1984).

forged a three-way agreement with publishers and labels. The suit was dropped, and the industry-sponsored compromise was presented to Congress as the Audio Home Recording Act of 1992.[60] The AHRA required that all digital recording devices incorporate SCMS—a special chip that allowed a first copy, but not further reproductions. In addition, the statute provided for manufacturers to pay royalties based on sales of both recording machines and blank DAT tapes, with proceeds to be distributed in designated percentages to publishers, composers, labels, and recording artists. Finally, as part of the compromise, copyright owners agreed to waive their right to sue consumers for infringement based on private copying.[61]

The compromise reflected in the AHRA had much to recommend it, but it was also flawed. First, although intentions were for a broad agreement that could usher music copyright into the digital age, the statute in fact was highly technology specific, and cloaked music copyright for the first time in the dense, technical, and arcane language of the computer age. Second, it was both early and late: the legal and legislative skirmishing had kept DAT products from the market for years after they were first available, so potential customers were aware the technology was being held back. Eventually, interest waned, and by the time the legislative compromise was implemented and the expensive machines came to market, the public was confused and complacent enough to simply bypass DAT as a consumer format. Although DAT technology found a lasting role in the recording studio, the consumer market never developed, and consequently the royalties distributed under the AHRA have remained modest: after peaking at $5.5 million a year in 2000, royalties have averaged around $3.5 million annually thereafter.[62]

37. Sample This

Digital music technology also enabled the explosion of a new art form based on "sampling," literally cutting and pasting segments of preexisting recordings (and the songs that underlie them) into new works. Sampling can also be accomplished "in analog," by splicing tape and manipulating vinyl records on a turntable, but digital techniques simplified the process and dramatically reduced its costs. Sampling is a matter of degree: a new work might utilize a single recognizable passage from an earlier work or, on the other end of the scale, incorporate dozens, hundreds, even thousands of snippets into a collage or pastiche of sound. The practice became prevalent in the late 1980s, with sampled loops serving as the backing tracks

---

60. 17 U.S.C. §§ 1001–1010.

61. *See* Paul Goldstein, Copyright's Highway: From Gutenberg to the Celestial Jukebox 128–33 (2003).

62. William W. Fisher III, Promises to Keep: Technology, Law and the Future of Entertainment 83–87 (2004).

for the lyrical rhyming and rapping of hip-hop. As the genre moved mainstream, the legalities of sampling came to the fore.

Sampling litigation came of age in a case called *Grand Upright* in 1991, in which the publisher of Gilbert O'Sullivan's well-known composition, "Alone Again (Naturally)," sued Warner Bros. Records for including an unlicensed sample of the song in the Biz Markie album, *I Need A Haircut*.[63] New York District Court Judge Kevin Duffy set the tone for his opinion with the biblical quote, "Thou shalt not steal," and it was downhill from there for Warner, whose activities were treated as "piracy" pure and simple. The opinion was notable in that it undertook no substantive infringement analysis, and cited no prior case law. On the other hand, Warner was not a sympathetic defendant: it cleared numerous samples for the album, but had not come to terms with Grand Upright. By moving ahead without permission, Warner was left with the meager excuse that "others in the 'rap music' business are also engaged in illegal activity," which the judge found "totally specious." Later courts, notably *Newton v. Diamond*,[64] took the view that a song sample could be so small—de minimis—as to avoid infringement, but in a series of cases now known by the lead plaintiff's name, Bridgeport Music, a stricter view of sampling *sound recordings* emerged in 2005.[65]

The Bridgeport plaintiffs commenced a massive litigation in May 2001, raising nearly 500 claims against 800 different defendants for using unlicensed samples in various rap recordings. The court separated the action into hundreds of individual suits, which meandered through various district courts before the claims made against Dimension Films reached the Sixth Circuit Court of Appeals. The specific facts involved the use of a sample from the George Clinton composition and sound recording "Get Off Your Ass and Jam," in the rap song "100 Miles and Runnin'." Dimension then included "100 Miles" in the soundtrack to the movie *I Got the Hook Up* in 1998, creating a sample within a sample. With regard to the recording, the trial court ruled for the filmmaker for the simple reason that the sampling was so minimal that it did not "rise to the level of a legally cognizable appropriation." The appeals court reversed, establishing a "bright line" test to the effect that *any* sound recording sample, regardless of length, could infringe.

In contrast to the *Grand Upright* decision, Circuit Judge Ralph B. Guy set forth a detailed analysis, pointing out important differences in the rights afforded to compositions as opposed to recordings. A composition could be infringed by a later song deemed "substantially similar," but not so for a sound recording. In granting protection against copying of sound recordings in the 1970s, Congress limited the owner's right to create "derivative works" to those in which "the *actual sounds fixed in the sound recording* are rearranged, remixed, or otherwise altered

---

63. Grand Upright Music Ltd. v. Warner Bros. Records, 780 F. Supp. 182 (S.D.N.Y. 1991).

64. *See* Newton v. Diamond, 349 F.3d 591 (9th Cir. 2003).

65. Bridgeport Music, Inc. v. Dimension Films, 410 F.3d 792 (6th Cir. 2005).

in sequence or quality." Further, according to the statute, a sound recording owner could not prevent another from "imitating or simulating" its sound, as long as the new recording consisted "*entirely* of an independent fixation of other sounds."[66] The court read these provisions to mean, as certain scholars had suggested, that sound recording copyright owners had the exclusive, indeed absolute, right to sample their own works, which was to be strictly enforced.

Thus the court drew a rare judicial "bright line," suggesting there was "much to recommend" its literal interpretation. First, there was the ease of enforcement— "Get a license or do not sample." Second, the market would control license fees, and third, "sampling is never accidental. It is not like the case of a composer who has a melody in his head, perhaps not even realizing that the reason he hears this melody is that it is the work of another which he had heard before. When you sample a sound recording you know you are taking another's work product." Judge Guy readily admitted there was no "Rosetta stone for interpreting the copyright statute," and also acknowledged that the "legislative history is of little help because digital sampling wasn't being done in 1971." But ultimately he put the burden on the industry itself, noting that "[i]f this is not what Congress intended or is not what they would intend now, it is easy enough for the record industry, as they have done in the past, to go back to Congress for a clarification or a change in the law." With that the court reversed the decision and sent the case back to the district, but with the following parting comment: "Since the district judge found no infringement, there was no necessity to consider the affirmative defense of 'fair use.' On remand, the trial judge is free to consider this defense and we express no opinion on its applicability to these facts."

The industry has not taken sampling issues to Congress, and the *Bridgeport* parties settled their dispute without testing the fair use defense. So the bright line test stands, as does the possibility that de minimis use of a sound recording sample could qualify as fair use. One artist who has proceeded boldly on this theory is the one-man "band," Gregg Gillis, who records as Girl Talk. Gillis' experiments in sampling yielded critically acclaimed albums in 2008 (*Feed the Animals*) and 2010 (*All Day*), consisting entirely of hundreds of overlapping samples, assembled using a laptop computer and relatively inexpensive software. None of the samples were licensed, putting the artist and his label (provocatively named "Illegal Art") at risk of hundreds of claims, yet none have materialized.[67]

---

66. 17 U.S.C. § 114(b).

67. In yet another *Bridgeport* ruling, the Sixth Circuit upheld a jury's rejection of the fair use defense in using the phrase "Bow wow wow, yippie yo, yippie yea," sampled from the George Clinton composition, "Atomic Dog." Bridgeport Music, Inc. v. UMG Recordings, Inc., 585 F.3d 267 (6th Cir. 2009). For a thoughtful and complete view of sampling issues, *see* KEMBREW MCLEOD & PETER DICOLA, CREATIVE LICENSE: THE LAW AND CULTURE OF DIGITAL SAMPLING (2011).

38. Holy Trinity of Music Copyright

Until 1994, there was no federal law against "bootlegging"—the unauthorized recording of a live musical performance. In that year, Congress passed the Uruguay Round Agreements Act, imposing both civil liability and criminal penalties for the practice.[68] As the name suggests, the amendment stemmed from attempts of the United States to satisfy its treaty obligations, as opposed to the expressed needs of the music industry; not surprisingly, the anti-bootlegging statute has rarely been invoked, and the few cases focus more on constitutional attacks on the law's validity than protecting the rights of performing artists.[69] Nevertheless, by the mid-1990s, related "performance" issues were again reaching a tipping point for the industry.

We have chronicled the long fight for recognition of a performance right in sound recordings. The frustrations of labels and recording artists continued when their efforts to make performance rights a part of the 1971 sound recording amendment, and the broader 1976 revisions, both failed. In 1978, New Jersey senator Harrison Williams introduced yet another performance royalty measure, which died in committee. Thereafter, following the trail blazed by Fred Waring, Paul Whiteman, and others, recording superstar Frank Sinatra entered the fray, organizing the Performers' Rights Society of America in 1989. Sinatra's personal attorney, Robert Finkelstein, acted as the group's spokesman, framing the issue as "a question of equity and justice and fairness."[70] "I think we recognize as a society that there exists a common right to the fruits of your labors," he insisted. "And this is really an anomaly . . . in our law, that performers have not shared in the payment of royalties." RIAA head Jay Berman was more pragmatic: "The time is right to try again, but getting it is another matter," he said. The performance right has "had political difficulty in the past because broadcasters are much more numerous than the rights holders, and broadcasters like getting their product for free." He was right. "We are opposed to performance royalties on the basis that [artists] have already been paid for recording the performance," said Bob Hallahan of the NAB. "Playing records on the air . . . also promotes the record," he added, "which stimulates record sales, which increases the popularity of an artist. That way, an artist can command more money [from a label] when he records something else."[71]

---

68. The URAA added Chapter 11 to the Copyright Act, 17 U.S.C. § 1101.

69. See United States v. Moghadam, 175 F.3d 1269 (11th Cir. 1999); KISS Catalog v. Passport Int'l Productions, 350 F. Supp. 2d 823 (C.D. Cal. 2004); United States v. Martignon, 492 F.3d 140 (2d Cir. 2007).

70. Russell Kishi, *A Question of Royalty*, UNITED PRESS INT'L, Feb. 3, 1989, available through http://www.highbeam.com/doc/1P2-3927617.html.

71. Zan Stewart, *Sinatra Heads Group Seeking Legislation for Performers' Royalties*, L.A. TIMES, Jan. 11, 1989.

Sinatra had the high-profile support of a select number of performers, including Ginny Mancini, the widow of composer and performer Henry Mancini, but without an effective lobbying strategy the group was no match for the NAB and its consistent refrain—free promotion in exchange for free music. Even as the effort faded, however, technology was changing the debate.

As of the early 1990s, terrestrial radio was no longer the only broadcast game in town. Traditional broadcasters were joined by a groundswell of "new media" entrepreneurs, heralding the beginning of a shift in music consumption from ownership of a physical product toward "music as a service," where consumer "subscribers" pay for access to broad libraries of recorded content. The new services made use of digital broadcast techniques to serve up music "streams" or "webcasts," also known as "Internet radio." Digital transmissions carried sound in perfect clarity, were more resistant to interference than analog sound waves, and required less power to broadcast. Moreover, digital broadcasters could offer highly specialized, "interactive" music formats, feeding music to listeners by genre, artist, and in some cases, specific tracks. The advances held great potential, but were also highly disruptive to the industry status quo. Through the RIAA, the labels expressed concern that streamed digital music was more easily captured and kept by listeners, creating, in effect, the ultimate "home-taping" dilemma: listeners could record "on-demand" streams directly to a computer hard drive, preserving their own copies in pristine digital sound, and eliminating the need to purchase physical copies from brick-and-mortar music merchants.

A 1991 Copyright Office study recognized that "digital audio transmissions" were a game changer, and recommended a broad-based performance right in response, the rationale being that performance royalties would offset lost sales. In 1993 performance right legislation was introduced in both houses of Congress. Sensing that digital broadcasting was fundamentally different, interested parties began a long series of private meetings, and for the first time, the performance right concept was met with something other than hostility and outright rejection by the broadcast community. Traditional terrestrial radio operators maintained that their analog broadcasts continued to perform the same promotional function as always, but the "promotion" argument was far more tenuous for digital broadcasters to make, as digital transmissions were seen as having the potential to "replace" music sales instead of promoting them. Based on these distinctions, a tentative agreement emerged, which served as the basis for revised performance legislation introduced by senators Orrin Hatch and Dianne Feinstein January 1995. A similar House bill followed in late June.

The congressional reports described a scenario where emerging technology enabled "pay-per-listen," "audio-on-demand," and similar "celestial jukebox" services, which expanded consumer choice and access to recorded music. But the pro-consumer developments also threatened the livelihoods of those "who depend upon revenues derived from traditional record sales." The House Report concluded that "recording artists and record companies cannot be effectively protected unless copyright law recognizes at least a limited performance right in sound recordings."[72] The resulting proposal called for the creation of "a carefully crafted and narrow performance right" for sound recordings. The legislation was complex, and like its digital predecessor, 1992's AHRA, buried music copyright further in the technical jargon of the computer age. But the bottom line was straightforward: when passed on November 1, 1995, the Digital Performance Right in Sound Recordings Act (DPRA) created a "public performance right" in sound recordings for the first time, marking a milestone many decades in the making. But the new right applied only to "digital audio transmissions." Traditional radio broadcasts, and other "analog" transmissions, were exempt.[73]

Digital broadcasters were concerned that their businesses would be stifled if they were required to negotiate with each major label, and thousands of independents, to license the breadth of sound recordings necessary for an attractive Internet radio offering. These concerns were addressed by creating a compulsory statutory license provision—the Section 114 license—allowing digital broadcasters to transmit any recordings they desired, so long as their services stayed within certain statutory guidelines and they contributed royalty payments into a general pool for distribution to rights holders. The guidelines were designed to make digital services less susceptible to home recording. To be eligible for the Section 114 license, a service could not publish program guides in advance, had to adhere to a "sound recording complement" that limited the number and frequency with which a particular artist's recordings could be played; most important, the service had to remain "noninteractive"—that is, listeners could not have the ability to call up particular songs at will.[74] Of all the new forms of digital transmission broadcasting, "interactive" services were viewed as the most likely to impact traditional record sales and, thus, they could not take advantage of the compulsory Section 114 license. Rather, launching an interactive service required negotiating separate licenses from each owner whose recordings would be included in the service, an onerous, time-consuming, and many times cost-prohibitive undertaking.

For services subject to the compulsory license, the DPRA established an arbitration procedure to set and periodically adjust applicable royalty rates. Currently, a three-judge panel known as the Copyright Royalty Board oversees rate-setting proceedings, which have themselves become hard-fought referenda on the elusive "value of music" in the digital environment. Finally, the DPRA set forth the manner in which royalties would be divided. Funds were to be distributed to sound

---

72. The House Report on the Digital Performance Right in Sound Recordings Act of 1995 (H.R. 1506), REP. No. 104–274, 104th Congress, 1st Session, p. 13.

73. 17 U.S.C. § 106(6). If retransmitted or "simulcast" over the Internet, traditional broadcast signals lose their exemption and fall within the Section 114 license. *See* Bonneville Int'l Corp. v. Peters, 347 F.3d 485 (3d Cir. 2003).

74. 17 U.S.C. § 114(d)(2).

recording copyright owners (typically record labels), who would keep 50 percent, with the remaining half passing through to the "featured artists" (45 percent) and nonfeatured musicians and vocalists (5 percent) appearing on the recordings.[75]

Two subsequent pieces of legislation completed the sound recording performance framework established by the DPRA. Congress passed the omnibus Digital Millennium Copyright Act in 1998, a controversial, dense, and expansive law making it illegal to circumvent copyright protection and management systems, and providing certain "safe harbor" provisions insulating Internet service providers from copyright liability for the infringing acts of their customers in posting user-generated content. The DMCA did not relate to music per se, but included last-minute amendments supplementing the licensing procedures and rate-setting standards established in the DPRA.[76] Finally, the Small Webcaster Settlement Agreement was put into place in 2002, whose primary function was to implement an agreed temporary fix for "small webcasters" who complained that statutory licensing rates were excessive. For recording artists, however, the SWSA took the significant step of mandating that their half of the Section 114 royalties be paid directly to them (through an independent collecting agent), instead of passing through the vague filters of major label accounting processes.

Whenever new pools of money are created, the question arises as to who will collect and distribute the funds. In the case of Section 114 royalties, this function has fallen to SoundExchange, a Washington, D.C.-based not-for-profit, which essentially acts as the sound recording equivalent of the performing rights organizations who collect on behalf of music publishers and composers—ASCAP, BMI, and SESAC. Formed in 1996 as an arm of the RIAA, SoundExchange was later spun off as a separate organization that now acts on behalf of labels and recording artists in collecting and distributing sound recording public performance royalties, and represents these constituents in rate proceedings. SoundExchange has come under criticism for an alleged lack of zeal in locating recording artists who are owed royalties, but to date more than $800 million has flowed to labels and artists through the "crack in the door" opened by what can be regarded as the holy trinity of sound recording copyright laws—the DPRA, DMCA, and SWSA. Sound recording copyright owners enjoy a consistent and increasing revenue stream, based on digital transmissions of their recordings by webcasters, satellite radio operators, digital cable services, and others who broadcast music digitally. Similarly, recording artists (and their estates) are the beneficiaries of a new intellectual property right—one "neighboring" on copyright, by which they earn royalties based on every digital "play" of their recorded performances. Recognition of a public perfor-

---

75. 17 U.S.C. § 114(g)(2).

76. *See* 2 Melville B. Nimmer & David Nimmer, Nimmer on Copyright § 8.21[C][2] (2011); *see also* Brian T. Yeh, *Copyright Licensing in Music Distribution, Reproduction, and Public Performance,* Congressional Research Service, Jan. 22, 2009, at 13–14.

mance right in sound recordings was a significant step, but at the same time, its narrow application in only the digital realm did little to alter traditional industry roles and relationships. In other words, the dichotomy between sound recordings and musical works remained essentially intact: publishers enjoyed a "full" and unfettered performance right, while label and artist rights were limited to digital performances. Thus, as we will see, the debates continue as to whether and when the U.S. will expand the performance right in sound recordings.

There is one more element of the DPRA that deserves our attention at this stage—its provisions that brought mechanical licensing into the digital era. The 1909 Copyright Act created a compulsory mechanical license reflected in Section 115, allowing any artist to create a new recording of a previously released composition, in return for payment of the statutory rate. The term itself referred to the "mechanical" means by which music was reproduced and formatted into "phonorecords"—the physical objects (piano rolls, cylinders, and discs, and thereafter, tapes and CDs) through which music is played back for personal enjoyment. In the digital realm, recordings could be made, reproduced, distributed, and played without manufacturing a physical object at all. Accordingly, as part of the DPRA, Congress added "digital phonorecord deliveries" to the mechanical license regime, such that purely digital recordings fell within the compulsory license. Since the definition of "phonorecord" contemplates a material object, the oxymoron of a "digital" version provides a good example of the breaking down of definitions, tied to the physical world, that formed the bedrock assumptions of music copyright since the advent of recorded sound. With the AHRA, followed by the DPRA and its related implementing legislation, lawmakers and rights holders began their struggle to maintain an integrated system of music copyright, one able to address and regulate a world in which musical art is created, distributed, and experienced in both physical and digital incarnations.

PART VI

The End of the World, Part 2

Kitty or devil? The logo for the original file-sharing
service, Napster, struck fear in the hearts of established
rights holders on its debut in 1999. The service was
enjoined in 2001, but survived in different incarnations
(and under various owners) until being absorbed into
the Rhapsody music service in 2011.

39. Party Like It's 1999

Recorded music sales approached $15 billion in 1999, the U.S. industry's biggest year ever. CDs accounted for almost 90 percent of purchases, the peak year for the format, with cassettes accounting for around 8 percent, and vinyl LPs less than 1 percent. Older catalog recordings were still being reissued en masse on CD, and in terms of new music, the boy-band craze was in full swing, with the Backstreet Boys' *Millennium* dominating the charts, alongside releases from Britney Spears and a rising rap star calling himself Eminem. And yet behind the euphoria were signs of weakness: less than 1 percent of CD titles released in 1999 sold more than 10,000 copies, making the business more hit-driven than ever, and according to RIAA figures, consumers over age thirty-five accounted for 35 percent of sales.[1] CDs were skewing to older consumers; more and more, the younger crowd was experimenting with the quickly evolving digital services.

By this time the U.S. recording industry had coalesced into five major labels—Warner Music Group, Sony Music Entertainment, Bertelsmann Music Group, EMI, and Universal Music Group. The industry had benefitted from a steady stream of copyright legislation following the recognition of sound recordings in 1971, with additional revisions implemented in 1976, 1984, 1992, 1994, 1995, and 1998. Nevertheless, the great unknown of digital distribution loomed before them. As one approach, in 1998 the labels formed a broad business consortium with technology companies, developing a program called the Secure Digital Music Initiative to promulgate encryption standards and "watermarking" techniques intended to control digital distribution.[2] The resulting standards were easily hacked, however, leading to an embarrassing legal run-in with a team of academics who threatened to publish their methods for cracking the codes. Attempts to corral the proliferation of digital music outside the legal process were not promising, and to make matters worse, rights holders were headed for a rare defeat in court as well.

Diamond Multimedia Systems, Inc. introduced the Rio PMP 300 in September 1998, a portable, lightweight music device that stored and played back music in a new format called "MP3." The term was shorthand for "Motion Picture Experts Group-1 Layer 3," in reference to the Geneva-based committee of engineers who in 1992 (ironically the same year as the AHRA) developed a method for compressing

---

1. Mark Coleman, Playback: From the Victrola to MP3, 100 Years of Music, Machines, and Money 174 (2003).
2. William W. Fisher III, Promises to Keep: Technology, Law and the Future of Entertainment 83–87 (2004).Fisher, pgs. 88–98.

digital video files. The audio version, MP3, soon followed, and became the format of choice for moving music files across the Internet and storing them on computer hard drives. Priced at $200, the Rio held an hour's worth of music, and came with a free software interface that converted CD tracks into MP3 files, which could then be moved from a computer hard drive to the device. MP3 files downloaded from the Internet could also be transferred to the Rio for playback, but importantly, the device itself could not record music.

In what it portrayed as an effort to "protect the creative content of the music industry," the RIAA sued Diamond in the Central District of California in October 1998, seeking an immediate injunction against sales of the Rio. The suit charged Diamond with encouraging consumers "to infringe the rights of artists by trafficking in unlicensed music recordings on the internet," and alleged specifically that the Rio player violated the 1992 Audio Home Recording Act by not incorporating the "Serial Copy Management System" required by the statute. Diamond and its supporters spoke out against the RIAA's action, citing statistics from Michael Robertson (whose company operated the popular MP3.com Web site) as to the growing number of artists authorizing the distribution of music in the MP3 format. Robertson would become a vocal RIAA gadfly in the coming decade, and a tenacious adversary in court. Bob Kohn, founder and chairman of the digital music service GoodNoise (and a foremost expert on music copyright and licensing)[3] called the suit "a smoke screen to slow down the digital distribution of music until the major labels are ready to capitalize on the revenues to be gained by the great momentum being created by the internet."[4]

District Court Judge Andrea Collins avoided the politics, denying the request for an injunction, basing her decision on the low likelihood that the RIAA would ultimately succeed. The RIAA appealed to the Ninth Circuit, where the panel included sixty-two-year-old Circuit Judge Diarmuid F. O'Scannlain, a Harvard law graduate appointed to the appellate bench by Ronald Reagan in 1986. Judge O'Scannlain delivered the opinion of the court on June 15, 1999, framing the issue as the (deceptively) simple question of whether the Rio was a "digital audio recording device" subject to the requirements of the AHRA.[5] As background, the court recounted the introduction of digital audio in the 1980s, the legislative history of the AHRA, the development of the MP3 compression algorithm, and the explosion of personal computing, all leading to the "brave new world of Internet music distribution." Because of its portability, the Rio device had "untethered" MP3 files from computers, a daunting development the RIAA could not live with. Echoing earlier

---

3. *See* AL KOHN & BOB KOHN, KOHN ON MUSIC LICENSING (4th ed. 2010).

4. Robert A. Starrett, *RIAA Loses Bid for Injunction to Stop Sale of Diamond Multimedia RIO MP3 Player,* EMEDIA PROFESSIONAL, Jan. 1999.

5. RIAA v. Diamond Multimedia Sys., Inc., 180 F.3d 1072 (9th Cir. 1999). The Alliance of Artists and Recording Companies, a nonprofit agency specializing in collecting and distributing royalties paid under the AHRA, joined the suit as a plaintiff.

claims, the RIAA predicted that "digital Internet piracy" losses would soon surpass the $300 million allegedly lost annually to "more traditional forms of piracy." Diamond criticized the estimates, arguing that the question of whether "piracy" (digital or otherwise) caused financial harm was unsettled.

Judge O'Scannlain meticulously pored through the "nested definitions" set forth in the AHRA, comparing them to the functions of the Rio. In the end, there was no way to categorize the player as a "digital audio recording device," as it did not record at all. The Rio could store music files transferred from a computer, but computers were exempt from the AHRA, because (unlike the DAT recorders that spawned the statute) their "primary purpose" was not making copies. The court went further, finding the Rio's operation "entirely consistent with the [AHRA's] main purpose—the facilitation of personal use." In practical terms, the device functioned to "space shift" music files already existing on the user's hard drive, much in the way home *video*tapers "time shifted" television programs using a VCR, a practice condoned by the Supreme Court's Betamax decision in 1984.

It has been reported that the Rio went on to sell 200,000 units, a respectable number, but not the category killer the RIAA feared.[6] Another source indicates that the RIAA cut a deal with Diamond in return for its assistance in with the Secure Digital Music Initiative.[7] If so, it would not be the last time big music attempted to "buy out" the perceived problem of digital music. In any event, the industry's first judicial attempt to control digital music had failed, caught up in the techno-speak of a narrowly drafted statute. At the risk of piling on the acronyms, we can say that when AHRA met MP3 it was bad for RIAA.

40. Hired or Fired?

Although sound recordings were recognized as copyrightable property in the 1971 amendment, the law sidestepped the thorny issue of authorship. Who owned a sound recording upon completion? Recordings were a product of multiple contributing "authors," including the musicians, of course, but also the producers, engineers, and label personnel who coordinated, produced, and finalized the product. Historically, labels paid advances to recording artists, covering studio time and related expenses, and those investments were often cited as a basis for extending copyright protection to recordings. The authorship issue was not addressed in the 1976 general copyright revisions, but two elements of the 1976 Act impacted the question—revisions to the termination right and the so-called work for hire doctrine.

---

6. STEVE KNOPPER, APPETITE FOR SELF-DESTRUCTION 166 (2009).
7. *See* EDWARD SAMUELS, THE ILLUSTRATED STORY OF COPYRIGHT 50–51 (2002).

The ability to terminate an assignment (transfer) of copyright is one of the most valuable rights held by an author; a successful termination results in all exclusive rights reverting to the original creator for the duration of the copyright, as if the assignment never occurred. The termination right was Congress' way of evening the playing field for individual authors, who have historically assigned their copyrights to businesses (book publishers, music publishers, and record companies, for example), and making them more able to exploit the works, in return for the payment of royalties. Oftentimes an author has little negotiating strength at the time of transfer; the termination right provides a "second bite at the apple"—the ability to renegotiate using the threat of termination as leverage. The termination right becomes available thirty-five years after the initial transfer.[8] This means that the initial works eligible for termination under the 1976 Act can revert to their original authors on January 1, 2013, thirty-five years from the effective date of the statute.[9]

The termination right does not apply to works "made for hire," a term first included (but not defined) in the 1909 Copyright Act. The clause provided that an "employer," not the individual, would be deemed the original author in cases where employees created copyrightable works within the scope of their day-to-day responsibilities. Over time, courts broadly construed the provision, finding that virtually any commissioned works qualified, even where there was no "employment" relationship. The 1976 revisions narrowed the definition of works made for hire to those made by an employee "in the scope of his employment," or to certain "specially ordered or commissioned works," which do not include sound recordings per se, but refer to "contributions to a collective work . . . as part of a compilation."[10] There is enough ambiguity in this language for labels to contend that, even though artists are not employees, their recorded performances are merely "contributions" to a collective work. Consistent with this background, major label artist contracts contain standard terms providing that recordings are works for hire, owned by the label as author and not subject to termination. As a belt-and-suspenders safeguard, the contracts also provide that to the extent the recordings are not works for hire, they are deemed assigned from the artist to the label, in which case the assignment could be terminated in thirty-five years. In this way, the incendiary issue of sound recording ownership has simmered between the lines of virtually every major label contract signed in the last forty years.[11] The powder reached a flashpoint as the millennium came to an end.

---

8. 17 U.S.C. § 203. The author must provide a termination notice within two and ten years before the end of the thirty-five-year period.

9. The termination right for works created before January 1, 1978, will go into effect no earlier than February 15, 2028, under 17 U.S.C. § 304.

10. The parties must agree in writing that a specially ordered or commissioned work will be treated as made for hire. 17 U.S.C. § 101.

11. See Mark Jaffe's excellent analysis in *Defusing the Time Bomb Once Again—Determining Authorship in a Sound Recording*, 53 J. COPYRIGHT SOC'Y USA 139 (Fall 2005–Winter 2006); *see also* Peter J. Strand, *What a Short Strange Trip It's Been: Sound Recordings and the Work Made for Hire Doctrine*,

A short item was attached to a giant omnibus appropriations bill passed by Congress in the rush to pass spending bills in the last hours of the first session of the 103rd Congress in November 1999. The provision added just four words—"as a sound recording"—to the list of commissioned works for hire set forth in the Copyright Act, and in so doing appeared to resolve the sound recording ownership issue in the labels' favor. The item was inserted in the unrelated "Satellite Home Viewer Improvement" section of the Intellectual Property and Communications Omnibus Reform Act of 1999. The omnibus bill was then added to the 90-page federal government appropriations bill, which in turn was folded into the huge omnibus spending bill of 1,174 pages. There were no hearings on the measure, and President Clinton signed the bill into law on November 29, 1999.

RIAA president Hilary Rosen said because record companies had long registered recordings with the Copyright Office as works-for-hire, "in everybody's view this was a technical issue." Well, not everybody. Led by artists Sheryl Crow and Don Henley, the artist community erupted in protest upon discovering the amendment, declaring the provision a substantive change to the law, a clandestine "pre-emptive strike" by the record companies to head off future litigation over the 2013 reversion of rights. Adding to the furor was the fact that the provision was not requested by a member of Congress. Instead, it was inserted into a final conference report on the satellite bill by a congressional staffer, Mitch Glazier, chief counsel to the subcommittee that passed the legislation, at the request of the RIAA. Making matters worse, the RIAA hired Mr. Glazier shortly after the controversial clause was added.

Register of Copyrights Marybeth Peters expressed concern that the provision was "suggested in the middle of the night," adding her view that the amendment was substantive, not technical in nature. Following a tension-filled hearing on May 25, 2000, the RIAA and artist groups announced a truce, and submitted a joint recommendation to Congress to repeal the amendment. The sides agreed on specific language to be inserted into the statute, confirming that in determining whether a particular work was made for hire, no effect or significance shall be given to the fact that Congress ever included or omitted sound recordings from the work for hire definition. When President Clinton signed the "Work Made for Hire and Copyright Corrections Act" in October, the industry officially deferred the ownership issue to another day, a day that is now fast approaching. The work for hire and termination debate is destined to become a major litigation battleground, with the stakes particularly high for labels, whose business is based entirely on the ownership and exploitation of sound recording assets. With physical

---

18 ENT. & SPORTS LAW, 12 (2000), and Stephen W. Tropp, *It Had to Be Murder or Will Be Soon—17 U.S.C. § 203 Termination of Transfers: A Call for Legislative Reform*, 51 J. COPYRIGHT SOC'Y USA 797 (Summer 2004).

distribution declining, label success is increasingly dependent on the ability to manage sound recording rights in the digital environment. The prospect of those underlying assets steadily reverting to individual artists is unsettling indeed.[12]

41. MP3.com

The recording industry's internal squabbles as to ownership had been deferred, but the spotlight remained on work for hire as the labels turned their attention back to the main millennial event, digital music. Of particular concern were the "music lockers" established by services such as MP3.com, headed by Michael Robertson, the Internet entrepreneur who had voiced support for Diamond Multimedia in the Rio litigation.[13] Around 1996 Robertson noticed increased search engine requests for "MP3" music, and in 1998 he turned it into a business—MP3.com, an advertising-supported clearinghouse for MP3 music files, mostly from independent artists not constrained by major label contract restrictions. Like many Internet start-ups, MP3.com lost money in its early years, but revenues hit $80 million in fiscal 2000, enough to get the attention of major labels, who perceived the company to be trafficking in illicit recordings. In the first month of the twenty-first century, Robertson added a service—MyMP3.com—that broke the camel's back and put the company on a fast track to litigation. Using the new service, consumers could listen to their own CD collection online by accessing designated personal "music lockers." Once a consumer's purchased CD was scanned into the system to verify ownership, the customer could access, listen to, and download MP3 versions of the same recordings, which the company had previously loaded into a master library. And there was the rub: to create the database, MP3.com had copied tens of thousands of major label CDs onto its servers.

Litigation commenced, and on May 4, 2000, Judge Jed Rakoff of the Southern District of New York delivered a crippling blow, commenting that the "complex marvels of cyberspatial communication may create difficult legal issues; but not in this case. Defendant's infringement of plaintiffs' copyrights is clear."[14] MP3.com ar-

---

12. In Fifty-Six Hope Road Music Ltd. v. UMG Recordings, Inc., 99 U.S.P.Q.2d 1735 (S.D.N.Y. 2010), the court held certain Bob Marley recordings to be works for hire, owned by Universal Music. Because of the age of the recordings, the court applied a more liberal work for hire standard under the 1909 Copyright Act, which would not apply to recordings made after January 1, 1978. With regard to publishing terminations, see Scorpio Music S.A. v. Victor Willis, 3:11-cv-01557, Dkt. 30 (S.D. Cal. May 7, 2012), finding that Village People member and co-songwriter Victor Willis successfully terminated his transfer of a partial interest in thirty-three compositions, including "YMCA," and "In the Navy."

13. *See* FISHER, *supra* note 2, at 98.

14. UMG Recordings, Inc. v. MP3.com, 92 F. Supp. 2d 349 (S.D.N.Y. 2000).

gued that its service was the "functional equivalent" of storing its subscribers' CDs, but "in actuality," said the court, the company was "replaying for the subscribers converted versions of the recordings it copied, without authorization." MP3.com also argued that its copying was protected as "fair use," to which the court responded that the "defense is indefensible." Judge Rakoff's ruling established liability as a matter of law, but left the question of damages lingering.

Over the next several months, Michael Robertson worked furiously to save his business, negotiating settlement terms with four of the five major labels.[15] The exception, Universal, pressed on with the litigation, leading to a three-day trial on the limited question of how damages would be calculated. On September 6, Judge Rakoff made an oral ruling that dealt a second harsh blow to MP3.com.[16] The infringement was deemed "willful," and the fair use defense "little more than a sham." Robertson and his colleagues had proceeded in the face of the known and recognized risk of infringement, and for this they were held accountable at the rate of $25,000 per CD, well within the court's discretion under the circumstances.[17] Judge Rakoff's reasoning was based in part on the perceived need for deterrence, noting that the evidence in the case "strongly suggests that some companies operating in the area of the Internet may have a misconception that, because their technology is somewhat novel, they are somehow immune from the ordinary applications of the laws of the United States, including copyright law. They need to understand that the law's domain knows no such limits." The only remaining issue was the number of CDs to be used as the multiplier: pursuant to the statute, damages could only be awarded for CDs the plaintiffs had actually registered as copyrights. MP3.com estimated that only 4,700 CDs were in issue, but even that number would yield $118 million in damages.

Judge Rakoff scheduled the final phase of the trial for November, and in the meantime Michael Robertson turned to Congress for relief. To his credit, Robertson gained the ear of Rick Boucher of Virginia, who introduced the Music Owners' Licensing Rights Act in late September, designed specifically to legalize the kind of music lockers provided by MP3.com. In the face of organized opposition by the RIAA and others, the bill died in committee.[18] With the damages trial approaching, MP3 made a last ditch effort to cast doubt on Universal's ownership of the copyrights in the CDs, arguing that Universal's copyrights had been improperly registered as works for hire. On November 2, just a week after President Clinton signed the work for hire repeal, Judge Rakoff denied Universal's request for a

---

15. FISHER, *supra* note 2, at 101.

16. UMG Recordings, Inc. v. MP3.com, 56 U.S.P.Q2d 1376 (S.D.N.Y. September 6, 2000).

17. In the only ruling that favored MP3.com, on July 31, 2000, Judge Rakoff denied plaintiffs' request to calculate damages *per song* as opposed to per CD, which could have multiplied the damage award exponentially. UMG Recordings, Inc. v. MP3.com, 109 F. Supp. 2d 223 (S.D.N.Y. 2000).

18. FISHER, *supra* note 2, at 101–02.

pretrial ruling that it owned the copyrights in question as works for hire.[19] With this window of leverage, MP3.com managed to negotiate settlements with Universal and the other major labels, but at a steep cost of around $160 million.

Following the settlement, a group of high-profile recording artists called the Recording Artists Coalition (including cofounders Sheryl Crow and Don Henley, along with Jackson Browne, Barry Gibb, Billy Joel, Bonnie Raitt, Clint Black, and Trisha Yearwood), submitted a letter to *Billboard* magazine, praising the result. RAC had remained neutral on the merits of the case, but saw a victory in Judge Rakoff's deferral of the work for hire issue. "This case represents a victory for all recording artists and especially the [Universal] recording artists. By allowing a judgment to be entered without ruling on whether a sound recording is a 'work made for hire' under the Copyright Act, the court has preserved for the [Universal] recording artists, and arguably all recording artists, the right to claim recapture of their copyrights at a later date. It is also quite gratifying that all recording artists will share in future royalties paid by MP3.com and that the [Universal] recording artists, pursuant to their contracts with [Universal], will receive no less than 50% of the monetary award paid by MP3.com."[20]

As for MP3.com, the company restarted its service on a subscription basis, but mountains of settlement debt weighed heavily on the bottom line. In May 2001 its main antagonist, Universal (by then owned by the French conglomerate, Vivendi), purchased the company for $350 million. Universal kept the site alive for a time, without the locker service, but sold the assets to CNET Networks in late 2003, where they languished and eventually went black. As noted by Terry Fisher, during the litigation Michael Robertson warned "presciently" that the labels' pursuit of locker services was shortsighted, and would push consumers toward more rogue digital services. "The labels made the decision to challenge a technology that will protect their intellectual property interests and grow their business. They will be left with copyright chaos."[21]

42. Learning to Share

The move from analog to digital music was a transformative change that brought near-term riches to the recording industry, but in the long run revealed itself as a Trojan horse.[22] When the doors opened, out poured foot soldiers in the form of digital downloads, MP3 compression, portable players, and music lockers. Then came the heavy artillery—a new form of digital music distribution called "P2P"—

---

19. *See* 112 (46) Billboard (Nov. 11, 2000).
20. 112 (48) Billboard (Nov. 25, 2000).
21. Fisher, *supra* note 2, at 102.
22. Coleman, *supra* note 1, at 177.

peer-to-peer file sharing across the outermost reaches of the Internet frontier. In 1998, a file-sharing service using the strange name "Napster" was hatched in the dorm room of Northeastern University freshman Shawn Fanning. After dropping out to pursue the project full-time, Shawn incorporated Napster with his uncle, John Fanning, in May 1999, and released a test version of their software in the summer. In simplest terms, Napster's free "MusicShare" software enabled a user to search for and download MP3 music files located on a "collective directory" consisting of the "shared" libraries of all other users logged on to the system. There was no charge for the service, or for music files shared with or by other users. It was, quite literally, a musical free-for-all. Not surprisingly, the service exploded in popularity; the Fannings enlisted another Boston-area teenager, the smooth-talking promoter Sean Parker, who began courting investors. They moved to Silicon Valley.

By October 1999 the fledgling service had gained 150,000 users, and the attention of the RIAA. The labels were in the midst of their litigation with both Diamond Multimedia and MP3.com, but wasted little time suing Napster as well, lodging the suit in San Francisco in early December. The case was assigned to Judge Marilyn Hall Patel, an experienced jurist and the first woman to serve as chief judge of the Northern District of California. The complaint was reminiscent of the suit Sammy Cahn had filed back in 1990, accusing Sony of "actively promoting" infringement by marketing DAT recorders. Like Sony, Napster was not copying or distributing music files—only its users were. Thus, the RIAA charged that by making its file-sharing technology available and managing the network, Napster was contributing to widespread copying in such a way that it became an infringer itself. Cahn's suit settled, but this one would not, setting up a test case for twenty-first century digital music issues, ranging from applicability of the DMCA and AHRA to "fair use" in the file-sharing context.

Despite the ongoing litigation, venture capital firm Hummer Winblad invested $13 million for a 20 percent interest in Napster in May 2000, installing partner Hank Barry as CEO. Judge Patel delivered a preliminary opinion the same month, denying Napster's request for an immediate legal declaration that its service fell within the "safe harbors" of the DMCA, which would likely have ended the case.[23] The opinion had little to do with copyright principles, and focused solely on the question of whether Napster was a "service provider" that could be insulated from contributory or vicarious liability. The answer was no. The DMCA had its own set of "nested definitions," like the AHRA terminology Judge O'Scannlain had wrestled with in the Rio matter, but in the end none applied to Napster; the service would face full scrutiny under substantive principles of copyright.

Following the unsuccessful gamble on a quick victory, Napster stocked its litigation war chest with fresh venture capital, and hired high profile attorney David Boies as its lead trial counsel in June 2000. The RIAA kept the pressure on by

---

23. A&M Records, Inc. v. Napster, Inc., 54 U.S.P.Q.2d 1746 (N.D. Cal. 2000).

requesting a preliminary injunction, seeking to enjoin the service from operating during the pendency of the case, based on the "irreparable harm" that would occur in the interim. Judge Patel's decision came down on July 26, 2000, granting the motion.[24] "The matter before the court concerns the boundary between sharing and theft, personal use and the unauthorized worldwide distribution of copyrighted music and sound recordings," the opinion said, setting an ominous tone for Napster. Procedurally, the judge clarified that a total of eighteen labels were co-plaintiffs, and they had been joined by a group of songwriters and music publishers, who alleged that their musical compositions—embedded in every recording—were also infringed by Napster. Both "sides" of the music industry were involved, and in theory, literally every music copyright—song *and* recording—was at stake.

The litigation had not slowed Napster's exponential growth. The service was growing by a mind-boggling 200 percent *monthly*, and according to its own documents, would have 75 million users by the end of 2000. Approximately 10,000 music files were shared per second using the system, and each second one hundred more users attempted to log on. The Napster service was itself a rock star, perceived by many as the Robin Hood of music, taking from rich labels and giving to poor individual consumers, lifting their burden of spending $18 on CDs containing only a few desired tracks. But cult status tends to dissipate in the courtroom, where bare facts mean more than public perception.

Napster argued that the system was "capable of commercially significant non-infringing uses," and that its users were making "fair use" of music copyrights, in that they were promoting new artists, "space shifting" music from CDs to computers (adopting the phrase coined in the Rio controversy), and merely "sampling" music prior to purchase. But the "new artist" program was anemic, and the AHRA was not invoked in the suit at all, so the space-shifting argument went nowhere. More important, there was strong evidence, in Napster executives' own words, that in contrast to providing samples, their primary goal was music world domination—taking over labels' traditional role as the promoters and distributors of popular music, bringing about the "death of the CD" in the process. Despite these admissions, Napster maintained that the system qualified as fair use. Judge Patel signaled her doubts, characterizing Napster's position as seeking to "expand" the fair use doctrine "to encompass the massive downloading of MP3 files by Napster users."

The fair use defense is a four-pronged inquiry taking into account the "purpose and character" of the unauthorized use, the nature of the copyrighted works in issue, the "amount" of those works used, and the effect of the use on the market for or value of the copyrighted works. In a clean sweep for the RIAA, Judge Patel found against Napster on every element. First, its use was unabashedly commercial. The service had no revenue, but it was venture-backed (valued at between $60 and $80 million), and there was every intention of monetizing the user base when

---

24. A&M Records, Inc. v. Napster, Inc., 114 F. Supp. 2d. 896 (N.D. Cal. 2000).

the time (and legal circumstances) were right. Second, the copyrighted works were "creative in nature; they constitute[d] entertainment," which cut against a finding of fair use.[25] Third, there was no disputing that downloading or uploading music files involved "copying the entire work." Finally, the court analyzed the effect Napster might have on the market for recorded music in general. The science was not definitive, but the RIAA had submitted expert opinions concluding that Napster reduced CD sales, particularly among college students. Further, by setting the price of digital music at zero, Napster made it more difficult for the labels to enter the digital download market themselves. Characterizing Napster as a "monster that is . . . devouring [plaintiffs'] intellectual property rights," Judge Patel issued a broad and onerous injunction, barring Napster from "engaging in, or facilitating others in copying, downloading, uploading, transmitting, or distributing plaintiffs' copyrighted musical compositions and sound recordings, protected by either federal or state law, without express permission of the rights owner." Further, the injunction applied to *all* copyrighted works owned by the plaintiffs, not just those listed in the complaint. "Plaintiffs have shown that they own the copyrights to more than seventy percent of the music available on the Napster system," the court concluded, and "[b]ecause defendant has contributed to illegal copying on a scale that is without precedent, it bears the burden of developing a means to comply with the injunction." For their part, the plaintiffs were required to file a written plan to help Napster identify their copyrights, and to post a $5 million bond to compensate Napster in the event the injunction was overturned. Napster immediately appealed to the Ninth Circuit, which stayed the injunction on July 28, 2000, the same day plaintiffs posted their bond.

The case was closely watched as it moved to the Ninth Circuit, and a veritable army of nearly fifty lawyers joined the proceedings, participating on behalf of the litigants and the various stakeholders and special interest groups who submitted "amicus" (friend of court) briefs supporting their particular points of view. The appeal was argued on October 2, 2000, and thereafter the parties waited four long months for a decision. In the interim, Napster lobbied record executives hard for a deal to keep major label recordings in the system in return for a substantial equity stake in the company. It was what one observer has called "the last chance for the record industry as we know it to stave off certain ruin," but the parties never got close.[26]

For all the waiting, Circuit Judge Robert R. Beezer's February 12, 2001, opinion was anticlimactic, more or less a garden variety affirmance of Judge Patel's decision.[27] In a few instances the appeals court said it may have reached different

---

25. Earlier in the opinion, Judge Patel described the plaintiffs' sound recordings as resulting from "a substantial investment of money, time, manpower, and" lastly, "creativity."

26. KNOPPER, *supra* note 6, at 141.

27. A&M Records, Inc. v. Napster, Inc., 239 F.3d 1004 (9th Cir. 2001).

conclusions had it evaluated the facts in the first instance, but that was not its job. Judge Patel's legal reasoning and factual findings were sound, and the substance of her decision would stand. Nevertheless, the *scope* of the injunction imposed was troubling, and would require tailoring. The Ninth Circuit found that the "mere existence" of the Napster system was not enough to impose contributory liability; it was the fact that Napster had not adequately monitored traffic on the system to control infringements. But it needed help. Plaintiffs should bear some of the responsibility by notifying Napster of specific copyrighted works on the system, and if Napster failed to remove them, it would become liable. The case returned to Judge Patel's courtroom, and on March 5, 2001, she modified the terms of the injunction as the Ninth Circuit prescribed. For three months the court monitored Napster's compliance (and the plaintiffs' obligations to identify infringing files), but despite a new "filtering system," infringements continued. Napster was not in satisfactory compliance, and the court issued a shutdown order, requiring Napster to disable the service until such time as compliance became possible. It was the final blow. On July 1, 2001, Napster ceased operations, but the company pursued another appeal, challenging the terms of the latest injunction. On March 25, 2002, Circuit Judge Beezer again affirmed Judge Patel's conclusions.[28]

Napster filed for bankruptcy in June 2002, and its assets were sold to Roxio Inc. for $5 million, the first in a series of transactions with owners, including Best Buy, the big box electronics retailer, who tried to resurrect the Napster name.[29] A decade later, Seattle-based Rhapsody acquired the assets, folding them into its ten-year-old subscription service effective December 1, 2011. "Digital music's most disruptive brand" was officially history.[30] Like the brand, however, the Napster litigation also had a long tail. For all the ups and downs between district and appeals courts, at the time of the Napster bankruptcy only a *preliminary* injunction was in place. The process of turning the injunction into a permanent and final judgment was complex and lengthy, with substantive legal issues still outstanding, including the important question of whether the labels in fact owned the recordings in issue. At one point Judge Patel recounted the "intriguing" history of the work for hire amendment, and concluded that "Napster has raised serious questions as to the validity of plaintiffs' claims of ownership as authors."[31] Napster also maintained other defenses, including the allegation that the labels had "misused" their copyrights by colluding in an effort to control and monopolize the market for digital music. In one of the more bizarre twists in the saga, Bertelsmann, the German media conglomerate and then-parent of major label BMG, invested a total of $85

---

28. A&M Records, Inc. v. Napster, Inc., 62 U.S.P.Q.2d 1221 (9th Cir. 2002).
29. Knopper, *supra* note 6, at 149.
30. David Downs, *Napster Laid to Rest . . . Inside Rhapsody*, Billboard.biz, Dec. 1, 2011.
31. *In re* Napster Copyright Litig., 191 F. Supp. 2d 1087 (N.D. Cal. 2002).

million in Napster in the form of convertible loans. After Napster went bankrupt, various labels sought damages against the still-solvent investors, including both Bertelsmann and Hummer Winblad. Thus, the waning days of the litigation pitted major labels against one another in an effort to recoup the exorbitant costs incurred in shutting down the Napster "monster."[32] But the file-sharing fights were just beginning.

Napster was not alone as a file-sharing pioneer; the clones had been multiplying and morphing into different configurations. Scournet.com, a multimedia search engine, was incubated at UCLA, and received an investment from former Disney executive Michael Ovitz in 1999. Nevertheless, its decision to add a file-sharing system in 2000 brought the wrath of more than thirty record labels, music publishers, and movie studios. The suit was lodged in July 2000, and by December Scournet.com's assets had been sold in bankruptcy.[33] Similarly, the Aimster service emerged in August 2000, and by the following April had over 4 million registered users.[34]

The next month forty media companies sued Aimster mastermind Johnny Deep and his far-flung corporate entities in a series of suits that were consolidated in the Chicago courtroom of Marvin Aspen of the Northern District of Illinois. The case followed the same pattern as Napster. On September 4, 2002, the court issued a broad preliminary injunction against the service, which was appealed to and affirmed by the Seventh Circuit on June 30, 2003, Circuit Judge Richard Posner writing for the court. In a chilling portent of what was soon to come for tens of thousands of individual file sharers, Judge Posner set the stage by noting that teenagers and young adults swapping music files "are ignorant or more commonly disdainful of copyright and in any event discount the likelihood of being sued" themselves. "Recognizing the impracticability or futility" of suing individual infringers, "the law allows a copyright holder to sue a contributor to the infringement instead."[35] Judge Posner has written extensively on economic analysis as a basis for judicial decision making, so it was not surprising that Aimster's product development costs were factored into his analysis. Aimster could not escape contributory liability, because it had not shown that the system was actually being used for any lawful purpose, or that it would have been "disproportionately costly" to design the system in a way that eliminated or reduced infringing uses. Johnny Deep declared bankruptcy and was unable to make good on his vow to take the file-sharing issue to the Supreme Court. Another of Napster's progeny would soon make the trip.

---

32. *In re* Napster Copyright Litig., 377 F.Supp. 2d 796 (N.D. Cal. 2005); *see also In re* Napster Copyright Litig., 80 U.S.P.Q.2d 1726 (N.D. Cal. 2006).

33. FISHER, *supra* note 2, at 112–14.

34. *Id.*

35. *In re* Aimster Copyright Litig., 67 U.S.P.Q.2d 1233 (N.D. Ill. 2003), aff'd 334 F.3d 643 (7th Cir. 2003).

43. . . . and Share Alike

The developers of the initial file-sharing services were held legally accountable due to the degree of control the systems exercised over individual users. In a word, they were "centralized"—all traffic passed through server farms operated by the services. The next generation of P2P was "decentralized," making the file sharing more remote from the system provider, and therefore even harder for rights holders to corral into the framework of copyright. Bay area computer programmer Justin Frankel was friendly with Shawn Fanning, and the two were aware of their mutual efforts in developing file-sharing software. In the spring of 2000, Frankel created a new program he called Gnutella, and posted it to the Web site of his employer's parent company, AOL. To users, Gnutella worked in much the same way as Napster, but there was a critical difference behind the screen: Gnutella did not operate from a central server; each user, or "node," functioned as its own.

AOL removed the Gnutella program almost immediately, dismissing it as an "unauthorized freelance project." But the proverbial (Trojan) horse had left the barn. Users around the world had already downloaded the software and were using it to develop their own systems, which soon emerged with cryptic names like LimeWire and BearShare.[36] In late 2000 another decentralized protocol called Fast-Track appeared, this time from KaZaA, a Dutch company. KaZaA offered users free access to its network, and later allowed access to two other companies, Stream-Cast Networks (the Morpheus service) and Grokster, respectively. Whereas Gnutella was an open source software project, KaZaA was proprietary, and its "licensees" were identifiable entities that were soon sued by a group of record labels, music publishers, and film studios for contributory and vicarious copyright infringement. As Terry Fisher has explained, the litigation was "jurisdictionally complicated" by the fact that KaZaA and Grokster were not U.S. companies, and indeed the Dutch Supreme Court refused to shutter KaZaA in a December 2002 ruling.[37] Eventually, in what became know as the "Grokster" case, Grokster and StreamCast were sued in the Central District of California courtroom of Judge Stephen Wilson. On April 25, 2003, Judge Wilson stunned the industry by ruling that neither service infringed.[38] Both were used for a variety of noninfringing purposes and, equally important, the decentralized structure of the networks meant that, unlike Napster, Aimster and others, they had little control over individual users' behavior. In the court's words, the plaintiffs refused to see the "seminal distinction" between

---

36. KNOPPER, *supra* note 6, at 148–49; FISHER, *supra* note 2, at 120–28.
37. FISHER, *supra* note 2, at 122.
38. Metro-Goldwyn-Mayer Studios v. Grokster, Ltd., 259 F. Supp. 2d 1029 (C.D. Cal. 2003).

Grokster/Streamcast and Napster: "Neither Grokster nor StreamCast provides the 'site and facilities' for direct infringement. Neither . . . facilitates the exchange of files between users the way Napster did. Users connect to the respective networks, select which files to share, send and receive searches, and download files, all with no material involvement of Defendants. If either Defendant closed their doors and deactivated all computers within their control, users of their products could continue sharing files with little or no interruption."

The RIAA looked to the Ninth Circuit Court of Appeals for relief, where Judge Beezer had issued the industry-friendly opinion in *Napster*. But on this occasion both the judge and the result were different. Appellate arguments were heard on February 3, 2004, and on August 19, Circuit Judge Sidney Runyan Thomas delivered the affirming opinion of the court. Judge Thomas lived up to his reputation for practical yet sometimes literary opinions, placing file sharing in the historical context of disruptive music industry technologies. "From the advent of the player piano," he wrote, "every new means of reproducing sound has struck a dissonant chord with musical copyright owners, often resulting in federal litigation. This appeal is the latest reprise of that recurring conflict."[39] From there he dove headlong into the technical particulars of file sharing, emphasizing the way Grokster was different—decentralization. Under the precedent set (by the Ninth Circuit itself) in *Napster*, Grokster could not be a contributory infringer unless it had "reasonable knowledge of specific infringement" on its system. The decentralized structure prevented such knowledge, insulating the services from liability. Judge Thomas returned to the historical context with the closing observation that "we live in a quicksilver technological environment with courts ill-suited to fix the flow of internet innovation. The introduction of new technology is always disruptive to old markets, and particularly to those copyright owners whose works are sold through well-established distribution mechanisms. Yet, history has shown that time and market forces often provide equilibrium in balancing interests, whether the new technology be a player piano, a copier, a tape recorder, a video reorder, a personal computer, a karaoke machine, or an MP3 player. Thus, it is prudent for courts to exercise caution before restructuring liability theories for the purpose of addressing specific market abuses, despite their apparent present magnitude." Judge Thomas' parting thoughts sent the case on its way to the Supreme Court, and his words had an eerie consistency with those of Justice Day nearly a hundred years before, when his opinion for the high court in *White-Smith v. Apollo* declared that piano rolls were not "copies" of sheet music. An astounding 1 million piano rolls were being produced each year, making the legal question of "very considerable importance, involving large property interests, and closely touching the rights of composers and music publishers."[40] Nevertheless, piano rolls were "not copies

---

39. Metro-Goldwyn-Mayer Studios v. Grokster, Ltd., 72 U.S.P.Q.2d 1244 (9th Cir. 2004).
40. *See* Chapter 12.

within the meaning of the copyright act." Was it possible that the Supreme Court would allow file sharing to go unchecked?

File sharing, seemingly destined for the Supreme Court from the beginning, had its day there on March 29, 2005, when the *Grokster* case was argued before a packed courtroom audience. On June 27, Justice David H. Souter delivered the opinion for a unanimous court, reversing the Ninth Circuit's decision. "We hold that one who distributes a device with the object of promoting its use to infringe copyright, as shown by clear expression or other affirmative steps taken to foster infringement, is liable for the resulting acts of infringement by third parties."[41]

The pithy holding seemed unconnected to the lower courts' opinions, which had turned on the fact that the systems' structures prevented defendants from having knowledge of specific instances of infringement. Justice Souter explained why. First, the opinion reviewed the structure and functions of the Grokster and StreamCast systems, noting their astounding popularity: 100 million copies of their software had been downloaded, and billions of files were shared across the networks each month. Since most shared files were conceded to be discrete unlawful acts, the "probable scope of copyright infringement," said the court, was "staggering." The opinion then turned to an issue that had been given short shrift below—the defendants' intentions in developing their business strategies. On that score, the factual record was "replete with evidence that from the moment Grokster and StreamCast began to distribute their free software, each one clearly voiced the objective that recipients use it to download copyrighted works, and each took active steps to encourage infringement." Both companies had aggressively pursued Napster users, StreamCast at one point proposing advertising copy reading: "Napster, Inc. has announced that it will soon begin charging you a fee. That's if the courts don't order it shut down first. What will you do to get around it?"

Continuing, Justice Souter explored the basic constitutional tension built into copyright administration: "The more artistic protection is favored, the more technological innovation may be discouraged." To address this tension, the court looked for guidance in the only recent case in which the Supreme Court had been called on to make a similar judgment, the *Sony* Betamax case, then twenty years old. The decision in *Sony*, said Justice Souter, "barred secondary liability based on presuming or imputing intent to cause infringement solely from the design or distribution of a product capable of substantial lawful use, which the distributor knows is in fact used for infringement." But the Ninth Circuit had interpreted *Sony* to mean that "whenever" a product was capable of substantial lawful use, "the producer can never be held contributorily liable for third parties' infringing use of it; [the Ninth Circuit] read the rule as being this broad, even when an actual purpose to cause infringing use is shown by evidence independent of design and distribution of the product, unless the distributors had 'specific knowledge of

---

41. Metro-Goldwyn-Mayer Studios v. Grokster, Ltd., 545 U.S. 913 (2005).

infringement at a time at which they contributed to the infringement, and failed to act on that information.'" The Ninth Circuit had misapplied the *Sony* precedent, and committed error by finding for Grokster on that basis. Further, the lower courts had erred in dismissing a different theory of secondary liability—the plaintiffs' claim that Grokster and StreamCast had actively "induced" their users to infringe. Where "active steps" are taken "to encourage direct infringement" by others, the inducer can also be liable—the equivalent of "aiding and abetting" criminal conduct. The lower courts had been too preoccupied with system architecture, and in the process overlooked the less technical, subjective question of the defendants' intentions. For this reason as well, the appellate decision was vacated and the case remanded to Judge Wilson in the district court.

Grokster quickly settled in the wake of the Supreme Court's ruling, leaving StreamCast as the only defendant when Judge Wilson's September 27, 2006, opinion completed the dramatic turnabout.[42] The plaintiffs had to show "only" that StreamCast distributed its product with the intent of encouraging infringement, and the evidence on that point was "overwhelming." From the beginning, StreamCast hoped to absorb the users who would be stranded if and when the Napster service went black, and the strategy had worked like a dream: as Napster's troubles deepened, StreamCast's fortunes improved. There was no denying the intent behind the plan—to gain file-sharing customers who were known to be trading copyrighted music files. Judgment was entered for the plaintiffs.

Even Grokster's trip to the Supreme Court and back did not exhaust the file-sharing litigation that dominated the early years of the twenty-first century. Still pending was the RIAA's suit against LimeWire, LLC, another of the decentralized sharing systems born of Gnutella in the summer of 2000. The LimeWire service was developed by Mark Gorton, and well financed through Tower Research Capital, which Gorton also founded. LimeWire forged ahead in the face of the *Grokster* decision, increasing its user base to 50 million in early 2006, absorbing millions of frustrated Grokster and StreamCast customers. The RIAA brought suit in 2006, and on May 11, 2010, Southern District of New York Judge Kimba Wood rendered her opinion that by distributing and maintaining LimeWire, the defendants (who included Mr. Gorton personally) had "intentionally encouraged direct infringement" by LimeWire users. Judgment was entered on the RIAA's claim of "inducement," again consistent with the *Grokster* precedent.[43] A year later, Judge Wood commenced a jury trial to determine damages. By this time, the Big Five RIAA major labels had become the Big Four—Warner, Universal, EMI, and Sony, the latter having bought out its joint venture partner, BMG, in 2008. Since the peak year of 1999, RIAA label sales had been cut nearly in half to under $8 billion, and the major label executives were lined up to blame LimeWire and its predecessors as

---

42. Metro-Goldwyn-Mayer Studios v. Grokster, Ltd., 454 F. Supp. 2d 966 (C.D. Cal. 2006).

43. Arista Records, LLC v. Lime Group, LLC, 2010 WL 1914816 (S.D.N.Y. May 11, 2010).

the leading cause. LimeWire pointed to other factors—increased competition for discretionary dollars and the demise of record store chains among them—but seeing the writing on the wall, LimeWire and Gorton abruptly settled for a reported $105 million, avoiding the possibility of a far greater jury award. Mitch Bainwol, head of the RIAA, hailed the settlement as "another milestone in the continuing evolution of online music to a legitimate marketplace that appropriately rewards creators."

♫ ♫♫ ♫

During the early years of the file-sharing litigation, the Pew Research Center conducted a series of surveys on the habits and attitudes of Internet users who downloaded music, and for rights holders, the results were quite disturbing. Between 2001 and 2003, file sharing rose steadily, and 67 percent of Internet users said they "did not care" whether the music they downloaded was copyrighted.[44] Bearing in mind that individual users were the "direct infringers" in the file-sharing cases, the RIAA embarked on an "educational" campaign critics decry as one of the worst public relations gaffes ever. Beginning in 2003, the RIAA sued more than 30,000 of its own customers for making copyrighted music files available for P2P sharing.[45] Locating individuals to sue was no easy task, but using a special section of the DMCA, the labels forced Internet service providers to reveal the identities of heavy file sharers. It was not a perfect science, and soon horror stories emerged documenting the RIAA's suits against unlikely candidates, from a twelve-year-old girl to elderly, even deceased individuals. The suits were processed in assembly-line fashion, with most defendants settling for a few thousand dollars to avoid further embarrassment and legal fees. But some hard-nosed defendants refused to settle on principle, and eventually two cases reached trial, those involving Joel Tenenbaum, a Boston area graduate student, and Jammie Thomas, a homemaker from small-town Minnesota. Both individuals lost at trial (in fact, Ms. Thomas was retried, and lost, three different times), and were subject to significant jury damage awards that are still on appeal today.[46] The RIAA announced an end to the campaign in 2008, but maintains that it "served as an essential educational tool," and helped foster a growing digital music market: "Where there was virtually no legal digital market before the lawsuits, today the market exceeds $3 billion annually, and revenue from online platforms will comprise more than 50% of total industry revenues [in 2011]. To boot, there are more than 400 licensed digital services worldwide, compared with fewer than 50 in 2003."[47]

---

44. FISHER, *supra* note 2, at 124.

45. *See generally* http://recordingindustryvspeople.blogspot.com.

46. *See* Sony BMG v. Tenenbaum, 2010 WL 2705499 (D. Mass); Capitol Records, Inc. v. Thomas-Rasset, 799 F. Supp. 2d 999 (D. Minn. 2011).

47. Liz Kennedy, RIAA Director of Communications, Letter to the Editor, *RIAA Largely Succeeds in Goal of Bringing Piracy under Control*, TENNESSEAN, Dec. 1, 2011.

The efficacy of litigation tactics can be debated in any context, but there are always two sides to tell. As Terry Fisher reminds us, "[t]here are no villains in this story. In seeking to protect their companies' sources of revenue . . . [technology resisters are] merely doing their jobs."[48] In the music industry in particular, rights holders' track record in court is nearly spotless. With the exception of the Supreme Court's *White-Smith* decision in 1908 (overturned by Congress the following year), it is hard to find a major legal battle in which established industry interests have not ultimately prevailed. Music copyrights are powerful bundles of rights, confirmed time and again since their first recognition in 1831. And yet the inherent tension in copyright administration does not create a zero-sum game: When rights are enforced, innovation suffers, but technology remains a powerful force, by its nature pushing the boundaries of what is "legal." Ultimately, as Judge Thomas recently reminded us, "history has shown that time and market forces often provide equilibrium in balancing interests," regardless of the form new technology takes. Despite "defeats" in court, new technologies have long since pushed the digital music genie out of its bottle, and there is no turning back. For their part, music rights holders have consistently proven themselves "right" in court, but nevertheless, market forces have cut their revenues in half in the last decade, causing upheaval and significant ongoing restructuring. No informed observer would say the major labels (now down to the Big Three) have the luxury of time in bringing their businesses into the digital age.

Opportunities are revealed in times of change, and in the legal chaos created by digital music technology, Steve Jobs and Apple Computer struck gold. Apple debuted its iTunes music store on April 28, 2003, selling fully licensed, single-track downloads for 99 cents. Conveniently, the downloads were formatted for use on the iPod portable music player, introduced in 2001. The store served its 16 billionth song in late 2011, and is now the largest music retailer in the country, in any format. For all its groundbreaking success, however, the iTunes store remains tied to the "old" model of buying and "owning" music. The newer model, born of the file-sharing phenomenon, is the concept of "renting" music: paying to "access" a library of recordings from a computer, phone, or other personal portable device. At age ten, Rhapsody is the grandfather of music streaming services, but there are many others, including Pandora, an Internet radio platform that went public in 2011, and the newest entry to gain prominence, Spotify, founded by twenty-eight-year-old entrepreneur Daniel Elk. These advertising and subscription-supported services offer differing degrees of customization and interactivity, but in broad terms they provide the same thing—"music as a service" instead of a "product." In their contrast with iTunes, they open a window into the myriad issues confronting music and copyright in the twenty-first century, as we will explore in our final chapters.

---

48. Fisher, *supra* note 2, at 133.

PART VII

Into the Cloud

In an age of copyright convergence, "used" digital
music reseller, ReDigi, is the latest advance in
music technology to be tested in court.

44. Convergence

Having come this far through the history of music and copyright, one would think we could explain the present. It is difficult. We live in a world where, in terms of music, the lines between physical and *meta*physical have blurred, where traditional definitions forming the bedrock principles of copyright are at risk of collapsing into themselves. Professor Nimmer calls this "convergence"—the state in which distinctions between types of copyrighted works begin to disappear, and in addition, the individual rights through which copyrights are exploited move toward "uniform wholeness."[1] As Nimmer points out, Congress grappled with this phenomenon when considering the DPRA back in 1995, which granted a limited "digital" performance right in sound recordings, after decades of effort by labels and artists. The Clinton administration produced a White Paper on these issues, analyzing the breakdown of copyright categories in the digital environment.[2] It was unclear at the time, for example, whether a digital "transmission," which implicates the *performance* right, might also involve a *distribution*, another exclusive right in the copyright owner's bundle. Congress did not clarify this conundrum in passing the DPRA, and its remains an example of the amorphous, metaphysical issues faced by creators, copyright owners, technologists, and, of course, courts in the twenty-first century.

One new business riding the rails of convergence is the Boston area start-up, ReDigi, Inc., which launched a "digital music resale" service in October 2011, the digital equivalent of a used record store. The ReDigi Web site proclaims itself "The Legal Alternative," explaining at length how its model complies with the first sale doctrine, codified in Section 109 of the Copyright Act. As we have seen, the doctrine permits the owner of a "particular copy" of a copyrighted work to resell that copy to another, as long as no additional copies are made in the process. ReDigi says the "genius" of its service is the ability "to facilitate the transfer of a digital music file from one user to another without copying or file sharing," thus creating a legitimate secondary market for "used" digital music. ReDigi earns a brokerage fee between 5 and 15 percent on files transferred for around 79 cents each.

The RIAA's cease-and-desist letter arrived within a few weeks of ReDigi's launch, accusing the company of "willful copyright infringement," asserting that the first sale doctrine does not permit the owner to "make another copy, sell the second copy and destroy the original." A federal lawsuit followed in January 2012,

---

1. MELVILLE NIMMER & DAVID NIMMER, NIMMER ON COPYRIGHT § 8.24[A] (2011).

2. Intellectual Property and the National Information Infrastructure: THE REPORT OF THE WORKING GROUP ON INTELLECTUAL PROPERTY RIGHTS (Bruce Lehman, Chair) (Sept. 1995).

alleging that tracks stored in the ReDigi "cloud" during the transfer process are "necessarily" copies. Users do not "sell" their original digital files, according to the complaint—they merely agree to their deletion after the file has been uploaded to the ReDigi cloud. After formally answering the complaint, ReDigi wrote to the court protesting that the claims against it "reflect a profound misunderstanding of how ReDigi works and have no merit." The letter explains in considerable technical detail how the service transfers files without making copies, and suggests that the case can be decided in summary fashion according to undisputable facts. "No copying takes place in the resale process at all," according to the letter, which adds however, that any copying that does take place is "obvious" fair use. The letter also points out that the current statute defines "copies" as "material objects," arguing that a "CD which contains digital files would be a 'material object' but the digital files themselves are not." Thus, the argument goes, ReDigi cannot infringe the distribution right, which applies only to "copies."

In presenting a modern twist on "first sale" doctrine, the ReDigi suit harkens back to *White-Smith v. Apollo* a century before, when the Supreme Court held that under the then-current statute, a piano roll was not an unlawful "copy" of a musical composition.[3] It took an act of Congress to overturn the ruling, putting the mechanical license in place. An adverse ruling in the ReDigi matter would certainly send rights holders to Congress once again, seeking legislation exempting digital music files from the first sale doctrine.[4] In the meantime, another new entrant is making similar waves. In January 2012, Madison, Wisconsin–based Murfie announced a funding round of $1.4 million to support its growing "used music" marketplace. Murfie's Web site promotes a service where users can "buy and sell music CDs, store your physical discs in our warehouse, and access rips and downloads via your online account." The distinguishing feature is that, as opposed to ReDigi, Murfie takes physical possession of a customer's CD collection, then rips the tracks into digital files and, on request, provides them back to the customer/ owner in the form of downloads. Stored CDs can be sold or traded to other Murfie users, who "take ownership of the physical disc," even though it stays "safe and sound" in the Murfie warehouse. The new owner can order downloads of the same tracks, but the seller is contractually required to delete them after the sale. Is Murfie making, distributing, or performing improper "copies"? The details will emerge soon enough, but the answers remain unclear.

♫♫ ♫♫ ♫♫

Another vexing question of convergence is presented in the "download as performance" debate. Can the distribution of a digital music file also be considered a

---

3. *See* Chapter 12.

4. As explored in Chapter 36, there is precedent for such a move in the Record Rental Amendment of 1984, which responded to the rise of record rental stores by modifying the first sale doctrine to prohibit the "rental, lease or lending" of phonorecords.

performance? The question was answered in the negative in 2007, in the context of a rate proceeding in which AOL, Yahoo!, and RealNetworks (owner of the Rhapsody music service) applied for a license to publicly perform the musical works in ASCAP's repertoire through their respective Internet services.[5] The parties were unable to agree on a fee, so the matter wound up before Judge William C. Conner in the Southern District of New York. Judge Conner was appointed to the federal bench in 1973, based on the perceived need for a judge with a background in intellectual property. During his thirty-five years on the bench he became known as the "ASCAP Judge" for his role in administering the terms of the ASCAP consent decree first imposed in 1941.[6]

The online services were not typical broadcasters: they provided hybrid services offering both Internet music "streams," as well as permanent song downloads for purchase. There was no question that ASCAP's constituent music publishers were entitled to performance fees when songs were streamed. And it was equally clear that paid downloads invoked a mechanical license, for which royalties were administered by a different collective, the Harry Fox Agency, but paid out to the same music publishers. Nevertheless, the unsettled issue emerged when ASCAP took the position that the distribution of a download also invoked the performance right, such that two rights (and royalty streams) were triggered whenever a download took place. The service providers called it "double-dipping," while publishers insisted it was the plain rule of law, so they sought a ruling on the specific question of whether a download constituted a "public performance" within the meaning of the Copyright Act. Judge Conner answered no, reasoning that a "performance" required "contemporaneous perceptibility," which was absent in the case of a pure download. ASCAP presented detailed arguments as to how the definitions and legislative histories of words like "transmit," "publicly," "render," and "perform" combined to create a dual distribution/performance right in downloads. The opinion references the Register of Copyrights' views on the subject, and those expressed in the Clinton administration's 1995 White Paper, but in the end Judge Conner seems to have relied on his own intuition in concluding that "the downloading of a music file is more accurately characterized as a method of *reproducing* that file," not performing it. But he hedged the bet, leaving the door open to future debates, with the footnoted comment that that he did "not mean to foreclose the possibility . . . that a transmission might, under certain circumstances, constitute both a stream *and* a download, each of which implicates a different right of the copyright holder." On September 28, 2010, the Second Circuit affirmed the holding, also repeating Judge Conner's cautionary footnote virtually word for word.[7]

Judge Conner continued to grapple with similar questions, addressing performance issues relating to "ringtone" and "ringback tone" previews, and in and setting

---

5. United States v. ASCAP, 485 F. Supp. 2d 438 (S.D.N.Y. 2007).

6. *See* Chapter 16.

7. United States v. ASCAP, 627 F.3d 64 (2d Cir. 2010).

ASCAP fees for performances through cell phones and other handheld devices, and on the YouTube video service, the latter less than two months before his passing at the age of eighty-nine in July 2009.[8] In October, Judge Denise Cote stepped into the role of rate court judge, adopting Judge Conner's prior reasoning in ruling that Verizon Wireless did not require a public performance license to sell ringtones to cell phone customers.[9] 2009 was indeed a year of convergence. In March, the Harry Fox Agency, a *mechanical* licensing agency, began collecting its first-ever statutory royalties for "limited downloads" and "on-demand streams"—the kind of digital music hybrids imagined in Judge Conner's footnote two years before.[10] And in August, the Second Circuit Court of Appeals rendered its opinion in *Arista Records, LLC v. Launch Media, Inc.*, weighing in on another perplexing issue, the definition of "interactive."[11]

As we have seen, the DPRA was enacted in 1995, giving sound recording owners a limited public performance right with respect to digital transmissions, implemented by the Section 114 statutory license. But a Section 114 license could be extended only to "noninteractive" services, where programming was controlled by the broadcaster. Services giving listeners discretion in designing their own playlists were deemed "interactive," unable to take advantage of the compulsory license. As webcasting services became more sophisticated in allowing listener input, the grey area of interactivity loomed large, and in 2001, a group of major labels sued Launch Media, alleging that its LAUNCHcast service crossed the line. After a jury declared the service noninteractive in 2007, the labels appealed, making the Second Circuit the first federal appellate court to determine "whether a webcasting service that provides users with individualized internet radio stations—the content of which can be affected by users' ratings of songs, artists, and albums—is an interactive service" within the meaning of Section 114.[12] Circuit Judge Richard C. Wesley wrote for the court in an opinion rendered August 21, 2009, confirming the jury's determination that the service was noninteractive. Reaching this conclusion required a Kafkaesque adventure into the convergence vortex.

The operative statutory language asked whether LAUNCHcast's Internet radio programs were "specially created" for the user, which the labels argued was a

---

8. *In re* Application of AT&T Wireless, 599 F. Supp. 2d 415 (S.D.N.Y. 2009); *In re* Application of AT&T Wireless, 607 F. Supp. 2d 562 (S.D.N.Y. 2009); *In re* Application of YouTube, LLC, 616 F. Supp. 2d 447 (S.D.N.Y. 2009).

9. *In re* Application of Cellco Partnership d/b/a Verizon Wireless, 663 F. Supp. 2d 363 (S.D.N.Y. 2009).

10. HFA has itself become a hybrid agency, collecting traditional mechanical royalties, as well as royalties based in part on "per play" allocations generated by online performances. *See* HFA Release, Oct. 22, 2008, "Royalty Rates for the Use of Musical Works in Services Providing Interactive Streaming and Limited Downloads."

11. Arista Records, LLC v. Launch Media, Inc., 578 F.3d 148 (2d Cir. 2009), *cert denied*, 103 S. Ct. 1290 (2010). Around the same time the suit was brought, Yahoo! had purchased Launch Media in a deal valued at $12 million.

12. Specifically, 17 U.S.C. § 114(j)(7).

simple, bright-line equation: if a service reflected *any* user input, it was "specially created" and therefore interactive. Seeing more subtlety in the issue, the court quoted Justice Oliver Wendell Holmes' observation that "a word is not a crystal, transparent and unchanged, it is the skin of a living thought and may vary greatly in color and content according to the circumstances and time in which it is used." Uncovering the meaning of "specially created" would therefore require an exploration of Congress' treatment of sound recordings, from the 1971 amendment to the limited performance right in 1995, and its modifications in the DMCA in 1998. After tracing this history, Judge Wesley concluded that Congress' overarching intention was to prevent "the diminution in record sales through outright piracy of music or new media that offered listeners the ability to select music in such a way that they would forego purchasing records." From there, he launched into the more daunting task of examining the "complex nature of the service LAUNCHcast provided." The explanation exceeded 2,000 words, delving into the minutiae of how user preferences and ratings combined with algorithmic calculations to create a 10,000-song "hashtable," then narrowed to a playlist of 50 by further criteria, including a final calculation confirming that "if a user rates five songs and ten others are implicitly rated—making a total of fifteen songs—then no more than one explicitly rated song can be selected $(3 \times (5 / [5 + 10]) = 3 \times \frac{1}{3} = 1$." "It is hard to think of a more complicated way to 'select songs'," the court observed, "but this is the nature of webcast music broadcasting in the digital age."

The exhausting analysis still was not complete. Given Congress' intention to avoid cannibalizing music sales, Judge Wesley pondered how "predictable" LAUNCHcast programming really was, finally concluding that there was no interactivity "because the webcasting service does not provide sufficient control to users such that playlists are so predictable that users will choose to listen to the webcast in lieu of purchasing music, thereby—in the aggregate—diminishing record sales." The case turned on language not found in the statute at all—the "predictability" of a user's experience. In this way, the question of interactivity was reduced to the practical (but still metaphysical) determination of when a music *service* could "replace" the purchase of a music *product*. But with each webcasting service operating a unique set of algorithmic calculations to create its own customized playlists, the decade-long litigation yielded only a thin precedent, limited to the specific LAUNCHcast music streams broadcast into the digital ether ending in 2001.[13]

---

13. The suit applied to digital broadcasts occurring between 1999 and 2001.

45. Performance under Pressure

The download-as-performance and interactivity debates suggest that "performance" may be the ultimate "converged" right for music copyright owners. If music rights are indeed collapsing into one, the logical endpoint—that place where we have anytime access to on-demand music—will be a universe of individualized, personal performances. It is not surprising, then, that in recent years significant resources have been devoted to proceedings involving the royalty rates paid in connection with sound recording public performance, as well the possible expansion of performance rights for recording owners and artists.

The Clinton administration's 1995 White Paper contained the first mention of a remote, heavenly body, beaming recorded music on demand. Presciently, the paper perceived that "[t]transmissions of sound recordings will certainly supplement and may eventually replace the current forms of distribution . . . In the very near future, consumers will be able to receive digital transmissions of sound recordings on demand—for performance in the home or downloading—from the so-called 'celestial jukebox.'" "The legal nature of such transmissions—whether they are performances or distributions—has been widely debated . . . However, many of these transmissions will clearly constitute exercise of the public performance right—a right which the Copyright Act fails to grant to copyright owners of sound recordings."[14]

Consistent with this vision, the White Paper recommended granting a full and unfettered performance right in sound recordings, equivalent to that enjoyed by publishers since 1897. The White Paper weighed in on the age-old promotion argument as well, noting that while broadcasting undoubtedly provided "free advertising" in some cases, it was "not a valid policy argument against providing sound recordings copyright owners with the full panoply of exclusive rights other copyright owners enjoy." "The copyright owners of sound recordings should be able to decide for themselves, as do all other copyright owners, if 'free advertising' is sufficient compensation for the use of their works. If the [broadcasters'] arguments regarding the benefit copyright owners derive from the public performance of their sound recordings are correct, [broadcasters] should be able to negotiate a very low rate for a license to do so." "There is no just reason to afford a lower level of protection to one class of creative artists," the paper concluded. "Further, *any* special limitations on this right weakens our position internationally. The digital communications revolution—the creation of advanced information infrastructures— is erasing the distinctions among different categories of protected works and the uses made of them."

---

14. The Report of the Working Group on Intellectual Property Rights, *supra* note 2, at 221–25.

Despite these recommendations the sound recording performance right extended in the DPRA in 1995 was limited to "digital audio transmissions."[15] Moreover, the statutory Section 114 license was made compulsory, meaning that if private negotiations failed, the royalty *rate* would be determined in public administrative proceedings before the Copyright Royalty Board (CRB). As a result, the question of extending the sound recording performance right to cover traditional terrestrial radio broadcasting has since simmered and occasionally boiled over. Further, with billions in royalty dollars at stake, the debates have brought the biggest lobbying guns to the battlefield, suggesting again that the future of music will be closely aligned with the exclusive right of public performance.

A decade later, labels, artists, and broadcasters were deeply embroiled in the battles anticipated in 1995, brought on by the realities of convergence. In July 2004, Copyright Office General Counsel David O. Carson appeared before a House subcommittee, commenting on the workings of the Section 114 license and the continued confusion over the concept of "interactivity"; he recommended that Congress "strike the proper balance in favor of a full performance right" for sound recordings.[16] The debate spilled over into the CRB rate proceeding initiated in early 2005, in which Section 114 royalty rates were established for the period 2006–2010. Millions in legal and expert fees and resources were devoted to the extensive administrative litigation process, involving testimony from dozens of witnesses presented by SoundExchange on behalf of labels and recording artists, on one hand, and through the Digital Media Association (DiMA) on behalf of the digital broadcast community.[17]

Nearly two years later, on March 2, 2007, the CRB issued a lengthy decision, essentially adopting the rate structure proposed by the labels, causing an immediate uproar from digital broadcasters.[18] As the July 15 implementation date for the new rates approached, the legal, lobbying, and public relations efforts went into full swing. Arguing that the new rates would put many of them out of business, webcasters asked the U.S. Court of Appeals for the District of Columbia Circuit to stay implementation pending their appeal, which was denied on July 11. A new grassroots organization, SaveNetRadio, was formed to advance small webcaster interests, which SoundExchange quickly accused of operating as a front for large webcasters trying to dodge increased rates. For their part, webcasters portrayed SoundExchange's efforts as a major label money grab—an attempt to revive a dying business model through exorbitant fee increases at the expense of technological developments and consumer interests.

---

15. *See* NIMMER & NIMMER, *supra* note 1, § 8.24[A], at 8–369.

16. Statement of David O. Carson, General Counsel, U.S. Copyright Office, Before the Subcommittee on Courts, the Internet and Intellectual Property of the House Committee on the Judiciary, 108th Congress, 2d Session, July 15, 2004.

17. *In re* Digital Performance Right in Sound Recordings and Ephemeral Recordings, Docket No. 2005–1, CRB DTRA (Mar. 2, 2007).

18. *Id.*

The activity continued at a fever pitch in the ensuing months, with congressional hearings, flurries of news releases, an organized "day of silence" for Internet radio, and the introduction of the Internet Radio Equality Act (IREA), designed to void the CRB rate decision. Under pressure from Congress, SoundExchange made a limited proposal to cap certain small webcaster fees while maintaining that commercial webcasters like Yahoo! and AOL should begin paying increased rates. DiMA accepted the offer, noting that the "agreement marks an important first step in the Internet radio royalty negotiation process." In the meantime, IREA was introduced in the Senate, leading to SoundExchange's offer to keep smaller webcasters' existing rates in place through 2010. A number of smaller webcasters embraced the offer, but many complained that it did not address the major issues in the royalty debate, would not allow them to properly grow their businesses, and simply amounted to SoundExchange "yet again pretending to offer us a deal so that Congress can see them as benevolent, while they're really just cornering the internet radio market to increase airplay for the major music labels."

In the wake of the continuing *rate* debate, the closely related issue of the *scope* of the performance right crept once again to the fore. In early 2006, Sound-Exchange celebrated a decade of digital performance rights by asserting that "the next step is to secure a full performance right"—to broaden the sound recording performance right to include payment for use by "radio and television stations, stadiums, and other commercial establishments that use music," creating true parity with music publishers and songwriters.[19] Positioning the issue as a matter of artist rights (as opposed to a music label income stream), SoundExchange Executive Director John Simson said, "We are determined not only to serve [recording artists], but to obtain for them what should rightfully be theirs. It is easy to see that songwriters, with a full performance right, can retire with royalties as their annuity, while most performers, without this right, must tour until they die." The dramatic words were not lost on the National Association of Broadcasters, whose president and CEO, David K. Rehr, spoke to the issue in his keynote address to the group's annual convention in April 2007. Mincing no words, Mr. Rehr returned, predictably, to the NAB's familiar refrain: Free music for free promotion. "Imagine the brazen greed it takes for the record companies to expect *us* to pay them for promoting *their* artists' music," he said. "It would make much more sense for us to charge *them* for our promotional efforts. We will advocate that Congress oppose this levy on the market. If successful, it would be a government imposed performance tax. And we will fight it with everything we have."[20] The NAB launched an equally blunt print advertising campaign, claiming that "[f]or decades, radio has been promoting new music free of charge, contributing to record sales and the

---

19. Press Release, SoundExchange, Tenth Anniversary Celebration, (Feb. 1, 2006) (on file with author).
20. Press Release, NAB, Rehr Delivers Opening Keynote Address at NAB 2007 (Apr. 16, 2007) (on file with author).

growth of new stars and new genres of music. But the international record label conglomerates have a problem—they haven't adapted to the digital age. Now they are asking Congress to tax local radio stations to subsidize their failing business model—to the tune of billions of dollars."[21] SoundExchange countered by helping establish the musicFIRST Coalition in June 2007. Using an acronym for "Fairness in Radio Starting Today," the organization positioned itself as a coalition of recording artists and recording industry organizations working together for broader rights, and in recent years has assumed the role of leading advocate for a full performance right.[22]

The "royalty rate" and "full performance right" debates coalesced further in 2007. In testimony before the House Subcommittee on Intellectual Property on July 31, recording artists Judy Collins and Sam Moore represented musicians' rights, while the NAB argued against the imposition of further royalties. In keeping with the Copyright Office's long-standing support for broader performance rights, Register of Copyrights Marybeth Peters noted that "terrestrial broadcasters have long enjoyed the freedom to use the newest record releases without any payment to the artists or the record companies. While in the past, broadcasters' argument that airplay promotes the sale of records may have had validity, such a position is hard to justify today in light of recent technological developments and the alternative sources of music from other music services, and declining record sales. So what is to be done?" Answering that query, she said, "in 1995, Congress accepted the notion that terrestrial over-the-air broadcasts offered no threat to the record industry and actually promoted the sales of records. The actual turn of events since that time, however, casts doubt on this premise . . . I strongly urge Congress to expand the scope of the performance right for sound recordings to cover all analog and digital by broadcasters as a way to enable creators of the sound recordings to adapt to the precipitous decline in revenue due to falling record sales. Such an approach has multiple benefits. It would provide performers and record producers with an ongoing and growing source of revenue, and it would also level the playing field between, on the one hand, digital music services and webcasters who today pay a performance royalty on each digital transmission and, on the other hand, broadcasters who pay nothing for their use of sound recordings when transmitted over the air."[23]

Sensing a shift in momentum, the NAB launched a legislative surprise attack on Halloween, introducing the Local Radio Freedom Act, a draft resolution declaring that "Congress should not impose any new performance fee, tax, royalty,

---

21. NAB print advertisement, "No performance tax on local radio," *see also* Letter from David K. Rehr to U.S. Senators (May 9, 2007), *both available* at www.nab.org.

22. *See* www.musicfirstcoalition.org.

23. Statement of Marybeth Peters, U.S. Register of Copyrights, before the Subcommittee on Courts, the Internet and Intellectual Property, House Committee on the Judiciary, 110th Cong., 1st Sess., July 31, 2007, *available at* http://www.copyright.gov/docs/regstat073107.html.

or other charge relating to the public performance of sound recordings on a local radio station for broadcasting sound recordings over the air, or on any business for such performance of sound recordings."[24] The NAB has made a ritual of introducing the same resolution in each congressional session since.[25]

In November 2007, Senator Patrick Leahy convened a hearing to explore the scope of performance rights in music. His introductory remarks framed the issue as one of "fairness" to musicians, a mantra then taken up in the testimony of recording artist Lyle Lovett, who urged lawmakers to eliminate the "incomprehensible anomaly" in performers' rights by expanding the sound recording public performance right to encompass broadcast radio. Performer Alice Peacock followed, calling the NAB's promotion argument "silly," and suggesting that "the concept of basic fairness" required payment of artists' royalties by traditional radio. On December 18, Representative Howard Berman introduced the Performance Rights Act of 2007 to the House Judiciary Committee, Subcommittee on Courts, the Internet, and Intellectual Property, and Senator Leahy introduced the Senate version the same day. With these measures, the recorded music industry officially called for an end to the broadcast radio exemption, seeking to apply the Section 114 license to traditional analog broadcasting.[26]

The year 2007 ended as it began, with emotionally charged rhetoric from both sides of the performance right debate. The NAB reacted to the proposed legislation with a seasonal reference, saying, "After decades of Ebenezer-Scrooge-like exploitation of countless artists, RIAA and the foreign-owned record labels are singing a new holiday jingle to offset their failing business model. NAB will aggressively oppose this brazen attempt to force America's hometown radio stations to subsidize companies that have profited enormously through the free promotion provided by radio airplay." In turn, the musicFIRST Coalition delivered a "holiday poem" to its "friends on Capitol Hill wishing them a happy holiday season." Penned to the cadence of "'Twas the Night before Christmas," the poem began: "'Twas the night before recess in the Senate and House / As our leaders worked hard to correct a great louse / A fair performance right danced in their mind / They could no longer leave the artists behind. . . ."

By the spring of 2008, the halls of Congress were again alive with the sound of music, with impromptu performances leading to further hearings in June. Recording artist Nancy Sinatra, known for her recordings of "These Boots Are Made for Walking," "Somethin' Stupid," and others, invoked the name of her famous father (and his own late-1980s' efforts to bring about the performance right) in speaking on behalf of thousands of "middle class" recording artists who, as a "matter of prin-

---

24. H. Con. Res. 244, 110th Cong. (2007).

25. *See* H. Con. Res. 21 and S. Con. Res. 7: Supporting the Local Radio Freedom Act, 112th Cong., 1st Sess. (2011).

26. H.R. 4789; S. 2500 110th Cong. (2007).

ciple or decency, . . . or simple fairness," should earn royalties from the broadcast-ing generated by their recorded art. Sinatra noted the Register of Copyrights' consistent support for full performance rights, a position joined by the outgoing Bush administration through a letter of support from the General Counsel of the Department of Commerce. The subcommittee approved the Performance Rights Act on June 26, moving it to the full committee for further action.

California Senator Dianne Feinstein took up the mantle in July 2008, chairing a hearing on "Music and Radio in the 21st Century." Reflecting on a changing in-dustry, Senator Feinstein noted that "[n]ew radio services are allowing users to do more than simply listen to music. What was once a passive listening experience has turned into a forum where users can record, manipulate, collect and create person-alized music libraries. As the modes of distribution change and the technologies change, so must our laws change." The hearing turned into a wide-ranging referen-dum on the state of the music industry, with record labels and digital broadcasters restating their opposing positions on the correct standards for setting royalties. Amidst the rancor, the testimony of songwriter and recording artist Matt Nathan-son emerged as a voice of moderation. Nathanson reflected on an Internet-enabled world that has "leveled the playing field for all artists," making "self-promotion" possible and allowing artists to achieve a level of independent success not previ-ously possible through a "bottlenecked" major label system. Internet radio, he said, "is a crucial part of this new business." In telling, direct, and sincere testimony, Nathanson acknowledged both the financial and promotional benefits of Internet radio, seeking a balance that will allow both to continue: "In contrast to some who try to maximize every revenue opportunity, it's more important to me, and I think to most artists at my level, to strike the right balance between promotional oppor-tunities and revenue opportunities. Royalties should be fair, but not so high that Internet radio has to struggle to stay alive and to grow." "We are entering a new phase of the way music is distributed and heard," he concluded, "and we need to work together to make it happen. The law is working from this fearful place of crushing technologies that have galloped ahead. You just can't do that."[27]

The debates continued into 2009, when the Performance Rights Act was rein-troduced in the 111th Congress.[28] On March 10, the House Judiciary Committee convened a three-and-a-half hour hearing, with committee members suggesting that the time had come for the legislation, and that the debate should turn to the "value" of a full performance right and the timing of its introduction. Echoing the position of generations of performing artists before him, Billy Corgan of Smashing Pumpkins fame testified as to the "longtime inequity" of the current, "outmoded"

---

27. Live testimony of Matt Nathanson before S. Comm. on the Judiciary, hearing on "Music and Radio in the 21st Century: Assuring Fair Rates and Rules Across Platforms" (July 29, 2008). Live and written testimony *available at* http://judiciary.senate.gov.

28. H.R. 848 and S. 379, 111th Cong., 1st Sess. (2009).

law, again calling it an "issue of fundamental fairness."[29] NAB witnesses countered that broadcast radio was in a decline, and that new royalties could put smaller market stations out of business. The legislation gathered enough momentum for congressional leaders to demand the presence of representatives with "decision-making authority" at a November 17 Capitol Hill session to hammer out the final text of a bill. The groups dutifully reported, but the talks fizzled.[30] The issue simmered until the spring of 2010, when the NAB blanketed the country with a sixty-second radio advertisement describing the performance royalty as a "tax" that would "bankrupt local radio stations" by forcing payments to "giant record companies, most of which are foreign owned." In response, the Music-FIRST Coalition launched a campaign of its own, with print ads depicting the NAB as a pig with an antenna for a tail and its head buried in a pail labeled "Bailout Funds." A local radio spot ran in Washington, D.C., and the group introduced a short-lived Web site, piggyradio.com.

With this name-calling, the debate reached a new low point, remote from any principled debate as to the constitutional mandate of promoting the arts. It was raw, sausage-making democracy in action, but not unprecedented in the history of music copyright. Indeed, the charges were reminiscent of the allegations that music publishers had combined with the Aeolian Company to form a "complete monopolistic octopus" one hundred years before, and the NAB's likening ASCAP to a rampaging Hitler in 1939.[31]

The debate regained a more rational footing on April 1, 2010, when Department of Commerce General Counsel Cameron Kerry expressed support for the Performance Rights Act in a letter to Senator Leahy, marking the Obama administration's first step toward backing performance right legislation. Suggesting that the legislation made sense as a matter of domestic and international policy, Mr. Cameron said the measure would address a "long-standing omission in U.S. copyright law that may have harmed American performers and record companies. Today, the United States stands alone among industrialized nations in not recognizing a public performance right in sound recordings," he noted. "Most of the other countries are parties to international treaties that require protection for performers and producers of sound recordings. All too often, however, American performers and producers have not benefitted from such protections because of the lack of reciprocal protection under U.S. copyright law. As a result, substantial royalties for the public performance of U.S. sound recordings abroad are either not collected at all or not distributed to American performers and record companies."

---

29. Live testimony of Billy Corgan before House Judiciary Committee Hearing on the Performance Rights Act, (Mar. 10, 2009).

30. Nate Anderson, *Congress Locks Radio Stations, Record Labels into Boardroom*, ARS TECHNICAL, LAW & DISORDER BLOG (Nov. 2, 2009), http://arstechnica.com/tech-policy/news/2009/11/congress-locks-radio-stations-music-labels-into-boardroom.ars.

31. *See* Chapters 12, 24.

The Performance Rights Act lay dormant until August 2010, when there was word of a possible breakthrough. On August 6, the NAB circulated a term sheet to its members, describing a compromise which, in return for yielding on the performance right, would cap royalties at 1 percent of broadcasters' revenue, and notably, require that all mobile phones be equipped with a chip making them capable of receiving FM radio signals. Technology associations quickly voiced their disapproval, calling it "simply wrong for two entrenched industries to resolve their differences by agreeing to burden a third industry—which has no relationship to or other interest in the performance royalty dispute—with a costly, ill-considered, and unnecessary new mandate."[32] The NAB issued a more specific "term sheet" on October 25, 2010, which was quickly rejected as an attempt to rewrite several aspects of the tentative agreement reached earlier in the year.[33] The deal was off.

On February 28, 2011, the NAB reintroduced the Local Radio Freedom Act, the latest incarnation of its anti–performance right resolutions.[34] In March, the Obama administration expressed further support for performance rights, as part of a broader set of recommendations from White House Intellectual Property Enforcement Coordinator Victoria Espinel. But the debates soon took a backseat to Congress's preoccupation with the budget issues that dominated the national political spotlight through the end of the new year. Performance rights remain on the domestic legislative agenda, but there seems little chance for the issue to rise above the rhetoric of the 2012 presidential election campaign. Nevertheless, like the individual questions of convergence, these broader debates center on the increasing value of public performance rights in the digital economy. Indeed, performance royalty income remains on the rise. CISAC, an international confederation of collecting societies across all artistic genres, recently reported that 2010 global royalty collections increased by 5.5 percent, part of a steady climb over the last seven years. Among the categories of collections, "public performance continued to provide the lions' share of revenues," rising by 7.5 percent to €5.5 billion, representing 73 percent of all revenues.[35]

In terms of sound recordings in particular, SoundExchange distributed $292 million to labels and artists in 2011, up an impressive 17 percent from the prior year.[36] But a much larger global revenue pool remains essentially closed to U.S. rights holders. As far back as 2007, the International Federation of the Phonographic Industry estimated that "societies around the world collected a total of

---

32. Anandashankar Mazumdar, *Proposed Performance Rights Compromise Triggers Objections from Phone Makers*, 80 P.T.C.J. 566 (Aug. 2010).

33. "Term Sheet for Performance Rights Agreement," Oct. 25, 2010.

34. H. Con. Res. 21 and S. Con. Res. 7: Supporting the Local Radio Freedom Act, 112th Cong., 1st Sess. (2011).

35. CISAC Press Release, Royalty Collections Climb to New Peak at €7.5 billion (Jan. 30, 2012) (release and full report available at http://www.cisac.org).

36. SoundExchange Press Release, SoundExchange Ends Record-Setting Year with $89.5 Million in Q4 2011 Distributions (Jan. 17, 2012).

$1.5 billion" on behalf of record companies and performers for licensing the use of sound recordings and music videos in broadcasting, public performance, and other collective licensing.[37] Although much of this income is derived from the foreign performance of American recordings, most remains uncollected by U.S. artists, due to the limited "digital only" reciprocal rights extended to foreign artists. In general, we can expect continued pressure on performance rights, exerted by those seeking to increase both the performance pie itself, and their portions of it.

46. Partly Cloudy

The 1995 White Paper anticipated the emergence of what we now call "cloud" services, the next generation of music lockers pioneered by MP3.com and others. The term refers generally to services providing remote storage of digital music (and other media/data), which can then be downloaded or streamed over the Internet to a customer's various devices. Copyright issues arise in the context of how users build their personal libraries, along with the performance and distribution implications of delivering music streams and downloads. The question of whether a particular service is shielded from liability under the DMCA also hangs overhead. In 2011 the cloud space became crowded with entries from heavyweights Google, Amazon, and Apple. As these businesses emerged, so did the war of words as to whether they could proceed without licenses from music labels. Apple launched its iCloud service in late 2011, with licenses from the Big Four. Google Music entered the scene with licenses from all majors except Warner. But after courting the labels for some time, Amazon launched its Cloud Drive service without any licenses, asserting that the service was not substantively different than existing media management applications. Sony said it was "keeping [its] legal options open," but no complaints were filed against these new players, perhaps because test cases were already underway.[38]

Michael Robertson had stayed busy in the years since MP3.com was shut down and sold to Universal. In February 2005, Robertson launched MP3Tunes.com, again selling music in the MP3 format. The service was soon supplemented by providing personal online storage lockers, from which customers could play and download their tracks to any Internet-enabled device. Other features allowed users to load music from third-party servers into their MP3Tunes locker. The functionality was quite similar to the ill-fated MP3.com, but unlike the original service, users

---

37. IFPI, *Spotlight Falls on Performance Rights Income*, 2008 Global Recording Industry in Numbers, at 16; *see also* Katie Allen, *Music Industry Sees Rise in Royalty Payments*, Guardian.co.uk, Oct. 14, 2009, estimating 2008 worldwide royalties of $1.5 billion, *available at* http://www.guardian.co .uk/business/2009/oct/14/music-industry-royalty-payment-revenue.

38. Ethan Smith, *Amazon in Big Push to Clinch Music Deals*, Wall St. J., Mar. 31, 2011.

loaded their own music—the service did not itself copy CDs or other files into a master database of stored music. In 2007 Capitol Records parent EMI sent MP3Tunes a series of "takedown notices" under the DMCA, demanding removal of allegedly infringing music files. MP3Tunes complied by removing the links through which those tracks had been loaded, but did not take the additional step of removing the songs from individual lockers. Unsatisfied, EMI (along with thirteen other labels and music publishers) filed suit in New York. After nearly four years of litigation, both sides asked Judge William H. Pauley for a judgment in their favor, without the necessity of a trial. (Mindful of the legal uncertainties surrounding its own music service, Google offered a "friend-of-court" brief in support of MP3Tunes.)

According to the court's order issued October 25, 2011, the case turned "in large part on whether MP3Tunes is eligible for protection under the safe harbors created by the Digital Millennium Copyright Act."[39] The service was indeed eligible, as it had implemented the necessary procedures to terminate the accounts of repeat infringers, and responded promptly to EMI's takedown notices. Presenting a question of "first impression," EMI argued that the DMCA did not apply to pre-1972 sound recordings, which were still protected under state law principles. But the court held otherwise, on the ground that limiting the DMCA to recordings after 1972 would cause "legal uncertainty and subject otherwise innocent service providers to liability for the acts of third parties." But there was a chink in MP3Tunes' DMCA armor—those songs it had failed to remove from users' individual lockers. For those, there was no DMCA safe harbor, so the court addressed the substantive allegations of contributory copyright infringement, finding the service liable.

EMI had made the litigation personal, accusing Michael Robertson of "direct" copyright infringement, based on recordings he had loaded into his own personal locker. Further, EMI argued that the MP3Tunes storage system violated its public performance rights as well, by using a "master copy" to rebroadcast songs to users who had uploaded different copies of the same track. The court found Robertson personally liable, but disagreed as to the performance claims. Unlike the ill-fated MP3.com, which created a master database by copying tens of thousands of discs into its system, MP3Tunes used a "data compression algorithm" that eliminated redundant data, while preserving the "exact digital copy" of each song uploaded into the system.[40]

There was something for both sides to cheer in Judge Pauley's order. Robertson declared a "victory for cloud music," adding that "those in the industry that are building or contemplating personal music services like Amazon, Google, Grooveshark and Dropbox will surely have renewed confidence in offering similar unlicensed services." For its part, EMI celebrated the limited findings of liability, but

---

39. Capitol Records v. MP3Tunes, LLC, 07 Civ. 9931 (S.D.N.Y.) Oct. 25, 2011 Amended Memorandum & Order.

40. *See* Cartoon Network, LP v. CSC Holdings, Inc., 536 F.3d 121 (2d Cir. 2008).

expressed disappointment in the DMCA-related holdings. "EMI believes that companies like MP3Tunes, which knowingly build a business based on stolen music, should not be entitled to any DMCA harbor defense, and we're evaluating our options to seek review of those portions of the decision. We will continue to fight—in this case and in the future—for the rights of our artists and writers, and to ensure that they are always properly compensated every time their music is used in a commercial setting." Objectively, the "win" seemed to go to MP3Tunes; its system, expertly engineered to fall under the DMCA, had been vindicated, and with a few tweaks could avoid liability altogether. But as EMI's statement confirmed, the case is not over. Various issues remain, and on this basis Judge Pauley recently denied EMI's request to allow an appeal of the DMCA issues before the case is fully decided.[41]

Following a pattern that has become familiar over a century's time, MP3Tunes declared bankruptcy in May 2012, founder Michael Robertson declaring that "four and a half years of legal torment" were too much for the company to bear. "[I]t is apparent to EMI that Robertson has finally realized that his case has no merit," the label responded. "While Robertson may believe that MP3Tunes will be able to escape liability in the upcoming trial through this bankruptcy, Robertson himself is still a named defendant in the case and the court has already determined that both he and MP3Tunes have infringed EMI's copyrights. EMI will continue to pursue its case against Robertson, to ensure that its songwriters and artists are properly compensated for their creative work."[42]

47. A Letter from Google

When we left ReDigi, the digital used music pioneer was asking the court for a quick, summary judgment in its favor on the claims brought by the RIAA. But the labels, led by Capitol Records, got aggressive as well, requesting a preliminary

---

41. Capitol Records v. MP3Tunes, LLC, 07 Civ. 9931 (S.D.N.Y.) Jan. 9, 2012 Memorandum & Order. Litigation also continues against Grooveshark, the cloud service mentioned in Michael Robertson's victory statement. As of December 2011, three major labels had joined suit against Grooveshark and its principals. The fourth, EMI, settled earlier litigation by extracting license fees from the service, but was reportedly pursuing a separate suit for unpaid royalties. Times were even tougher for Kim Schmitz (aka "Kim Dotcom"), who was jailed in New Zealand for his role in operating MegaUpload, a popular "locker-and-links" service that authorities allege is a front for a massive piracy operation. On January 22, 2012, the FBI took down the site and jailed Dotcom and other company executives in perhaps the largest criminal copyright case ever brought by the United States. The case is bound to raise compelling copyright issues, as some commentators liken MegaUpload to similar cloud services that are used for a variety of legitimate purposes.

42. Timothy B. Lee. "Music Labels Force Pioneering MP3Tunes Into Bankruptcy," Ars Technica, May 14, 2012, 2:15PM CDT, http://arstechnica.com/tech-policy/2012/05/music-labels-force-pioneering-mp3tunes-into-bankruptcy/.

injunction that would shutter the service while the litigation made its way to trial. In early February 2012, Google tried to insert itself into the case, with a letter asking permission to submit a friend-of-court brief (as it had done in the MP3Tunes litigation), "in order to highlight the importance of the copyright law questions" raised in the case.[43] At first blush it seemed odd that Google would concern itself with a used music service, but in barely three pages Google's counsel showed that in a converged world nearly every digital music fact pattern involves the same series of overlapping metaphysical questions, and therefore the potential to impact every cloud service.

Google claimed to be objective on the ultimate merits of the case, but asked that its perspective be heard in light of its "specific and vital interest in the legal doctrines underpinning the 'cloud computing' industry," an estimated "$41 billion dollar global market that depends in large part on a few key legal principles" raised by the case. To illustrate these principles, Google referred to the Second Circuit's holding in the *Cartoon Network* case, another "cloud" controversy, involving the remote storage of television recordings by customers on a cable service provider's central servers.[44] According to Google, *Cartoon Network* established that a service provider does not directly infringe copyright by operating a service that permits users to make copies, even if some of those copies may be infringing; and second, that a performance is not "public" if it is "transmitted from a copy of the work that is uniquely identified to a particular user, even if other users receive transmissions of the same work from different copies." Google submitted that the ReDigi case ran the risk of "blurring these clear rules" to the extent it seeks to hold the service directly liable "for copying that users may initiate and for publicly performing copyrighted sound recordings by streaming songs to a single user from her own private 'locker.'"

Google also warned that "fair use," principles were in play, suggesting the court be mindful of the "time shifting" precedent set by the Supreme Court in the Betamax case,[45] as supplemented by the Ninth Circuit's "space shifting" holding in the Diamond Rio litigation.[46] "With the rise of digital technologies," the letter continued, "'space shifting'—copying purchased files onto computer hard drives, backup drives, or music players like iPods—has been widely accepted as a fair use." According to Google, Capitol had "challenge[d] the scope of fair use as it relates to space shifting in cloud storage services."

Google's final concern involved the first sale doctrine. Google maintained that Capitol had taken contradictory positions by first arguing "that the first sale doctrine—which permits the owner of a lawfully-made copy . . . to sell it without

---

43. February 1, 2012, letter to Judge Richard J. Sullivan from Kathryn J. Fritz of Fenwick & West LLP, on behalf of Google, Inc. Capitol Records' response, also dated February 1, 2012, is from Richard S. Mandel of Cowan, Liebowitz & Latman, P.C.

44. Cartoon Network LP v. CSC Holdings, Inc., 536 F.3d 121 (2d Cir. 2008).

45. *See* Sony Corp. of Am. v. Universal City Studios, Inc., 464 U.S. 417 (1984).

46. *See* RIAA v. Diamond Multimedia Sys., Inc., 180 F.3d 1072, 1079 (9th Cir. 1999); *see* Chapter 40.

needing the copyright owner's permission—cannot apply to this case because no material objects change hands. But it also argues that ReDigi infringes Capitol's exclusive right to 'distribute copies . . . ', despite its admission that no material objects are distributed. Either both provisions apply, and ReDigi's service may be protected by the first sale doctrine, or neither applies, and ReDigi's service does not infringe the distribution right. Google takes no position on which outcome is correct but urges the Court to reject an internally inconsistent argument that would weaken the statutory restrictions on the distribution right." In closing, Google warned against a "premature decision on incomplete facts," which "could create unintended uncertainties for the cloud computing industry," urging the Court "to proceed to a full consideration on the merits, applying a steady and un-hurried hand to the legal principles that have been the foundation of an unprece-dented groundswell of productive economic activity."

Capitol's attorneys responded to these high-minded admonitions by suggesting that Google mind its own business. "After echoing ReDigi's admiration for 'cloud computing,'" said the response, "Google worries that Capitol's efforts would 'blur' the legal rules regarding public performance and 'challenge the scope of fair use' relating to cloud storage services. None of these concerns are remotely justified." Capitol insisted that the case was about little more than ReDigi "copying files for purposes of transfer and sale, for profit," arguing that the other legal principles raised by Google were specific issues applying "only to the very unique fact pattern of ReDigi's conduct and implicate no particular interest of Google." "Likewise, Google's nearly verbatim rehash of ReDigi's argument that ReDigi either distrib-utes no copies or is entitled to a first sale defense adds nothing to what the parties have already briefed. Google identifies no interest or additional 'perspective'" that entitles it to invade what is a private dispute between Capitol and ReDigi." "ReDigi is a profiteer," the letter concluded, "trying to earn money by processing sales of infringing copies of Capitol's sound recordings."

Judge Sullivan was of the same mind, at least insofar as Google's interests were concerned. He abruptly denied Google's request to submit a brief, confirming that the parties should report as scheduled on February 6, 2012, to square off on the substance of their pending motions. But Google's letter had already served its in-tended purpose, heightening the court's sensitivity to the tricky, complex, and far-reaching issues implicated by virtually any digital music controversy in the age of convergence.

48. Saving Prokofiev

It is fitting that the last case we will explore on our journey is the Supreme Court's latest pronouncement on music and copyright, its decision in *Golan v. Holder*.[47] It is appropriate, too, that *Golan* returns us to the root of the story, the founding principles of copyright recognized in Section 8 of Article I of the Constitution, which vested in Congress the power "To promote the Progress of Science and Useful arts, by securing for limited Times to Authors and Inventors the exclusive Right to their respective Writings and Discoveries." *Golan* recalls Noah Webster and his son-in-law, Representative William W. Ellsworth, whose efforts to extend the copyright period came to fruition in 1831, when the term was extended to twenty-eight years, renewable for an additional fourteen. The same Act of Congress recognized "musical compositions" as a new category of copyrightable works, creating the legal foundation for the business of music, and putting us on the course we have followed into the digital present. "Times," quite literally, have changed. And *Golan* harkens back to the same era in another way, by reminding us of the early–nineteenth century music publishers who made a habit of distributing foreign compositions. It made business sense for them to do so, as there were no royalty obligations on foreign works not protected under U.S. law.[48] By reconnecting with a familiar childhood favorite, Sergei Prokofiev's *Peter and the Wolf*, we will see that those times have changed, too.

We earlier visited the anti-bootlegging provisions of the Uruguay Round Agreements Act, passed in 1994 to bring the U.S. into compliance with the Berne Convention, the international copyright treaty established in 1886, which the U.S. joined belatedly in 1989.[49] To establish the necessary degree of reciprocity under Berne, URAA Section 514 established U.S. copyrights in certain foreign works that were protected in the author's home country, but not in the U.S. In turn, American authors received reciprocal protection in Berne member countries. Implementing Section 514 proved controversial, as it had the effect of "restoring" the copyrights in a large number of foreign works that had previously been in the public domain. Those accustomed to exploiting such works free of charge—orchestra conductors, musicians, publishers, and others—were suddenly required to pay for using the same works. As a consequence, a group of these stakeholders sued Attorney General Eric Holder, alleging that Congress had exceeded its constitutional authority in passing Section 514, violating in the process the group's First Amendment rights to continue using works formerly in the public domain.

---

47. Golan v. Holder, 565 U.S. __, No. 10–545 (Jan. 18, 2012).
48. *See* Chapter 1.
49. *See* Chapter 38.

The district court agreed with plaintiffs, holding that copyright "restoration" violated the First Amendment and could not be justified by a legitimate federal interest. The Tenth Circuit Court of Appeals reversed, setting up a sequel to the Supreme Court's 2003 decision in *Eldred v. Ashcroft*,[50] which affirmed the constitutionality of a previous extension of copyright terms. (Under current law, the copyright term for an individual is the author's life plus 70 years. Where a corporation is deemed author, protection exists for the shorter of 95 years after publication, or 120 years from creation.[51])

Section 514 applies to all categories of works, and has restored copyrights in works of fine art and literature by Pablo Picasso, Virginia Wolf, and many others. But the musical centerpiece of the *Golan* dispute was the symphonic favorite, *Peter and the Wolf*, written by Russian composer Sergei Prokofiev in 1936. Commissioned as a musical symphony for children, the enthusiastic composer completed the piece in just four days, creating a lively score to be accompanied by the narrated story of Peter, who lives at his grandfather's home in a forest clearing. When Peter is scolded for being outside unsupervised, he defiantly says he is "not afraid of wolves," before being taken back inside behind a locked gate. Soon afterward a ravenous wolf emerges from the forest, quickly swallowing a duck and threatening Peter's cat. Witnessing the mayhem, Peter fetches a rope and climbs over the garden wall into a tree, and succeeds in lowering a noose that catches the wolf by its tail. When the hunters who have been tracking the wolf appear and prepare to shoot, Peter persuades them to lay down their guns and lead a victory parade to the wolf's new home at the local zoo. The happy ending is tempered by the grumbling grandfather, who wonders "What if Peter *hadn't* caught the wolf? What then?" and the narrator's reminder of the forest dangers—"If you listen very carefully, you'd hear the duck quacking inside the wolf's belly, because the wolf in his hurry had swallowed her alive."

Despite its dark edges, the story was an immediate hit with audiences of all ages, and quickly became one of the most performed and recorded works of its day. Taking advantage of the story being in the public domain, Walt Disney produced an animated version of *Peter and the Wolf* in 1946,[52] and thereafter the recordings multiplied further, eventually numbering more than 400 in a dozen languages, including performances by an eclectic cast of narrators including Eleanor Roosevelt, Sir Alec Guinness, Sir Peter Ustinov, Basil Rathbone, Sophia Loren, Boris Karloff, "Weird Al" Yankovic, and Ziggy Stardust himself, David Bowie.[53]

---

50. Eldred v. Ashcroft, 537 U.S. 186 (2003).

51. 17 U.S.C. § 302.

52. Disney has deftly played on both sides of the public domain. The copyright term extensions at issue in *Eldred* have been called the "Mickey Mouse extensions," as they came just in time to prevent the Disney character from falling into the public domain.

53. Michael Biel, *The Recordings of* Peter and the Wolf, THREE ORANGES J. (Nov. 2006), *available at* http://www.sprkfv.net/journal/three12/summary12.html.

Over the decades, *Peter and the Wolf* has become one of the most frequently performed classical compositions of all time, performed around the world by groups ranging from local school districts to the world's greatest conductors and orchestras—Leonard Bernstein and the New York Philharmonic, Arthur Fiedler, Leopold Stokowski, Andre Previn, and Keith Lockhart and the Boston Pops among them. Like Disney, these orchestras paid nothing to publicly perform *Peter and the Wolf*, or to use the work in educational and other settings. But all this changed with the passage of Section 514, which "restored" Prokofiev's most cherished work to the property of his heirs (the composer having died in 1953). Thus, *Golan v. Holder.*

Supreme Court Justice Ruth Bader Ginsburg wrote for the majority, ruling that Congress was within its authority in enacting the law, as "Congress determined that U.S. interests were best served by our full participation in the dominant system of international copyright protection." The net effect was to give foreign authors full reciprocal treatment, putting them on the same footing as U.S. creators. "Prokofiev's 'Peter and the Wolf' could once be performed free of charge," observed the court, but after the new law, "the right to perform it must be obtained in the marketplace. This is the same marketplace, of course, that exists for the music of Prokofiev's U.S. contemporaries: works of Copland and Bernstein, for example, that enjoy copyright protection, but nevertheless appear regularly in the programs of U.S. concertgoers." The First Amendment argument was a nonstarter for the Supreme Court, which observed that by its nature, "[s]ome restriction on expression is the inherent and intended effect of every grant of copyright." As long as the "traditional contours" of copyright were not invaded, Congress had broad discretion in deciding how long exclusive rights could last, and even the authority to pluck works from public domain and restore them to protected status, if necessary, to realize the broader policy objectives of international copyright cooperation.

Some point to the *Eldred* and *Golan* decisions as evidence that copyright is "broken," and that Congress itself is complicit in rights holders' inexorable march toward "perpetual copyright." Justice Ginsberg reasoned that "Congress can hardly be charged with a design to move stealthily toward a regime of perpetual copyrights," finding legitimate policy goals in "aligning the United States with other nations bound by the Berne Convention, and thereby according equitable treatment to once disfavored foreign authors." At a minimum, though, *Golan* is another judicial affirmation of the *strength* of copyright, as well as the *length* of its term. As we have seen in the patterns that have emerged in our story, courts tend to uphold copyrights in the face of new technology, and failing that, Congress has routinely passed legislation at the industry's behest.

Whether we have reached another watershed moment when our copyright regime requires wholesale, omnibus revision is not for us to say, but it would not be the first time, of course. Without weighing in on that ultimate question, it is within our province to observe that the power of convergence is forcing the entire creative community to confront the digital future, testing copyright every day in the process. But there is plenty of evidence to suggest that copyright will survive in some form, and help propel us deeper into the new millennium. According to Paul Goldstein, copyright is well-suited to the task at hand. "Some years into the twenty-first century," he wrote in 2003, "the celestial jukebox [is] still unrealized, its promise clouded in no small part by the fear of copyright owners—the Napster experience fresh in their minds—that they, and not consumers, would ultimately pay the price for putting copyrighted works on line. But behind the clouds it was possible to discern the legal, institutional, and business structures that would in time restore stability to copyright markets even as it transformed them."[54] Indeed, he said, "unlike such earlier technologies as photocopiers and VCRs, which threatened to undermine copyright incentives, the celestial jukebox has the capacity to secure them. As revolutionary as the celestial jukebox may be, its demands on copyright lawmaking are modest, and certainly do not require such regulatory excesses as those embodied in the DMCA. [A]dherence to copyright's traditional strictures in the digital marketplace offer the surest prospect for the production and consumption of creative work in the widest possible variety and at the lowest price."

In practical terms, we are already managing music copyrights more efficiently. In today's jargon, the focus is on "rights management," which is the province of both independent artists and entrepreneurs and their larger, more traditional counterparts. After BMG Music exited the traditional label business in 2008, "BMG Rights Management" arose in its wake, a joint venture between Bertelsmann AG and investment bankers Kohlberg Kravis Roberts & Co. The company has moved aggressively in managing and acquiring publishing and sound recording copyrights, but performs few of the "traditional" label functions. Similarly, in his company-wide e-mail announcing the transfer of control to Citigroup in 2011, EMI chief executive Roger Faxon referred three times to his strategy of building a "global rights management" business, telling his troops flatly: "global rights management is the future."[55] Large or small, those who can facilitate the billions of transactions that together create a "pool of money," and a "fair way to allocate it," to borrow the motto of digital music guru Jim Griffin, will form the backbone of the Celestial Jukebox we have been dreaming of.[56]

---

54. Paul Goldstein, Copyright's Highway: From Gutenberg to the Celestial Jukebox 185, 188 (2003).

55. E-mail from Roger Faxon to all EMI Music Staff globally, *available at* http://www.guardian.co.uk /media/2011/feb/07/emi-roger-faxon-email. Faxon insisted this was a reason EMI's publishing and recorded music assets would be kept together, as opposed to being carved up and sold in pieces to different bidders, but in the end the two segments of the business were sold to Sony and Universal, respectively.

56. Jim Griffin interview at Greplaw.org, Nov. 28, 2003, *available at* http://grep.law.harvard.edu /articles/03/11/28/095219.shtml; *see also* Al Kohn & Bob Kohn, Kohn on Music Licensing 61 (4th ed. 2010). One recent entrepreneurial success story is that of the rights management startup, RightsFlow, acquired by Google in late 2011.

Before we leave our final case, we should remind ourselves that *Golan* is about "foreign" as well as domestic works. Music copyright is increasingly a global issue. The Internet knows no bounds, and neither legal nor geographic "territories" will foster the global community's goal of anytime access to any and all musical creations. Parochialism will not carry the day in the digital age. If it is to be complete, the Celestial Jukebox must hold all 400+ recordings of *Peter and the Wolf*, adjacent to the collected works of Peter Gabriel (rock); Peter Tosh (reggae); Peter Rowan (country); Peter, Paul and Mary (folk), and all the other "Peters" who have contributed to the massive database that is the entire history of recorded music. And finally, the example of reciprocity set by *Golan* reminds us that when we access these recordings, the artists responsible for them, domestic and foreign, must be treated with absolute parity.

49. Beautiful Future of Music

As we entered the second decade of the twenty-first century, Vivendi's Universal Music Group remained the market leader, controlling almost 30 percent of the U.S. market in 2011, with Sony running a close second, followed by Warner with 19 percent and EMI slightly under 10 percent, leaving 10 percent to the vast sea of independents. The two leaders remained cocooned within much larger corporate conglomerates, but EMI struggled under a crushing debt load, causing its largest creditor, Citigroup, Inc., to seize control of the company in early February 2011. Only a few months later, on May 6, 2011, Warner announced its merger agreement with Access Industries, headed by Russian billionaire Len Blavatnik, in an all-cash transaction valued at $3.3 billion. Rumors swirled that EMI would be Access' next target in a massive music rollup strategy, but as it happened, EMI was divided and sold in two pieces in the fall of 2011—publishing assets to Sony, and its recorded music division to Universal. Some, including exiting Warner chairman Edgar Bronfman, vowed to fight the merger, but in all likelihood, we will soon be down to the Big Three—Sony, Warner, and Universal—completing a wholesale reordering of the major label music business not seen since the 1920s. The reorganization of the twenties was brought on by the advent of recorded music, accelerated by a disruptive technology called radio, but in time these changes proved to be the catalysts for the rise of the independent labels in the forties and fifties, and ultimately the Golden Age of recorded music that peaked in 1999. Then, as now, the industry remained engulfed in litigation, but through the haze a new era emerged.

Similarly, the chaotic developments of the last decade have marked a new beginning, turning 2011 into a year of promise for the future of music. In 2011, for the first time in history, digital music purchases accounted for more than half (50.3 percent) of U.S. music sales.[57] "The music business has clearly hit bottom and the resurrection is here," proclaimed independent music veteran Tom Silverman. "After ten years of decline, the music business hit bottom in the second week of February 2010 and began to rise."[58] Reflecting on the preceding decade, Silverman noted that in 2003 "there were virtually no single sales as the labels stopped manufacturing them to drive buyers to higher priced albums to get the song they wanted. In 2004, iTunes changed all that and for the first time music lovers could buy not only the radio single, but also every track on the album separately for only 99 cents. Digital singles exploded, soon surpassing total album sales, physical and digital combined." Indeed, in 2011, digital singles sales increased another 8.5 percent, representing growth of over 100 million singles year-over-year, to a total of 1.27 billion tracks, growth coming in all genres and including both new music and "catalog" staples.

In addition, "digital album" sales took their second biggest jump ever, increasing by 16.8 million units, and marking another important metric—2011 was the first year the *increase* in digital album sales exceeded the *decrease* in the sale of physical CDs. Despite this, Silverman also found it noteworthy that with "CD sales still running almost 69% of album sales seven years into the iTunes era, it is clear that people still want physical CDs." Indeed, physical formats demonstrated their staying power in the new millennium. The last piano roll came off the presses in 2008, more than a century after its introduction.[59] And in 2011, sales in the sixty-year-old vinyl LP format, while small as a percentage, surged by a whopping 37 percent. Even the almost-forgotten cassette tape saw a revival of sorts, with the emergence of "cassette only" independent labels, preserving a more tactile, analog

---

57. The Nielsen Company & Billboard's 2011 Music Industry Report, Jan. 5, 2012, available at http://www.businesswire.com/news/home/20120105005547/en/Nielsen-Company-Billboard%E2%80%99s-2011-Music-Industry-Report.

58. *Tom Silverman: 1st Anniversary of the Resurrection of the Music Business*, Hypebot.com Guest blog, Jan. 27, 2012, http://www.hypebot.com/hypebot/2012/01/tom-silverman-on-the-music-business-resurrection.html.

59. On New Year's Eve 2008, the last piano roll came off the assembly line at QRS Music Technologies in Buffalo, New York. The tune embedded in the roll was "Spring Is Here," a 1938 classic from the songwriting team of composer Richard Rodgers and lyricist Lorenz Hart, written for the musical *I Married an Angel*, and recorded in subsequent years by an array of popular artists, ranging from Ella Fitzgerald to Frank Sinatra, from the Supremes to Carly Simon, from Chet Baker to John Coltrane. Thus ended the run of the only continuously operating mass producer of piano rolls in the world, a company founded in Chicago at the turn of the twentieth century by Melville Clark, a piano designer and inventor, who engineered a method of making rolls to supply content to the burgeoning market for "player pianos." QRS carried on with production of its more current products—digitized and computerized player piano technology, digital self-playing violins and the like—but its sales of old-fashioned rolls had fallen to around 50,000 units annually, no longer enough to justify production. Still, its 108-year run of roll manufacturing was testimony to a remarkably resilient music format.

past. In the new millennium, "indie" artists, labels and creative entrepreneurs seem well poised for another renaissance, if not a revolution.[60]

Silverman also saw improvement along the digital frontier of music performance, noting that in 2011, "$95 million more dollars were collected by Sound-Exchange than in 2010 and projections for 2012 show growth into the mid $400 million mark." A variety of interactive audio and video services were also contributing new dollars to the industry. "A decade of adjustment is over and it is clear that we are on the brink of the next big growth era of the music business," he concluded. "Welcome to the resurrection. Have a nice day."

Grizzled major label veteran Doug Morris was also optimistic about the future of music. After years of running the world's largest music enterprise, CEO Doug Morris moved from Universal to Michael Jackson's label, Sony, in what some mocked as a game of musical chairs between dinosaur major labels. Upon arrival, Morris, who long ago admitted his technological handicaps, confirmed his unwavering commitment to the major label business model: "Our core focus still needs to be developing hits," he insisted. "That's the only constant amidst all the change.[61] So if you don't get that right it doesn't matter how revolutionary the distribution model is or how many revenue streams you have. You still have to have the hits."

Sean Parker, the cofounder of Napster (and early Facebook investor), who at age thirty-two is a veteran of a decade of "music wars," found himself in strange alignment with his former major label nemesis. Appearing at the e-G8 Conference in Paris in May 2011, Parker explained the motivation behind his participation in an unsuccessful bid to acquire Warner Music (sold earlier that month to Access Industries). "I think that there is a pretty dramatic change in the way music is monetized that is on the cusp of happening," he said. "Back catalogs of record labels are going to become extremely valuable, just as music publishers' back catalogs have become more valuable. If you believe this transformation is occurring, if you believe the broken distribution systems are on the verge of being fixed, those recordings are dramatically undervalued."[62] Parker bridged the gap between the traditional business and the new, opining that the "old model" of iTunes sells a lot of singles and Top 40 hits, but for cutting-edge music services like Spotify (in which he is also an investor), "it's the back catalog that is driving the consumption."

---

60. *See* Greg Kot, Ripped: How the Wired Generation Revolutionized Music (2009); *see also* Damian Kulash, Jr., "The New Rock Star Paradigm, Wall St. J., Dec. 17, 2010. Of his band, OK Go, Mr. Kulash says, "We once relied on investment and support from a major label. Now we make a comparable living raising money directly from fans and through licensing and sponsorship."

61. Morris might have mentioned another constant—radio airplay still drives hits. A joint NPD Group and NARM study released in November 2011 concluded that traditional radio remains the most important method of new music discovery. Reported at Digital Music News, Nov. 13, 2011, http://digital musicnews.com/permalink/2011/111113fmradio.

62. Tim Bradshaw, *Sean Parker, Scourge of Record Labels, Calls the Bottom of the Music Industry*, Fin. Times Blog, May 25, 2011.

Parker believes that services like Spotify represent a "paradigm shift" in music consumption, bringing us closer to our celestial destination. "In the last 10 years we have presided over the greatest destruction in value in the history of the music industry," he continued, noting the $45 billion industry worldwide had been reduced to $12 billion. "Assuming we can stabilize things and restore growth, it shouldn't be that difficult to preside over the greatest increase in value in the history of the recorded music industry."

Observers outside the industry are reaching the same conclusions. In their 2012 report, "The Sky Is Rising," Michael Masnick and Michael Ho conclude that the overall entertainment industry, including music, is growing and producing more content than ever before, presenting an "age of amazing new opportunity" for individual artists, as well as traditional middlemen and gatekeepers-cum-enablers who have the courage and foresight to navigate the shifting terrain.[63] The twin disruptive forces of digitization and the Internet continue to reshape the industry in the age of convergence, and the pace of change can be dizzying, but with history as our guide, we—creators, entrepreneurs and consumers alike—can participate in the greatest artistic and commercial rise the music industry has ever seen. Music is online, in the satellite, and in the cloud, but these are not celestial bodies. And yet, if indeed the sky is rising, there is no reason to abandon our quest for the beautiful future of music, traveling another day, another mile on the long road to the Celestial Jukebox.

---

63. Michael Masnick & Michael Ho, *The Sky Is Rising: A Detailed Look at the State of the Entertainment Industry* (Jan. 2012), *available at* http://www.techdirt.com/skyisrising/.

EPILOGUE: LONG LIVE THE KING!

The sad tale of Michael Jackson's demise reached closure in late 2011 with the sentencing of Conrad Murray, the private physician convicted of involuntary manslaughter for administering a lethal dose of propofol, intended as a sleep aid, at the weary singer's request. But Jackson's legacy lives on. Following his death, Jackson's heirs set another music industry record, signing a $250 million record deal with Sony Music, covering ten albums over seven years, using both a cache of unreleased recordings and new combinations of previously released material. Given the state of the recorded music business, the deal was especially striking, causing some to conclude that the arrangement underscored the fact that "the biggest acts are becoming even more essential to record labels, as individual fans purchase fewer albums each year."[1]

Such words are a challenge to "album" buyers, so I set out in search of Michael Jackson. Downtown Chicago was once a retail music mecca, populated by chains and independents alike, but those days are gone. With the closings of Tower Records, followed by Virgin Music and most recently Borders, the pickings are getting thin. But within a few blocks sat a stalwart independent, Reckless Records, and a fine used copy (courtesy of the first sale doctrine!) of what I regard as the King of Pop's finest work, 1979's breakthrough solo effort, *Off the Wall*. "Lovely, is the feelin' now," begins the vocal, as strings swirl around a funked-up dance groove, punctuated by brass periods and commas, and Jackson's trademark "ooh." The album was a coming-of-age statement by an artist transitioning from the earlier era of Jackson 5 Motown records. Now performing his own compositions, along with personal interpretations of songs from Paul McCartney, Stevie Wonder, and Rod Temperton, and marking a new production partnership with Quincy Jones, Jackson conceived an immaculate groove. Fans flocked to the record, sensing the renewed passion and exuberance in Jackson's vocals, a barely contained sexuality balanced by a naiveté that would soon get left behind in the heady, jaded days of *Thriller* and beyond, when the trappings of Jackson's own persona overshadowed the great art he continued to make.

But "finding" Michael Jackson is only the tip of my musical iceberg.

---

1. Wall St. J., Mar. 16, 2010, at A1.

My friend Richard Weize runs Bear Family Records, a prolific and perfection-ist reissue label that has kept the flame of traditional American music burning for thirty-five years, releasing lavish boxed sets containing multi-CD historical retro-spectives of some of this country's best-known artists, and giving the same treat-ment to obscure, but talented performers. One of his latest projects is "The Bristol Sessions," a 5-CD collection celebrating "The Big Bang of Country Music," the 1927–1928 Victor sessions marking the earliest recordings of Jimmie Rodgers and the Carter Family, among many others, made at the dawn of the radio age. I have pored over the hardcover book that comes with this set, replete with vintage pho-tographs and historical notes from the leading lights of music writers. I can't say I've given all 124 tracks their proper due, but I will soon, honest.

Last spring I attended the ReThink Music conference in Boston, an impressive enclave of musicians, academics, entrepreneurs, and attorneys focused on finding the best ways forward in the challenging business of music. An opening night acoustic performance by Metric, coupled with the band's perspective on indepen-dent music-making and promotion, turned into a conference highlight. Fortunately, Boston's record retailing institution, Newbury Comics, was close by, providing easy access to *Fantasies*, Metric's self-produced release from 2009. And what a pre-cious and complete record it is, the breathless, sometimes haunting vocals of Emily Haines fronting superbly produced modern rock.

Like most new cars these days, ours came with satellite radio, and a free ninety-day trial. Suddenly I was looking for excuses to drive, making my way through hundreds of commercial-free channels, enough music to impress even the quirki-est, most jaded fan. I dutifully extended the trial into a paying subscription, which provided access to and perspective on the music of the forties, fifties, and sixties as those sections of this book were in progress. Here's a tip: *Little Steven's Under-ground Garage* (Channel 21) is a wonderfully eclectic, well-curated trip between the fifties and now. Despite the new car, however, I remain a dedicated train com-muter, making the twenty-minute trip to Chicago and back each workday. I don't always listen to music on the commute, but when the mood strikes I use an iPod, which, at less than half capacity, holds more than 6,000 tracks—easily 300 hours of music. At that rate I could surround myself with personalized playlists for the next 900 train rides, never repeating a track.

My three teenagers are building their own music libraries. None have much use for CDs, but Santa brings them anyway, knowing the tracks will wind up on their own iPod playlists (as well as his). Last year my eldest, nineteen, received the latest from Bon Iver, and the youngest, fourteen, a copy of Adele's *21*, the year's biggest mainstream breakthrough, from that rare artist who, as one friend put it, "lives up to the hype." At seventeen, my son is the middle child, a budding drum-mer and guitarist who is coming of age musically at a wonderful time. He has ac-cess to and enjoys the classic rock of his parents' generation, the alternative rock of his, and the incredible cache of popular music that came in between. Santa delivered him a colored vinyl edition of *Suburbia: I've Given You All and Now I'm Nothing*, from Philadelphia's The Wonder Years, a song series said to be inspired by Allen Ginsberg's 1956 poem "America." Regardless, *Suburbia* flat out rocks the basement speakers, played on a turntable that, at the flip of switch, will turn those warm analog tracks into portable digital files.

Newfangled music services Spotify and Pandora populate my computers, but the family van came equipped (in 2002) with a cassette deck, a throwback to the fading era of analog sound. These days the only "cassette" we use contains not music, but a technical tether to iPods and iPhones, in turn connecting to the myriad playlists, applications and services available on the digital frontier.

I am surrounded by an embarrassment of musical riches, a veritable Celestial Jukebox.

♪♪ ♫♫ ♪♪

As it was at the beginning of our journey, so it is now. The caveman's flute echoes again, the melody emerging from the depths and joining the music recorded in the centuries since, which together makes its way through the villages and cities, then turning upward through the clouds and beyond the satellites, to its ultimate destination among the stars. And when it is delivered down again, on demand, it will pass through layers of technological miracles, filtered and monitored seamlessly, so that when it reaches our ears it is greeted in the same way the caveman's audience responded to the flutist's call—with the wonder and excitement that raises us to new levels of communication and consciousness, through one of the rare and pure beauties of this life—music.

TIMELINE

1787   Section 8 of Article I of the Constitution grants Congress "the power . . . To promote the Progress of Science and Useful arts, by securing for limited Times to Authors and Inventors the exclusive Right to their respective Writings and Discoveries."

1790   First U.S. copyright statute enacted.

1831   Recognition of "musical compositions" as copyrightable subject matter, granting the "sole right and liberty of printing, reprinting, publishing, and vending."

1844   *Millett v. Snowden*. First case to enforce rights against making copies of a musical composition.

1845   *Reed v. Carusi*. First case to find infringement based on "substantial similarity" to an earlier composition.

1888   *Kennedy v. McTammany*. "Organette rolls" do not infringe the copyright in musical compositions embedded therein.

1891   Congress extends first international copyright protection to authors in reciprocating countries.

1893   Columbian Exposition in Chicago. With promotional support from performances by John Philip Sousa, sheet music sales of Charles K. Harris's "After the Ball" are propelled to unprecedented international success.

1897   The exclusive right of public performance is extended to musical compositions.

1901   *Stern v. Rosey*. Wax cylinder recordings do not infringe the copyright in musical compositions embedded therein.

1908   *White-Smith Music Pub. Co. v. Apollo Co*. Landmark Supreme Court decision holds that piano rolls do not infringe the copyright in musical compositions embedded therein.

1909   Omnibus Copyright Act of 1909 reverses *White-Smith* precedent, but includes compulsory "mechanical license" provision to avoid music monopoly. Act also adds "for profit" restriction on exclusive right of public performance. Fledgling jukebox industry exempted from paying performance royalties.

1913   American Society of Composers, Authors and Publishers (ASCAP) founded to license and collect performance royalties for music publishers and composers.

1917   *Herbert v. Shanley Co.* In a decision authored by Oliver Wendell Holmes, Jr. the U.S. Supreme Court finds Shanley's restaurant liable for infringement based on hired orchestra's public performance of Victor Herbert's "Sweethearts" without an ASCAP license.

1922   *Harms v. Cohen.* Performing composition in movie theater constitutes infringing public performance for profit.

1923   *M. Witmark & Sons v. L. Bamberger & Co.* Radio broadcasting constitutes infringing public performance for profit.

1931   *Buck et al. v. Jewell-La Salle Realty Co.* U.S. Supreme Court finds that piping music throughout hotel as "background music" constitutes infringing public performance for profit.

1931   Broadcast Music, Inc. (BMI) founded by broadcasting interests to break the hegemony of ASCAP.

1936   *Waring v. WDAS Broadcasting Station, Inc.* Pennsylvania state court upholds Fred Waring's property interest in his recorded performances.

1940   *RCA Mfg. Co., Inc. v. Whiteman.* Second Circuit Court of Appeals essentially overrules *Waring* decision in terms of federal law. Recording artist unable to prevent broadcasting of his records.

1948   *Alden-Rochelle, Inc. v. ASCAP.* ASCAP movie licensing structure found to violate antitrust laws. Public performance right no longer exercised with respect to movie theaters.

1955   *Capitol Records, Inc. v. Mercury Record Corp.* Contract battle over distribution rights points up void in copyright protection for sound recordings.

1964   *Capitol Records, Inc. v. Greatest Records, Inc.* Copying of Beatles recordings enjoined on theories of unfair competition.

1972   Federal copyright protection extended to sound recordings in Sound Recording Amendment of 1971. Law upheld against challenge in *Shaab v. Kleindienst.*

1973   *Goldstein v. California,* U.S. Supreme Court rules that state law remains applicable to "pre-1972" sound recordings.

1976   General revision of copyright law in Copyright Act of 1976. Includes repeal of "for profit" restriction on public performance, and repeal of jukebox exemption. "Fair use" codified.

1984   Record Rental Amendment passed, modifying "first sale" doctrine with respect to phonorecords.

1984   *Sony Corp. of America v. Universal City Studios.* U.S. Supreme Court decides the "Betamax case," establishing concept of "time shifting" as fair use.

1991   *Grand Upright Music Ltd. v. Warner Bros. Records.* "Sampling" of composition found to infringe copyright.

1992   Audio Home Recording Act of 1992 (AHRA) passed, requires that digital recording devices include chip limiting copies; creates royalty system for recording devices and blank digital audio tapes.

1995   Digital Performance Right in Sound Recordings Act (DPRA) passed, recognizes a performance right in sound recordings for the first time, limited to noninteractive "digital audio transmissions." Section 114 license created, royalties payable 50 percent to sound recording copyright owners, 50 percent to recording artists.

1998   Digital Millennium Copyright Act (DMCA) passed, creates "safe harbors" insulating Internet service providers from liability from user-generated content. DPRA licensing provisions adjusted.

1999   *RIAA v. Diamond Multimedia Systems, Inc.* "Rio" portable MP3 player held not to infringe.

1999   Sound recording work-for-hire provisions included in Intellectual Property and Communications Omnibus Reform Act; repealed in Work Made for Hire and Copyright Corrections Act in 2000.

2000   *UMG Recordings, Inc. v. MP3.com.* MP3.com music locker service found infringing.

2000   *A&M Records, Inc. v. Napster, Inc.* Napster file-sharing service found infringing.

2002   Small Webcaster Settlement Act (SWSA) passed, requires direct payment of recording artists' 50 percent of Section 114 license royalties.

2005   *Metro-Goldwyn-Mayer Studios v. Grokster, Ltd.* U.S. Supreme Court finds Grokster decentralized file-sharing service infringing.

2009   *Arista Records v. Launch Media, Inc.* Webcasting service not "interactive," may utilize Section 114 license.

2010   *U.S. v. ASCAP.* Second Circuit Court of Appeals affirms holding that music download does not constitute a public performance.

2011   *Capitol Records v. MP3Tunes LLC.* In a mixed ruling, MP3Tunes "cloud" service found eligible for DMCA safe harbor protection, but certain features infringe.

2012   RIAA sues "used" digital music reseller, ReDigi.

2012   *Golan v. Holder.* U.S. Supreme Court holds Congress within its authority in allowing "restoration" of certain works previously in the public domain.

INDEX

About the ABA Section of Intellectual Property Law

From its strength within the American Bar Association, the ABA Section of Intellectual Property Law (ABA-IPL) advances the development and improvement of intellectual property laws and their fair and just administration. The Section furthers the goals of its members by sharing knowledge and balanced insight on the full spectrum of intellectual property law and practice, including patents, trademarks, copyright, industrial design, literary and artistic works, scientific works, and innovation. Providing a forum for rich perspectives and reasoned commentary, ABA-IPL serves as the ABA voice of intellectual property law within the profession, before policy makers, and with the public.

ABA Section of Intellectual Property Law
Order today! Call 1-800-285-2221
Monday-Friday, 7:30 a.m. – 5:30 p.m., Central Time
or Visit the ABA Web Store: www.ShopABA.org

Qty	Title	Regular Price	ABA Member Price	ABA-IPL Member Price	Total
_____	ADR Advocacy, Strategies, and Practice in Intellectual Property Cases (5370195)	$139.95	$129.95	$114.95	$_____
_____	ANDA Litigation (5370199)	$299.00	$299.00	$249.00	$_____
_____	Annual Review of Intellectual Property Law Developments 2011 (5370196)	$169.95	$149.95	$134.95	$_____
_____	Annual Review of Intellectual Property Law Developments 2010 (5370191)	$149.95	$127.95	$119.95	$_____
_____	Annual Review of Intellectual Property Law Developments 2009 (5370169)	$149.95	$127.95	$119.95	$_____
_____	Computer Games and Virtual Worlds (5370172)	$69.95	$59.95	$55.95	$_____
_____	Distance Learning and Copyright (5370163)	$89.95	$89.95	$79.95	$_____
_____	Fundamentals of Intellectual Property Valuation (5370143)	$69.95	$59.95	$49.95	$_____
_____	The Intellectual Property Handbook (5620116)	$110.00	$100.00	$90.00	$_____
_____	IP Attorney's Handbook for Insurance Coverage in Intellectual Property Disputes (5370168)	$129.95	$110.95	$103.95	$_____
_____	A Lawyer's Guide to Section 337 Investigations Before the U.S. International Trade Commission (5370171)	$89.95	$76.95	$71.95	$_____
_____	A Legal Strategist's Guide to Trademark Trial and Appeal Board Practice, Second Edition (5370200)	$169.95	$169.95	$129.95	$_____
_____	New Practitioner's Guide to Intellectual Property (5370198)	$89.95	$89.95	$69.95	$_____
_____	The Patent Infringement Litigation Handbook (1620416)	$149.95	$129.95	$129.95	$_____
_____	Patent Obviousness in the Wake of KSR International Co. v. Teleflex Inc. (5370189)	$129.95	$110.95	$103.95	$_____
_____	Preliminary Relief in Patent Infringement Disputes (5370194)	$119.95	$109.95	$94.95	$_____
_____	Settlement of Patent Litigation and Disputes (5370192)	$179.95	$159.95	$144.95	$_____
_____	The Tech Contracts Handbook (5370188)	$89.95	$76.95	$71.95	$_____
_____	Trademark and Deceptive Advertising Surveys (5370197)	$179.95	$179.95	$134.95	$_____

* Tax
DC residents add 6%
IL residents add 9.50%

Payment
❑ Check enclosed payable to the ABA
❑ VISA ❑ Mastercard ❑ American Express

* Tax $_____
** Shipping/Handling $_____
TOTAL $_____

**Shipping/Handling
Up to $49.99 .... $5.95
$50 to $99.99 .... $7.95
$100 to $199.99 .... $9.95
$200 to $499.99 .... $12.95
$500 to $999.99 .... $15.95
$1,000 and above $18.95

Name_____

Firm/Organization_____

Address_____

City_____ State_____ Zipcode_____

Phone_____ E-mail_____
(in case of questions about your order)

Please allow 5 to 7 business days for UPS delivery. Need it sooner? Ask about overnight delivery. Call the ABA Service Center at 1-800-285-2221 for more information.

Guarantee: If – for any reason – you are not satisfied with your purchase, you may return it within 30 days of receipt for a complete refund of the price of the book(s). No questions asked!

Please mail your order to:
ABA Publication Orders, P.O. Box 10892, Chicago, Illinois 60610-0892
Phone: 1-800-285-2221 or 312-988-5522 • Fax: 312-988-5568
E-mail: orders@abanet.org

Thank you for your order!

Section of Intellectual Property Law